THE BOOK OF THE SACRED MAGIC OF ABRAMELIN THE MAGE

BOOKS I, II AND III

AS DELIVERED BY ABRAHAM THE JEW UNTO HIS SON LAMECH, A.D. 1458. TRANSLATED FROM THE ORIGINAL HEBREW INTO THE FRENCH, AND NOW RENDERED FROM THE LATTER LANGUAGE INTO ENGLISH. FROM A UNIQUE AND VALUABLE MS. IN THE "BIBLIOTHÈQUE DE L'ARSENAL" AT PARIS.
By

S. L. MAC GREGOR MATHERS

AUTHOR OF "THE KABBALAH UNVEILED," "THE KEY OF SOLOMON," "THE TAROT," ETC.
PUBLISHED JOHN M. WATKINS, LONDON
ORIGINALLY PUBLISHED IN 1900

ISBN: 978-1-963956-99-3

Contents

INTRODUCTION,
BY

S. L. MAC GREGOR MATHERS.

O WING perhaps to the circumstance that the indispensable "Bædecker" accords only a three or four line notice to the "Bibliothèque de l'Arsenal"; but few English or American visitors to Paris are acquainted with its name, situation, or contents, though nearly all know at least by sight the "Bibliothèque Nationale" and the "Bibliothèque Mazarin".

This "Library of the Arsenal," as it is now called, was founded as a private collection by Antoine René Voyer D'Argenson, Marquis de Paulny; and was first opened to the public on the 9th Floréal, in the fifth year of the French Republic (that is to say, on 28th April, 1797), or just a century ago. This Marquis de Paulny was born in the year 1722, died in 1787, and was successively Minister of War, and Ambassador to Switzerland, to Poland, and to the Venetian Republic. His later years were devoted to the formation of this Library, said to be one of the richest private collections known. It was acquired in 1785 by the Comte D'Artois, and to-day belongs to the State. It is situated on the right bank of the Seine, in the Rue de Sully, near the river, and not far from the Place de la Bastille, and is known as the "Bibliothèque de l'Arsenal". In round numbers it now possesses 700,000 printed books, and about 8000 manuscripts, many of them being of considerable value.

Among the latter is this Book of the Sacred Magic of Abra-Melin, as delivered by Abraham the Jew unto his son Lamech; which I now give to the public in printed form for the first time.

Many years ago I heard of the existence of this manuscript from a celebrated occultist, since dead; and more recently my attention was again called to it by my personal friend, the well-known French author, lecturer and poet, Jules Bois, whose attention has been for some time turned to occult subjects. My first-mentioned informant told me that it was known both to Bulwer Lytton and Éliphas Lévi, that the former had based part of his description of the Sage Rosicrucian Mejnour on that of Abra-Melin, while the account of the so-called Observatory of Sir Philip Derval in the "Strange Story" was to an extent copied from and suggested by that of the Magical Oratory and Terrace, given in the Eleventh Chapter of the Second Book of this present work. Certainly also the manner of instruction applied by Mejnour in "Zanoni" to the Neophyte Glyndon, together with the test of leaving him alone in his abode to go on a short journey and then returning unexpectedly, is closely similar to that employed by Abra-Melin to Abraham, with this difference, that the latter successfully passed through that test, while Glyndon failed. It would also be especially such experiments as those described at length in the Third Book, which the author of the "Strange Story" had in view when he makes Sir Philip Derval in the MS. history of his life speak of certain hooks describing occult experiments, some of which he had tried and to his surprise found succeed.

This rare and unique manuscript of the Sacred Magic of Abra-Melin, from which the present work is translated, is a French translation from the original Hebrew of Abraham the Jew. It is in the style of script usual at about the end of the seventeenth and beginning of the eighteenth centuries, and is apparently by the same hand as another MS. of the Magic of Picatrix[1] also in the "Bibliothèque de l'Arsenal". I know of no other existing copy or replica of this Sacred Magic of Abra-Melin, not even in the British Museum, whose enormous collection of Occult Manuscripts I have very thoroughly studied.

Neither have I ever heard by traditional report of the existence of any other copy.[2] In giving it now to the Public, I feel, therefore, that I am conferring a real benefit upon English and American students of Occultism, by placing within their reach for the first time a Magical work of such importance from the Occult standpoint.

The Manuscript is divided into three Books, each with its separate Title Page, surrounded by an ornamental border of simple design, in red and black ink, and which is evidently not intended to be symbolical in the slightest degree, but is simply the work of a conscientious caligraphist wishing to give an appearance of cleanness and completeness to the Title Page. The wording of each is the same: "Livre Premier (Second or Troisième, as the case may be) de la Sacrée Magie que Dieu donna à Moyse, Aaron, David, Salomon et à d'autres Saints Patriarches et Prophetes qui enseigne la vraye sapience Divine laissée par Abraham à Lamech son Fils traduite de l'hébreu 1458". I give the translated title at the commencement of each of the Three Books.

On the fly-leaf of the original MS. is the following note in the handwriting of the end of the eighteenth century:--

"This Volume contains 3 Books, of which here is the first.--The Abraham and the Lamech, of whom there is here made question, were Jews of the fifteenth century, and it is well known that the Jews of that period possessing the Cabala of Solomon passed for being the best Sorcerers and Astrologers." Then follows in another and recent hand:--

"Volume composed of three parts--

1st	part	102	pages.
2nd	"	194	"
3rd	"	<u>117</u>	"
		413	"

June,
1883."

The style of the French employed in the text of the MS. is somewhat vague and obscure, two qualities unhappily heightened by the almost entire absence of any attempt at punctuation, and the comparative rarity of paragraphic arrangement. Even the full stop at the close of a sentence is usually omitted, neither is the commencement of a fresh one marked by a capital letter. The following example is taken from near the end of the Third Book: "Cest pourquoy la premiere chose que tu dois faire principalement ates esprits familiers sera de leur commander de ne tedire jamais aucune chose deuxmemes que lorsque tu les interrogeras amoins queles fut pour tavertir des choses qui concerne ton utilite outon prejudice parceque situ ne leur limite pas leparler ils tediront tant etdesi grandes choses quils tofusquiront lentendement et tu ne scaurois aquoy tentenir desorte que dans la confusion des choses ils pourroient te faire prevariquer ettefaire tomber dans des erreurs irreparables ne te fais jamais prier en aucune chose ou tu pourras aider et seccourir tonprochain et nattends pas quil tele demande mais tache descavoir afond," etc. This extract may he said to give a fair idea of the average quality of the French. The style, however, of the First

[1] Probably the same as Gio Peccatrix the Magician, the author of many Manuscripts on Magic.

[2] Since writing the above, I have heard casually that a copy of at least part, or perhaps of the whole, is said to exist in Holland.

Book is much more colloquial than that of the Second and Third, it being especially addressed by Abraham to Lamech, his son, and the second person singular being employed throughout it. As some English readers may be ignorant of the fact, it is perhaps as well here to remark that in French "tu," thou, is only used between very intimate friends and relations, between husband and wife, lovers, etc.; while "vous," you, is the more usual mode of address to the world in general. Again, in sacred books, in prayers, etc., "vous" is used, where we employ "thou" as having a more solemn sound than "tu". Hence the French verb "tutoyer," = "to he very familiar with, to be on extremely friendly terms with any one, and even to be insolently familiar". This First Book contains advice concerning Magic, and a description of Abraham's Travels and experiences, as well as a mention of the many marvellous works he had been able to accomplish by means of this system of Sacred Magic. The Second and Third Books (which really contain the Magic of Abra-Melin, and are practically based on the two MSS. entrusted by him to Abraham, the Jew, but with additional comments by the latter) differ in style from the former, the phraseology is quaint and at times vague, and the second person plural, "vous," is employed for the most part instead of "tu".

The work may then be thus roughly classified.--

First Book:=Advice and Autobiography; both addressed by the Author to his son Lamech.

Second Book:=General and complete description of the means of obtaining the Magical Powers desired.

Third Book:=The application of these Powers to produce an immense number of Magical results.

Though the chapters of the Second and Third Books have special headings in the actual text, those of the First Book have none; wherefore in the "Table of Contents" I have supplemented this defect by a careful analysis of their subject matter.

This system of Sacred Magic Abraham acknowledges to have received from the Mage Abra-Melin; and claims to have himself personally and actually wrought most of the wonderful effects described in the Third Book, and many others besides.

Who then was this Abraham the Jew? It is possible, though there is no mention of this in the MS., that he was a descendant of that Abraham the Jew who wrote the celebrated Alchemical work on twenty-one pages of bark or papyrus, which came into the hands of Nicholas Flamel, and by whose study the latter is said eventually to have attained the possession of the "Stone of the Wise". The only remains of the Church of Saint Jacques de la Boucherie which exists at the present day, is the tower, which stands near the Place du Châtelet, about ten minutes' walk from the Bibliothèque de l'Arsenal; and there is yet a street near this tower which bears the title of "Rue Nicolas Flamel," so that his memory still survives in Paris, together with that of the Church close to which he lived, and to which, after the attainment of the Philosopher's Stone, he and his wife Pernelle caused a handsome peristyle to be erected.

From his own account, the author of the present work appears to have been born in. A. D. 1362, and to have written this manuscript for his son, Lamech, in 1458, being then in his ninety-sixth year. That is to say, that he was the contemporary both of Nicholas Flamel and Pernelle, and also of the mystical Christian Rosenkreutz, the founder of the celebrated Rosicrucian Order or Fraternity in Europe. Like the latter, he appears to have been very early seized with the desire of obtaining Magical Knowledge; like him and Flamel, he left his home and travelled in search of the Initiated Wisdom; like them both, he returned to become a worker of wonders. At this period, it was almost universally believed that the Secret Knowledge was only really obtainable by those who were willing to quit their home and their country to undergo dangers and hardships in its quest; and this idea even obtains to an extent in the present day. The life of the late Madame Blavatsky is an example in point.

This period in which Abraham the Jew lived was one in which Magic was almost universally believed in, and in which its Professors were held in honour; Faust (who was probably also a contemporary of our author), Cornelius Agrippa, Sir Michael Scott, and many others I could name, are examples of this, not to mention the celebrated Dr. Dee in a later age. The history of this latter Sage, his association with Sir Edward Kelly, and the part he took in the European politics of his time are too well known to need description here.

That Abraham the Jew was not one whit behind any of these Magicians in political influence, is evident to an one who peruses this work. He stands a dim and shadowy figure behind e tremendous complication of central European upheaval at that terrible and instructive epoch; as Adepts of his type always appear and always have appeared upon the theatre of history in great crises of nations. The age which could boast simultaneously three rival claimants to the direction of two of the greatest levers of the society of that era--the Papacy and the Germanic Empire--when the jealousies of rival Bishoprics, the overthrow of Dynasties, the Roman Church shaken to her foundations, sounded in Europe the tocsin of that fearful struggle which invariably precedes social reorganisation, that wild whirlwind of national convulsion which engulfs in its vortex the civilisation of a yesterday, but to prepare the reconstitution of a morrow. The enormous historical importance of such men as our Author is always underrated, generally doubted; notwithstanding that like the writing on the wall at Belshazzar's feast, their manifestation in the political and historical arena is like the warning of a MENE, MENE TEKEL, UPUARSIN, to a foolish and undiscerning world.

The full and true history of any Adept could only be written by himself, and even then, if brought before the eyes of the world at large, how many persons would lend credence to it? and even the short and incomplete statement of the notable events of our Author's life contained in the First Book, will be to most readers utterly incredible of belief. But what must strike all alike is the tremendous faith of the man himself, as witnessed by his many and dangerous journeyings for so many years through wild and savage regions and places difficult of access even in our own day with all the increased facilities of transit which we enjoy. This faith at length brought him its reward, though only at the moment when even he was becoming discouraged and sick at heart with disappointed hope. Like his great namesake, the forefather of the Hebrew race, he had not in vain left his home, his "Ur of the Chaldees," that he might at length discover that Light of Initiated Wisdom, for which his soul had cried aloud within him for so many years. This culmination of his wanderings was his meeting with Abra-Melin, the Egyptian Mage. From him he received that system of Magical instruction and practice which forms the body of the Second and Third Books of this work.

In the Manuscript original this name is spelt in several different ways, I have noted this in the text wherever it occurs. The variations are: Abra-Melin, Abramelin, Abramelim, and Abraha-Melin. From these I have selected the orthography Abra-Melin to place on the title page, and I have adhered to the same in this Introduction.

As far as can be gathered from the text, the chief Place of residence of Abraham the Jew after his travels was Würzburg, or, as it was called in the Middle Ages, "Herbipolis". He appears to have married his cousin, and by her to have had two sons, the elder, named Joseph, whom he instructed in the Mysteries of the Holy Qabalah, and Lamech, the younger, to whom he bequeaths this system of Sacred Magic as a legacy, and to whom the whole of the First Book is addressed. He speaks further of three daughters, to each of whom he gave 100,000 golden florins as a dowry. He expressly states that he obtained both his wife, and a treasure of 3,000,000 golden florins, by means of some of the Magical Operations described in the Third Book. He further admits that his first inclination to Qabalistical and Magical studies was owing to certain instructions in the Secrets of the Qabalah, which he received when young from his father, Simon; so that after the death of the latter his most earnest desire was to travel in search of an Initiated Master.

To the sincere and earnest student of Occultism this work cannot fail to be of value, whether as an encouragement to that most rare and necessary quality, unshaken faith; as an aid to his discrimination between true and false systems of Magic; or as Presenting an assemblage of directions for the production of Magical effects, which the Author of the book affirms to have tried with success.

Especially valuable are the remarks of Abraham the Jew on the various Professors of the "Art which none may name" in the course of his wanderings and travels; the account of the many wonders he worked; and, above all, the careful classification of the Magical Experiments in the Third Book, together with his observations and advice thereon.

Not least in interest are the many notable persons of that age for or against whom he performed marvels: The Emperor Sigismund of Germany: Count Frederic the Quarreller: the Bishop of his city (probably either John I., who began the foundation of the Würzburg University in 1403 with the authorisation of Pope Boniface IX., or else Echter von Mespelbrunn, who completed the same noble work): the Count of Warwick: Henry VI. of England: the rival Popes--John XXIII., Martin V., Gregory XII., and Benedict XIII.: the Council of Constance: the Duke of Bavaria: Duke Leopold of Saxony: the Greek Emperor, Constantine Palæologos: and probably the Archbishop Albert of Magdeburg: and also some of the Hussite Leaders--a roll of names celebrated in the history of that stirring time.

Considering the era in which our Author lived, and the nation to which he belonged, he appears to have been somewhat broad in his religious views; for not only does he insist that this Sacred system of Magic may be attained by any one, whether Jew, Christian, Mahometan, or Pagan, but he also continually warns Lamech against the error of changing the religion in which one has been brought up; and he alleges this circumstance as the reason of the occasional failures of the Magician Joseph of Paris (the only other person he mentions besides himself and Abra-Melin who was acquainted with this particular system of Magic), namely that having been brought up a Christian, he had renounced that faith and become a Jew. At first sight it does not seem clear from the Occult Point of view what particular Occult disadvantage should be attached to such a line of action. But we must remember, that in his age, the conversion to another religion invariably meant an absolute, solemn and thorough renunciation and denial of any truth in the religion previously professed by the convert. Herein would be the danger, because whatever the errors, corruption, or mistakes in any particular form of religion, all are based on and descended from the acknowledgment of Supreme Divine Powers. Therefore to deny any religion (instead of only abjuring the mistaken or erroneous parts thereof) would be equivalent to denying formally and ceremonially the truths on which it was originally founded; so that whenever a person having once done this should begin to practise the Operations of the Sacred Magic, he would find himself compelled to affirm with his whole will-force those very formulas which he had at one time magically and ceremonially (though ignorantly) denied; and whenever he attempted to do this, the occult Law of Reaction would raise as a Ceremonial Obstacle against the effect which he should wish to produce, the memory of that Ceremonial Denial which his previous renunciation had firmly sealed in his atmosphere. And the force of this would be in exact Proportion to the manner and degree in which he had renounced his former creed. For of all hindrances to Magical action, the very greatest and most fatal is unbelief, for it checks and stops the action of the Will. Even in the commonest natural operations we see this. No child could learn to walk, no student could assimilate the formulas of any science, were the impracticability and impossibility of so doing the first thing in his mind. Wherefore it is that all Adepts and Great Teachers of Religion and of Magic have invariably insisted on the necessity of faith.

But though apparently more broad in view in admitting the excellence of every religion, unfortunately he shows the usual injustice to and jealousy of women which has distinguished men for so many ages, and which as far as I can see arises purely and simply from an innate consciousness that were women once admitted to compete with them on any plane without being handicapped as they have been for so many centuries, the former would speedily prove their superiority, as the Amazons of old did; which latter (as the writings even of their especial enemies, the Greeks, unwillingly admit) when overcome, were conquered by superior numbers, not by superior valour. However, Abraham the Jew grudgingly admits that the Sacred Magic may he attained by a virgin, while at the same time dissuading any one from teaching it to her! The numerous advanced female occult students of the present day are the best answer to this.

But notwithstanding the forementioned shortcomings, his advice on the manner of using Magical Power, when acquired, to the honour of God, the welfare and relief of our neighbour, and for the benefit of the whole Animate Creation, is worthy of the highest respect; and no one can peruse it without feeling that his highest wish was to act up to his belief.

His counsel, however, of a retired life after attaining Magical Power by his system (I do not speak of the retirement during the six months' preparation for the same) is not borne out by his own account of his life, wherein we find him so constantly involved in the contests and convulsions of the time. Also, however much the life of a hermit or anchorite may appear to be advocated, we rarely, if ever, find it followed by those Adepts whom I may perhaps call the initiated and wonder-working medium between the Great Concealed Adepts and the Outer World. An example of the former class we may find in our Author, an example of the latter in Abra-Melin.

The particular scheme or system of Magic advocated in the present work is to an extent "sui generis," but to an extent only. It is rather the manner of its application which makes it unique. In Magic, that is to say, the Science of the Control of the Secret Forces of Nature, there have always been two great schools, the one great in Good, the other in Evil the former the Magic of Light, the latter that of Darkness the former usually depending on the knowledge and invocation of the Angelic natures, the latter on the method of evocation of the Demonic races. Usually the former is termed White Magic, as opposed to the latter, or Black Magic.

The invocation of Angelic Forces, then, is an idea common in works of Magic, as also are the Ceremonies of Pact with and submission to the Evil Spirits. The system, however, taught in the present work is based on the following conception: (α) That the Good Spirits and Angelic Powers of Light are superior in Power to the Fallen Spirits of Darkness. (β) That these latter as a punishment have been condemned to the service of the Initiates of the Magic of Light. (This Idea is to be found also in the Kôran; or, as it is frequently and perhaps more correctly written, "Qûr-an".) (γ) As a consequence of this doctrine, all ordinary material effects and phenomena are produced by the labour of the Evil Spirits under the command usually of the Good. (δ) That consequently whenever the Evil Demons can escape from the control of the Good, there is no evil that they will not work by way of vengeance. (ϵ) That therefore sooner than obey man, they will try to make him their servant, by inducing him to conclude Pacts and Agreements with them. (ζ) That to further this project, they will use every means that offers to obsess him. (η) That in order to become an Adept, therefore, and dominate them; the greatest possible firmness of will, purity of soul and intent, and power of self-control is necessary. (θ) That this is only to be attained by self-abnegation on every plane. (ι) That man, therefore, is the middle nature, and natural controller of the middle nature between the Angels and the Demons, and that therefore to each man is attached naturally both a Guardian Angel and a Malevolent Demon, and also certain Spirits that may become Familiars, so that with him it rests to give the victory unto the which he will. (κ) That, therefore, in order to control and make service of the Lower and Evil, the knowledge of the Higher and Good is requisite (i.e., in the language of the Theosophy of the present day, the knowledge of the Higher Self).

From this it results that the magnum opus propounded in this work is: by purity and self-denial to obtain the knowledge of and conversation with one's Guardian Angel, so that thereby and thereafter we may obtain the right of using the Evil Spirits for our servants in all material matters.

This, then, is the system of the Secret Magic of Abra-Melin, the Mage, as taught by his disciple Abraham the Yew; and elaborated down to the smallest points.

Except in the professed Black Magic Grimoires, the necessity of the invocation of the Divine and Angelic Forces to control the Demons is invariably insisted upon in the operations of evocation described and taught in Mediæval Magical Manuscripts and published works. So that it is not so much, as I have before said, this circumstance, as the mode of its development by the Six Moons' preparation, which is unusual; while again, the thorough and complete classification of the Demons with their offices, and of the effects to be produced by their services, is not to be found elsewhere.

Apart from the interest attaching to the description of his travels, the careful manner in which Abraham has made note of the various persons he had met professing to be in the possession of Magical powers, what they really could do and could not do, and the reasons of the success or failure of their experiments, has a particular value of its own.

The idea of the employment of a Child as Clairvoyant in the invocation of the Guardian Angel is not unusual; for example, in the "Mendal," a style of Oriental Divination familiar to all readers of Wilkie Collins' novel, "The Moonstone," ink is poured into the palm of a Child's hand, who, after certain mystical words being recited by the Operator, beholds visions clairvoyantly therein. The celebrated evocation at which the great Mediæval Sculptor, Benvenuto Cellini, is said to have assisted, also was in part worked by the aid of a Child as Seer. Cagliostro[3] also is said to have availed himself of the services of Children in this particular. But for my part I cannot understand the imperative necessity of the employment of a Child in the Angelic evocation, if the Operator be pure in mind, and has developed the clairvoyant faculty which is latent in every human being, and which is based on the utilisation of the thought-vision. This thought-vision is exercised almost unconsciously by every one in thinking of either a place, person, or thing, which they know well; immediately, coincident with the thought, the image springs before the mental sight; and it is but the conscious and voluntary development of this which is the basis of what is commonly called clairvoyance. Among the Highlanders of Scotland, the faculty, as is well known, is of common manifestation; and by the English it is usually spoken of as "Second-Sight".

Unfortunately, like far too many modern Occultists, Abraham the Jew shows a marked intolerance of Magical systems differing from his own; even the renowned name of Petrus di Abano[4] is not sufficient to save the "Heptameron or Magical Elements" from condemnation in the concluding part of the Third Book. Works on Magic, Written Conjurations, Pentacles, Seals, and Symbols, the employment of Magical Circles, the use of any language but one's mother tongue, appear at first sight to be damned wholesale, though on a more careful examination of the text I think we shall find that it is rather their abuse through ignorance of their meaning which he intends to decry, than their intelligent and properly regulated use.

It will be well here to carefully examine these points from the occult standpoint of an Initiate, and for the benefit of real students.

Abraham in several places insists that the basis of this system of Sacred Magic is to be found in the Qabalah. Now, he expressly states that he has instructed his eldest son, Joseph, herein as being his right by primogeniture, even as he himself had received somewhat of Qabalistic instruction from his father, Simon. But this system Magic he bequeaths to his younger son, Lamech, expressly as a species of recompense to him for not being taught the Qabalah, his status as a younger son being apparently a serious traditional disqualification. This being so, the reason is evident why he warns Lamech against the use of certain Seals, Pentacles, incomprehensible words, etc.; because most of these being based on the secrets of the Qabalah, their use by a person ignorant hereof might he excessively dangerous through the not only possible but probable perversion of the Secret Formulas therein contained. Any advanced student of Occultism who is conversant with Mediæval works on Magic, whether MS. or printed, knows the enormous and incredible number of errors in the Sigils, Pentacles, and Hebrew or Chaldee Names, which have

3   See Appendix B.
4   Born about 1250.

arisen from ignorant transcription and reproduction; this being carried to such an extent that in some cases the use of the distorted formulas given would actually have the effect of producing the very opposite result to that expected from them. (I have commented at length on this subject in my notes to the "Key of Solomon," published by me a few years ago.) Wherefore Abraham the Jew it appears to me, in his anxiety to save his son from dangerous errors in Magical working, has preferred to endeavour to fill him with contempt for any other systems and methods of operation than the one here laid down. For also besides the unintentional perversions of Magical Symbols I have above mentioned, there was further the circumstance not only possible but probable of the many Black Magic Grimoires falling into his hands, as they evidently had into Abraham's, the Symbols in which are in many cases intentional perversions of Divine Names and Seals, so as to attract the Evil Spirits and repel the Good.

S	A	L	O	M
A	R	E	P	O
L	E	M	E	L
O	P	E	R	A
M	O	L	A	S

For the Third Book of this work is crowded with Qabalistic Squares of Letters, which are simply so many Pentacles, and in which the Names employed are the very factors which make them of value. Among them we find a form of the celebrated SATOR, AREPO, TENET, OPERA, ROTAS, which is one of the Pentacles in the "Key of Solomon" Abraham's formula is slightly different:--and is to be used for obtaining the love of a maiden.

The Pentacle in my "Key of Solomon the King" is classed under Saturn, while the above is applied to the nature of Venus. I give the Hebrew form (see Appendix A, Table of Hebrew and Chaldee Letters) of Equivalents:--Or in Latin Letters:--

S	A	T	O	R
A	R	E	P	O
T	E	N	E	T
O	P	E	R	A
R	O	T	A	S

Sh	A	Th	V	R
A	R	H	P	V
Th	H	N	H	Th
V	P	H	R	A
R	V	Th	A	Sh

In the Key of Solomon it is (as being a Pentacle) inscribed within a double circle, wherein is written the following versicle from Psalm lxxii., v. 8: "His dominion shall be also from the one sea unto the other, and from the flood unto the world's end". In the Hebrew, this versicle consists of exactly twenty-five letters, the number of the letters of the square. It will be at once noticed that both this form and that given by Abraham the Jew are perfect examples of double Acrostics, that is, that they read in every direction, whether horizontal or perpendicular, whether backwards or forwards. But the form given as a Pentacle in the "Key of Solomon the King" is there said to be of value in adversity, and for repressing the pride of the Spirits.

This example therefore shows clearly that it is not so much the use of Symbolic Pentacles that Abraham is opposed to, as their ignorant perversions and inappropriate use.

It is also to be observed, that while many of the Symbolic Squares of Letters of the Third Book present the nature of the double Acrostic, there are also many which do not, and in the case of a great number the letters do not fill up the square entirely, but are arranged somewhat in the form of a gnomon, etc. Others again leave the centre part of the square blank.

In Appendix C[5] to the Introduction I will, for the sake of comparison, give some examples of Angelic invocation taken from other sources.

Abraham the Jew repeatedly admits, as I have before urged, that this particular System of the Sacred Magic of Abra-Melin has its Basis in the Qabalah. It is well to examine what is here meant. The Qabalah itself is divided into many parts; the great bulk of it is of a mystic doctrinal nature, giving the inner Occult meaning to the Jewish Sacred Writings. Also it employs the numerical values of the Hebrew Letters, to draw analogies between words, the total numerical value of whose letters is the same; this branch alone is a most complicated study, and it will be foreign to our purpose to go into it here; the more so as my work, the "Kabbalah Unveiled," treats at length of all these points. The so-called Practical Qabalah is the application of the mystic teachings to the production of Magical ejects. For the classification of Divine and Angelic Names; of Hosts and Orders of Angels, Spirits, and Demons; of particular Names of Archangels, Angels, Intelligences, and Demons, is to be found carried out even to minute detail in the Qabalah, so that the knowledge hereof can give a critical appreciation of the correspondences, sympathies, and antipathies obtaining in the Invisible World. Therefore what Abraham means is, that this system of Sacred Magic is thoroughly reliable, because correct in all its attributions, and that this being so, there is no chance of the Operator using Names and Formulas on wrong occasions and in error.

But also it is notable that Abraham the Jew (probably again with the intent of confusing Lamech as little as possible) speaks only of two great classes of Spirits: the Angels and the Devils; the former to control, the latter to be controlled; and leaves entirely out of consideration, or rather does not describe that vast race of beings, the Elemental Spirits, who in themselves comprise an infinitude of various divisions of classification, some of these being good, some evil, and a great proportion neither the one nor the other. Evidently, also, many of the results proposed to be attained in the Third Book, would imply the use of the Elemental Spirits rather than that of the Demons. No advanced Adept, such as Abraham evidently was, could possibly be ignorant of their existence, power, and value; and we are therefore forced to conclude either that he was unwilling to reveal this knowledge to Lamech; or, which is infinitely more probable, that he feared to confuse him by the large amount of additional instruction which would be necessary to make him thoroughly understand their classification, nature, and offices. This latter line of action would be the less imperative, as the correctness of the symbols of the Third Book would minimise chances of error; and what Abraham is undertaking to teach Lamech, is how to arrive at practical Magical results; rather than the Secret Wisdom of the Qabalah.

It is entirely beyond the scope of this Introduction for me to give here any lengthy dissertation on the natures, good or evil, of Spiritual beings. I will therefore, only state briefly and concisely the principal differences between Angels, Elementals, and Devils.

We may then conclude that Angels, though themselves divided into numerous orders and classes, possess generally the following characteristics: That they are entirely good in nature and operation, the conscient administrators of the Divine Will upon the plane of the material universe; that they are responsible, not irresponsible agents, and therefore capable of fall; and that they are independent of the currents of the infinite Secret Forces of Nature, and can therefore act beyond them, though their classification and qualities will cause them to be more sympathetic with certain among these forces than with the rest, and this in varying degree. Also that they are superior in power to Men, Spirits, Elementals, and Devils.

---

5   See Appendix C, "Examples of Angelic Invocation".

The Elementals on the other hand, though consisting of an infinitude of classes, are the Forces of the Elements of Nature, the administrators of the currents thereof; and can therefore never act beyond and independently of their own particular currents. In a sense, therefore, they are irresponsible for the action of a current as a whole, though responsible for the part thereof in which they Immediately act. Therefore also they are at the same time subject to the general current of the Force, wherein they live, move, and have their being; though superior to the immediate and particular part of it which they direct. Such races, superior to man in intuition, and magical powers; inferior to him in other ways; superior to him in their power in a particular current of an Element; inferior to him in only partaking of the nature of that one Element; are of necessity to be found constantly recurring in all the Mythologies of Antiquity. The Dwarfs and Elves f the Scandinavians; the Nymphs, Hamadryads, and Nature Spirits of the Greeks; the Fairies good and bad of the legends dear to our childish days; the host of Mermaids, Satyrs, Fauns, Sylphs, and Fays; the Forces intended to be attracted and propitiated by the Fetishes of the Negro-Race; are for the most part no other thing than the ill-understood manifestations of this great class, the Elementals. Among these, some, as I have before observed, are good; such are the Salamanders, Undines, Sylphs, and Gnomes, of the Rosicrucian Philosophy; many are frightfully malignant, delighting in every kind of evil, and might easily be mistaken for Devils by the uninitiated, save that their power is less; a great proportion are neither good nor evil, irrationally working either; just as a monkey or a parrot might act; in fact such closely resemble animals in their nature, and especially combinations of animals, in which forms distorted and mingled, would lie their symbolic manifestation. Another very large class, would not act irrationally in this manner; but with intent, only always following the predominant force either good or evil in their then entourage; a spirit of this kind, for example, attracted into an assembly of good persons would endeavour to excite their ideas towards good; attracted among evil-minded persons would incite them mentally to crime. Among how many criminals is not their only excuse that "they thought they kept hearing something telling them to commit the crime"! Yet these suggestions would not always arise from Elementals alone, but frequently from the depraved astral remnants of deceased evil persons.

Devils, on the other hand, are far more powerful than Elementals, but their action for Evil is parallel to that of the Good Angels for Good; and their malignancy is far more terrible than that of the Evil Elementals, for not being, like them, subjected to the limits of a certain current, their sphere of operation extends over a far greater area; while the Evil they commit is never irrational or mechanical, but worked with full consciousness and intent.

I do not agree entirely with the manner of behaviour, advised by Abraham towards the Spirits; on the contrary, the true Initiates have always maintained that the very greatest courtesy should be manifested by the Exorciser, and that it is only when they are obstinate and recalcitrant that severer measures should he resorted to; and that even with the Devils we should not reproach them for their condition; seeing that a contrary line of action is certain to lead the Magician into error. But, perhaps, Abraham has rather intended to warn Lamech against the danger of yielding to them in an Exorcism even in the slightest degree.

The word "Demon" is evidently employed in this work almost as a synonym of Devil; but, as most educated people are aware, it is derived from the Greek "Daimon," which anciently simply meant any Spirit, good or bad.

A work filled with suggestive Magical references is the well-known "Arabian Nights," and it is interesting to notice the number of directions in the Third Book of this work for producing similar effects to those there celebrated.

For example, the ninth chapter of the Third Book gives the symbols to be employed for changing human beings into animals, one of the commonest incidents in the "Arabian Nights," as in the story of the "first old man and the hind," that of the "three Calendars and the five ladies of Bagdad," that of "Beder and Giauhare," etc., etc.; as distinct from the voluntary transformation of the Magician into another form, as exemplified in the "story of the Second Calendar," the symbols for which are given in the twenty-first chapter of our Third Book.

Again these chapters will recall to many of my readers the extraordinary magical effects which Faust is said to have produced; who, by the way, as I have before remarked, was in all probability contemporary with Abraham the Jew.

But the mode of their production as given in this work is not the Black Magic of Pact and Devil-worship, against which our Author so constantly inveighs, but instead a system of Qabalistic Magic, similar to that of the "Key of Solomon the King" and the "Clavicles of Rabbi Solomon," though differing in the circumstance of the prior invocation of the Guardian Angel once for all, while in the works I have just mentioned the Angels are invoked in each Evocation by means of the Magical Circle. Such works as these, then, and their like, it could not be the intention of Abraham to decry, seeing that like his system they are founded on the Secret Knowledge of the Qabalah; as this in its turn was derived from that mighty scheme of Ancient Wisdom, the Initiated Magic of Egypt. For to any deep student at the same time of the Qabalah and of modern Egyptology, the root and origin of the former is evidently to be sought in that country of Mysteries, the home of the Gods whose symbols and classification formed so conspicuous a part of the Sacred Rites; and from which even to the present day, so many recipes of Magic have descended. For we must make a very careful distinction between the really Ancient Egyptian Magic, and the Arabian ideas and traditions prevailing in Egypt in recent times. I think it is the learned Lenormant who points out in his work on Chaldean Magic, that the great difference between this and the Egyptian was that the Magician of the former School indeed invoked the Spirits, but that the latter allied himself with and took upon himself the characters and names of the Gods to command the Spirits by, in his Exorcism; which latter mode of working would not only imply on his part a critical knowledge of the nature and power of the Gods; but also the affirmation of his reliance upon them, and his appeal to them for aid to control the forces evoked; in other words, the most profound system of White Magic which it is possible to conceive.

The next point worthy of notice is what Abraham urges regarding the preferability of employing one's mother tongue both in prayer and evocation; his chief reason being the absolute necessity of comprehending utterly and thoroughly with the whole soul and heart, that which the lips are formulating. While fully admitting the necessity of this, I yet wish to state some reasons in favour of the employment of a language other than one's own. Chief, and first, that it aids the mind to conceive the higher aspect of the Operation; when a different language and one looked upon as sacred is employed, and the phrases in which do not therefore suggest matters of ordinary life. Next, that Hebrew, Chaldee, Egyptian, Greek, Latin, etc., if properly pronounced are more sonorous in vibration than most modern languages, and from that circumstance can suggest greater solemnity. Also that the farther a Magical Operation is removed from the commonplace, the better. But I perfectly agree with Abraham, that it is before all things imperative that the Operator should thoroughly comprehend the import of his Prayer or Conjuration. Furthermore the words in these ancient languages imply "formulas of correspondences" with more ease than those of the modern ones.

Pentacles and Symbols are valuable as an equilibrated and fitting basis for the reception of Magical force; but unless the Operator can really attract that force to them, they are nothing but so many dead, and to him worthless, diagrams. But used by the Initiate who fully comprehends their meaning, they become to him a powerful protection and aid, seconding and focussing the workings of his Will.

At the risk of repeating what I have elsewhere said, I must caution the Occult student against forming a mistaken judgment from what Abraham the Jew says regarding the use of Magic Circles and of Licensing the Spirits to Depart. It is true that in the Convocation of the Spirits as laid down by him, it is not necessary to form a Magic Circle for defence and protection; but why?--Because the whole group of the Bedchamber, Oratory, and Terrace, are consecrated by the preparatory Ceremonies of the previous Six Moons; so that the whole place is protected, and the Magician is, as it were, residing constantly within a Magic Circle. Therefore also the Licensing to Depart may be to a great extent dispensed with because the Spirits cannot break into the consecrated limit of the periphery of the walls of the house. But let the worker of ordinary Evocations be assured that were this not so, and the Convocation was performed in an unconsecrated place, without any Magical Circle having been traced for defence, the invocation to visible appearance of such fearful potencies as Amaymon, Egyn, and Beelzebub, would probably result in the death of the Exorcist on the spot; such death presenting the symptoms of one arising from Epilepsy, Apoplexy, or Strangulation, varying with the conditions obtaining at the time. Also the Circle having been once formed, let the Evocator guard carefully against either passing, or stooping, or leaning beyond, its limits during the progress of the Exorcism, before the license to depart has been given. Because that, even apart from other causes, the whole object and effect of the Circle working, is to create abnormal atmospheric conditions, by exciting a different status of force within the Circle to that which exists without it; so that even without any malignant occult action of the Spirits, the sudden and unprepared change of atmosphere will seriously affect the Exorciser in the intensely strained state of nervous tension he will then be in. Also the License to Depart should not be omitted, because the Evil Forces will be only too glad to revenge themselves on the Operator for having disturbed them, should he incautiously quit the Circle without having previously sent them away, and if necessary even forced them to go by contrary conjurations.

I do not share Abraham's opinion as to the necessity of withholding the Operation of this Sacred Magic from a Prince or Potentate. Every great system of Occultism has its own Occult Guards, who will know how to avenge mistaken tampering therewith.

At the risk of repeating myself I will once more earnestly caution the Student against the dangerous automatic nature of certain of the Magical Squares of the Third Book; for, if left carelessly about, they are very liable to obsess sensitive persons, children, or even animals.

Abraham's remarks concerning the errors of Astrology in the common sense, and of the attribution of the Planetary Hours are worthy of careful note. Yet I have found the ordinary attribution of the Planetary Hours effective to an extent.

In all cases where there is anything difficult or obscure in the text, I have added copious explanatory notes; so many indeed as to form a species of commentary in parts. Especially have those on the Names of the Spirits cost me incredible labour, from the difficulty of identifying their root-forms. The same may be said of those on the Symbols of the Third Book.

Wherever I have employed parentheses in the actual text, they shew certain words or phrases supplied to make the meaning clearer.

In conclusion I will only say that I have written this explanatory Introduction purely and solely as a help to genuine Occult students; and that for the opinion of the ordinary literary critic who neither understands nor believes in Occultism, I care nothing.

87 RUE MOZART, AUTEUIL, PARIS.

APPENDIX A.
HEBREW AND CHALDEE ALPHABET

Number.	Sound or Power.	Hebrew and Chaldee Letters.	Numerical Value.	How expressed in this work by Roman Letters.	Hebrew Name of Letter.	Signification of Name.
1.	a (soft breathing).	א	1 1	A.	Aleph.	Ox, also Duke, or Leader.
2.	b, bh (v).	ב	2	B.	Beth.	House.
3.	g (hard), gh.	ג	3	G.	Gimel.	Camel.
4.	d, dh (flat th).	ד	4	D.	Daleth.	Door.
5.	h (rough breathing).	ה	5	H.	Hé.	Window.
6.	v, u, o.	ו	6	V.	Vau.	Peg, Nail.
7.	z, dz.	ז	7	Z.	Zayin.	Weapon, Sword.
8.	ch (guttural).	ח	8	Ch	Cheth.	Enclosure, Fence.
9.	t (strong).	ט	9	T.	Teth.	Serpent.
10.	i, y (as in yes).	י	10	I.	Yōd.	Hand.
11.	k, kh.	כ Final = ך	20 Final = 500	K.	Kaph.	Palm of the hand.
12.	l.	ל	30	L.	Lamed.	Ox-Goad.
13.	m.	מ Final = ם	40 Final = 600	M.	Mem.	Water.
14.	n.	נ Final = ן	50 Final = 700	N.	Nun.	Fish.
15.	s.	ס	60	S.	Samekh.	Prop, Support.
16.	o, aa, ng (guttural).	ע	70	O.	Ayin.	Eye.
17.	p, ph.	פ Final = ף	80 Final = 800	P.	Pé.	Mouth.
18.	ts, tz, j.	צ Final = ץ	90 Final = 900.	Tz.	Tzaddi.	Fishing-hook.
19.	q, qh (guttural).	ק	100 2	Q.	Qoph.	Back of the head.
20.	r.	ר	200	R.	Resh.	Head.
21.	sh, s.	ש	300	Sh.	Shin.	Tooth.
22.	th, t.	ת	400	Th.	Tau.	Sign of the Cross.

NOTE:--It is to be remembered that in Hebrew the Vowels are supplied by certain points and marks added to the letters; and that the Transliteration into Roman Letters given in the fifth column of this Table is not intended to give the full power of the Hebrew letters; which is shewn in column two.

APPENDIX B.
EMPLOYMENT OF A CHILD-CLAIRVOYANT BY CAGLIOSTRO

THE well-known Joseph Balsamo, Count Cagliostro, is said to have been born at Palermo in 1743. On his trial at Rome in 1790, and at Zurich in 1791, he was accused of "having practised all kinds of impositions; of gold making, and of possessing the secret of prolonging life; of teaching Cabalistic Arts; of summoning and exorcising Spirits; of having actually foretold future things especially in small and secret assemblies, and chiefly by means of a little boy whom he took aside with him into a separate room, in order to fit him for divining".

With regard to the manner in which he employed this Child-Clairvoyant, the documents of the trial give the following information:-

-"This Child had to kneel before a small table, on which a vessel of water and some lighted candles were placed.

He then instructed the boy to look into the vessel of water, and so commenced his conjurations; he next laid his hand on the head of the Child, and in this position addressed a prayer to God for a successful issue of the experiment. The Child now became clairvoyant, and said at first that he saw something white; then that he saw visions, an Angel, etc."

Again the documents say, "That he worked through the usual ceremonies, and that all was wonderfully corroborated through the appearance of the Angel".

Cagliostro is also said at Milan to have availed himself of the services of an orphan maiden of marriageable age as clairvoyant.

It will be remarked that this modus operandi differs strongly from that employed by the mesmerists and hypnotists of to-day with their clairvoyants.

For here the whole force of the Operator was concentrated on a magical ritual of evocation, the hand being merely laid on the child's head to form a link; and it in no way appears that the child was reduced to the miserable condition of automatic trance now practised, and which a really advanced Occultist would be the first to condemn, as knowing its dangers.

On the other hand, there seems to be a distinct similarity between Cagliostro's method, and the system of Oriental Divination called the Mendal, to which I have previously referred.

APPENDIX C.

EXAMPLES OF OTHER METHODS OF ANGELIC EVOCATION

FOR the benefit of the Occult Student I here give two other systems of Angelic Evocation. The first is taken from that part of the Book called "Barrett's Magus" (1801), which is entitled "the Key to Ceremonial Magic". The second is copied from my Key of Solomon the King".

From
The Perfection and Key of . . . Ceremonial Magic";
being the second part of the second Book of
"The Magus
or
Celestial Intelligencer";[6]
by
Francis Barrett, F.R.C.

"The good Spirits may be invoked of us, or by us, divers ways, and they in sundry shapes and manners offer themselves to us, for they openly speak to those that watch, and do offer themselves to our sight, or do inform us by dreams and by oracle of those things which we have a great desire to know. Whoever therefore would call any good Spirit to speak or appear in sight, he must particularly observe two things; one whereof is about the disposition of the invocant, the other concerning those things which are outwardly to be adhibited to the invocation for the conformity of the Spirit to be called.

"It is necessary therefore that the invocant religiously dispose himself for the space of many days to such a mystery, and to conserve himself during the time chaste, abstinent, and to abstract himself as much as he can from all manner of foreign and secular business; likewise he should observe fasting, as much as shall seem convenient to him, and let him daily, between sun-rising and setting, being clothed in pure white linen, seven times call upon God, and make a deprecation unto the Angels to be called and invocated, according to the rule which we have before taught. Now the number of days of fasting and preparation is commonly one month, i.e., the time of a whole lunation. Now, in the Cabala, we generally prepare ourselves forty days before.

"Now concerning the place, it must be chosen clean, pure, close, quiet, free from all manner of noise, and not subject to any stranger's sight. This place must first of all be exorcised and consecrated; and let there be a Table or Altar placed therein, covered with a clean white linen cloth, and set towards the east: and on each side thereof place two consecrated wax-lights burning, the flame thereof ought not to go out all these days. In the middle of the Altar let there be placed lamens, or the holy paper we have before described, covered with fine linen, which is not to be opened until the end of the days of consecration. You shall also have in readiness a precious perfume and a pyre anointing oil. And let them both be kept consecrated. Then set a censer on the head of the Altar, wherein you shall kindle the holy fire, and make a precious perfume every day that you pray.

"Now for your habit, you shall have a long garment of white linen, close before and behind, which may come down quite over the feet, and gird yourself about the loins with a girdle. You shall likewise have a veil made of pure white linen on which must be wrote in a gilt lamen, the name Tetragrammaton; all which things are to be consecrated and sanctified in order. But you must not go into this holy place till it be first washed and covered with a cloth new and clean, and then you may enter, but with your feet naked and bare; and when you enter therein you shall sprinkle with holy water, then make a perfume upon the altar; and then on your knees pray before

6   Published originally by Lackington & Allen, London, 1801; but reprinted and re-issued by Bernard Quaritch, Piccadilly, some years since.

the altar as we have directed.

"Now when the time is expired, on the last day, you shall fast more strictly; and fasting on the day following, at the rising of the sun, enter the holy place, using the ceremonies before spoken of, first by sprinkling thyself, then, making, a perfume, you shall sign the cross with holy oil on the forehead, and anoint your eyes, using prayer in all these consecrations. Then open the lamen and pray before the Altar upon your knees; and then an invocation may be made as follows:--

AN INVOCATION OF THE GOOD SPIRITS.

"IN the Name of the Blessed and Holy Trinity, I do desire ye, strong and mighty Angels (here name the Spirit or Spirits you would have appear), that if it be the Divine Will of Him Who is called Tetragrammaton, etc., the Holy God, the Father, that ye take upon ye: some shape as best becometh your celestial nature, and appear to us visibly here in this place, and answer our demands, in as far as we shall not transgress the bounds of the Divine mercy and goodness, by requesting unlawful knowledge; but that thou wilt graciously shew us what things are most profitable for us to know and do, to the glory and honour of His Divine Majesty Who liveth and reigneth world without end. Amen.

"Lord, Thy Will be done on earth as it is in heaven--make clean our hearts within us, and take not Thy Holy Spirit from us. O Lord, by Thy Name we have called them, suffer them to administer unto us.

"And that all things may work together for Thy Honour and Glory, to Whom with Thee, the Son and blessed Spirit, be ascribed all might, majesty, and dominion, world without end. Amen.

"The Invocation being made, the Good Angels will appear unto you which you desire, which you shall entertain with a chaste communication, and licence them to depart.

"Now the Lamen which is used to invoke. any Good Spirit must be made after the following manner: either in metal conformable or in new wax mixed with convenient spices and colours; or it may be made with pure white paper with convenient colours, and the outward form of it may be either square, circular, or triangular, or of the like sort, according to the rule of the numbers; in[7] or character of six corners; in the middle thereof write the Name and Character of the Star, or of the Spirit his Governor, to whom the Good Spirit that is to be called is subject. And about this Character let there be placed so many Characters of five corners, or pentacles[8] as the Spirits we would call together at once. But if we should call only one, nevertheless there must be made four pentagons, wherein the name of the Spirit or Spirits with their characters are to be written. Now this Lamen ought to be composed when the Moon is in her increase, on those days and hours which agree to the Spirit; and if we take a fortunate planet therewith, it will be the better for the producing the effect; which Table or Lamen being rightly made in the manner we have fully described, must be consecrated according to the rules above delivered.

"And this is the way of making the general Table or Lamen for the invocating of all Spirits whatever; the form whereof you may see in plates of pentacles, seals, and lamens.

"We will yet declare unto you another rite more easy to perform this thing: Let the Man who wishes to receive an oracle from a Spirit, be chaste, pure, and sanctified; then a place being chosen pure, clean, and covered everywhere with clean and white linen, on the Lord's-day in the new of the Moon, let him enter into that place clothed with white linen; let him exorcise the place, bless it, and make a circle therein with a consecrated coal; let there be written in the outer part of the Circle the Names of the Angels; in the inner part thereof write the Mighty Names of

---

7   Probably an error for "hexagram, or "hexangle".

8   Probably an error for "pentagrams," or "pentangles".

God; and let be placed within the Circle, at the Four Parts of the World,[9] the vessels for the perfumes. Then being washed and fasting, let him enter the place, and pray towards the East this whole Psalm:--"Blessed are the undefiled in the way, etc.". Psalm cix. Then make a fumigation, and deprecate the Angels by the said Divine Names, that they will appear unto you, and reveal or discover that which you so earnestly desire; and do this continually for six days washed, and fasting. On the seventh day being washed and fasting, enter the Circle, perfume it, and anoint thyself with holy oil upon the forehead, eyes, and in the palms of both hands, and upon the feet; then with bended knees, say the Psalm aforesaid, with Divine and Angelical Names. Which being said, arise, and walk round the Circle from East to West, until thou shalt be wearied with a giddiness of thy head and brain, then straightway fall down in the Circle, where thou mayest rest, and thou wilt be wrapped up in an ecstasy; and a Spirit will appear and inform thee of all things necessary to be known. We must observe also, that in the Circle there ought to be four holy God, I the Minister and faithful Servant of the Most High conjure ye, let God Himself, the Existence of Existences, conjure ye to come and be present at this Operation; I the Servant of God, most humbly entreat ye. Amen.

"After which thou shalt incense it with the incense proper to the Planet and the Day, and thou shalt replace the Book on the aforesaid table, taking heed that the Fire of the Lamp be kept up continually during the operation, and keeping the curtains closed. Repeat the same Ceremony for seven days, beginning with Saturday, and perfuming the Book each day with the Incense proper to the Planet ruling the day and hour, and taking heed that the Lamp shall burn both day and night; after the which thou shalt shut up the Book in a small Drawer under the table, made expressly for it, until thou shalt have occasion to use it; and every time that thou wishest to use it, clothe thyself with thy vestments, kindle the lamp, and repeat upon thy knees the aforesaid prayer, 'ADONAI, ELOHIM,' etc.

"It is necessary also in the Consecration of the Book, to summon all the Angels whose Names are written therein in the form of Litanies, the which thou shalt do with devotion; and even if the Angels and Spirits appear not in the Consecration of the Book, be not thou astonished thereat, seeing that they are of a pure nature, and consequently have much difficulty in familiarising themselves with men who are inconstant and impure, but the Ceremonies and Characters being correctly carried out, devoutly, and with perseverance, they will be constrained to come, and it will at length happen that at thy first invocation thou wilt be able to see and communicate with them. But I advise thee to undertake nothing unclean or impure, for then thy importunity, far from attracting them will only serve to chase them from thee; and it will be thereafter exceedingly difficult for thee to attract them for use for pure ends." candles burning at the Four Parts of the World, which ought not to want light for the space of a week.

"And the manner of fasting is this: to abstain from all things having a life of sense, and from those which do proceed from them, let him drink only pure running water; neither is there any food or wine to be taken till the going down of the Sun.

"Let the perfume and the holy anointing oil be made as is set forth in Exodus, and other holy books of the Bible. It is also to be observed, that as often as he enters the Circle he has upon his forehead a golden lamen, upon which must be written the Name Tetragrammaton, in the manner we have before mentioned."

In "The Key of Solomon the King"[10] (Book II.--Chapter XXI.) will be found other directions for invoking spirits as follows:--

"Make a small Book containing the Prayers for all the Operations, the Names of the Angels in the form of Litanies, their Seals and Characters; the which being done thou shalt consecrate

---

9   I.e., The Cardinal Points, or Quarters.

10   Published by G. Redway, London, 1889.

the same unto God and unto the pure Spirits in the manner following:--

"Thou shalt set in the destined place a small table covered with a white cloth, whereon thou shalt lay the Book opened at the Great Pentacle which should be drawn on the first leaf of the said Book; and having kindled a lamp which should be suspended above the centre of the table, thou shalt surround the said table with a white curtain;[11] clothe thyself in the proper vestments, and holding the Book open, repeat upon thy knees the following prayer with great humility:--

THE PRAYER.

ADONAI, ELOHIM, EL, EHEIEH ASHER EHEIEH, Prince of Princes, Existence of Existences, have mercy upon me, and cast Thine eyes upon Thy servant (N.) who invoketh Thee most devoutly, and supplicateth Thee by Thy Holy and tremendous Name, Tetragrammaton, to be propitious and to order Thine Angels and Spirits to come and take up their abode in this place; O ye Angels and Spirits of the Stars, O all ye Angels and Elementary Spirits, O all ye Spirits present before the Face of

---

11   So as to make a species of small tabernacle around the altar.

THE FIRST BOOK

OF THE

HOLY MAGIC,

WHICH GOD GAVE UNTO MOSES, AARON, DA-VID, SOLOMON, AND OTHER

SAINTS, PATRIARCHS AND PROPHETS; WHICH TEACHETH

THE TRUE DIVINE WISDOM.

BEQUEATHED BY ABRAHAM UNTO LAMECH HIS SON.

TRANSLATED FROM THE HEBREW.

1458

THE FIRST BOOK OF THE HOLY MAGIC.

ALTHOUGH this First Book serveth rather for prologue than for the actual rules to acquire this Divine and Sacred Magic nevertheless, O! Lamech, my son, thou wilt therein find certain examples and other matters[12] which will be none the less useful and profitable unto thee than the precepts and dogmas which I shall give thee in the Second and Third Books. Wherefore thou shalt not neglect the study of this First Book, <u>which shall serve</u> thee for an introduction[13] unto the Veritable and Sacred Magic, and unto the practice of

12   Des exemples et des circonstances.

13   D'acheminement.

that which I, ABRAHAM, THE SON OF SIMON, have learned, in part from my father, and in part also from other Wise and faithful Men, and which I have found true and real, having submitted it unto proof and experiment. And having written this with mine own hand, I have placed it within this casket, and locked it up, as a most precious treasure; in order that when thou hast arrived at a proper age thou mayest be able to admire, to consider, and to enjoy the marvels of the Lord; as well as thine elder brother Joseph, who, as the first-born, hath received from me the Holy Tradition of the Qabalah.[14]

THE FIRST CHAPTER

LAMECH, if thou wishest to know the reason wherefore I give unto thee this Book, it is that if thou considerest thy condition, which is that of being a last-born Son, thou shalt know wherefore it appertaineth unto thee; and I should commit a great error should I deprive thee of that grace which God hath given unto me with so much profusion and liberality. I will then make every effort to avoid and to fly prolixity of words in this First Book; having alone in view the ancientness of this Venerable and Indubitable Science. And seeing that TRUTH hath no need of enlightenment and of exposition, she being simple and right; be thou only obedient unto all that I shall say unto thee, contenting thyself with the simplicity thereof, be thou good and upright, [15] and thou shalt acquire more wealth than I could know how to promise unto thee. May the Only and Most Holy God grant unto all, the grace necessary to be able to comprehend and penetrate the high Mysteries of the Qabalah and of the Law; but they should content themselves with that which the Lord accordeth unto them; seeing that if against His Divine Will they wish to fly yet higher, even as did Lucifer, this will but procure for them a most shameful and fatal fall. Wherefore it is necessary to be extremely prudent, and to consider the INTENTION which I have had in describing this method of operation; because in consideration of thy great youth I attempt no other thing but to excite thee unto the research of this Sacred Magic. But the manner of acquiring the same will come later, in all its perfection, and in its proper time; for it will be taught thee by better Masters than I, that is to say, by those same Holy Angels of God. No man is born into the World a Master, and for that reason are we obliged to learn. He who applieth himself thereunto, and studieth, learneth; and a man can have no more shameful and evil title [16]than that of being an Ignorant person.

THE SECOND CHAPTER

THEREFORE do I confess, that I, even I also, am not born a MASTER; neither have I invented this science of my own proper Genius; but I have learned it from others in the manner which I will hereafter tell thee, and in truth.

My father, SIMON, shortly before his death, gave me certain signs and instructions concerning the way in which it is necessary to acquire the Holy Qabalah; but it is however true that he did not enter into the Holy Mystery by the true Path, and I could not know how to understand the same sufficiently and perfectly as Reason demanded. My father was always contented and satisfied with

---

14   I consider this a truer orthography of the word than the usual rendering of "Cabala".

15   Réel.

16   This is identical with the Oriental doctrine that Ignorance is in itself evil and unhappiness.

such a method of understanding the same, and he sought out no further the Veritable Science and Magical Art, which I undertake to teach thee and to expound unto thee.

After his death, finding myself twenty years of age, I had a very great passion to understand the True Mysteries of the Lord; but of mine own strength I could not arrive at the end which I intended to attain.

I learned that at Mayence there was a Rabbi who was a notable Sage, and the report went that he possessed in full the Divine Wisdom. The great desire which I had to study induced me to go to seek him in order to learn from him. But this man also had not received from the Lord the GIFT, and a perfect grace; because, although he forced himself to manifest unto me certain deep Mysteries of the Holy Qabalah, he by no means arrived at the goal; and in his Magic he did not in any way make use of the Wisdom of the Lord, but instead availed himself of certain arts and superstitions of infidel and idolatrous nations, in part derived from the Egyptians,[17] together with images of the Medes and of the Persians, with herbs of the Arabians, together with the power of the Stars and Constellations; and, finally, he had drawn from every people and nation, and even from the Christians, some diabolical Art. And in everything the Spirits blinded him to such an extent, even while obeying him in some ridiculous and inconsequent matter, that he actually believed that his blindness and error were the Veritable Magic, and be therefore pushed no further his research into the True and Sacred Magic. I also learned his extravagant experiments, and for ten years did I remain buried in so great an error, until that after the ten years I arrived in Egypt at the house of an Ancient Sage who was called ABRAMELIM, who put me into the true Path as I will declare it unto thee hereafter, and he gave me better instruction and doctrine than all the others; but this particular grace was granted me by the Almighty Father of all Mercy, that is to say, ALMIGHTY GOD, who little by little illuminated mine understanding and opened mine eyes to see and admire, to contemplate, and search out His Divine Wisdom, in such a manner that it became possible unto me to further and further understand and comprehend the Sacred Mystery by which I entered into the knowledge of the Holy Angels, enjoying their sight and their sacred conversation, from whom[18] at length I received afterwards the foundation of the Veritable Magic, and how to command and dominate the Evil Spirits. So that by way of conclusion unto this chapter I cannot say that I have otherwise received the True Instruction save from ABRAMELIM, [19] and the True and Incorruptible Magic save from the Holy Angels of God.

THE THIRD CHAPTER

I HAVE already said in the preceding chapter that shortly after the death of my father, I attached myself unto the research of the True Wisdom, and of the Mystery of the Lord. Now in this chapter I will briefly mention the places and countries by which I have passed in order to endeavour to learn those things which are good. And I do this in order that it may serve thee for a rule and example not to waste thy youth in petty and useless pursuits, like little girls sitting round the fireplace. For there is nothing more deplorable and more unworthy in a man than to find himself ignorant in all circumstances. He who worketh and travelleth learneth much and he who knoweth not how to conduct and govern himself when far from his native land,

17   Yet the true Qabalah is undoubtedly derived from the Egyptian and Eastern Wisdom.

18   I.e. from the Angels.

19   This name is spelt "Abramelin" in some places, and "Abramelim" in others. I have consequently carefully in all cases put the orthography as it there occurs in the MS.

will know still less in his own house how to do so. I dwelt then, after the death of my father, for four years with my brothers and sisters, and I studied with care how to put to a profitable use what my father had left me after his death; and seeing that my means were insufficient to counterbalance the expenses which I was compelled to be at, after having set in order all my affairs and business as well as my strength permitted; I set out, and I went into Vormatia[20] to Mayence, in order to find there a very aged Rabbi named Moses, in the hope that I had found in him that which I sought. As I have said in the preceding chapter, his Science had no foundation such as that of the True Divine Wisdom. I remained with him for four years, miserably wasting all that time there, and persuading myself that I had learned all that I wished to know, [21] and I was only thinking of returning to my paternal home, when I casually met a young man of our sect, named SAMUEL, a native of Bohemia, whose manners and mode of life showed me that be wished to live, walk, and die in the Way of the Lord and in His Holy Law; and I contracted so strong a bond of friendship with him that I showed him all my feelings and intentions. As he had resolved to make a journey to Constantinople, in order to there join a brother of his father, and thence to pass into the Holy Land wherein our forefathers had dwelt, and from the which for our very great errors and misdeeds we had been chased and cast forth by God. He, [22] having so willed it, the moment that he [23] had made me acquainted with his design, I felt an extraordinary desire to accompany him in his journey, and I believe that Almighty God wished by this means to awaken me, for I could take no rest until the moment that we mutually and reciprocally passed our word to each other and swore to make the voyage together.

On the 13th day of February, in the year 1397, we commenced our journey, passing through Germany, Bohemia, Austria, and thence by Hungary and Greece unto Constantinople, where we remained two years, and I should never have quitted it, had not death taken Samuel from me at length through a sudden illness. Finding myself alone, a fresh desire for travel seized me, and so much was my heart given thereto, that I kept wandering from one place to another, until at length I arrived in Egypt, where constantly travelling for the space of four years in one direction and another, the more I practised the experiments of the magic of RABBIN MOSES, the less did it please me. I pursued my voyage towards our ancient country, where I fixed my residence for a year, and neither saw nor heard of any other thing but misery, calamity, and unhappiness. After this period of time, I there found a Christian who also was travelling in order to find that which I was seeking also myself Having made an agreement together, we resolved to go into the desert parts of Arabia for the search for that which we ardently desired; feeling sure that, as we had been told, there were in those places many just and very learned men, who dwelt there in order to be able to study without any hindrance, and to devote themselves unto that Art for which we ourselves were seeking; but as we there found nothing equivalent to the trouble we had taken, or which was worthy of our attention, there came into my head the extravagant idea to advance no farther, but to return to my own home. I communicated my intention to my companion, but he for his part wished to follow out his enterprise and seek his good fortune; so I prepared to return,

---

20   " Vormatie"; that is to say, the district under the government of the town of Worms, called in Latin "Vormatia" anciently.

21   in the previous chapter he says that he remained in this path of study for ten years.

22   I.e., God.

23   Samuel.

THE FOURTH CHAPTER

IN my return journey I began to reflect on the time which I had lost in travelling, and on the great expense which I had been at without any return, and without having made any acquisition of that which I wished for and which had caused me to undertake the voyage. I had, however, taken the resolution of returning to my home on quitting Arabia Deserta by way of Palestine, and so into Egypt; and I was six months on the way. I at length arrived at a little town called ARACHI, situated on the bank of the Nile, where I lodged with an old Jew named AARON, where indeed I had already lodged before in my journey; and I communicated unto him my sentiments. He asked me how I had succeeded, and whether I had found that which I wished. I answered mournfully that I had done absolutely nothing, and I made him an exact recital of the labours and troubles which I had undergone, and my recital was accompanied by my tears which I could not help shedding in abundance, so that I attracted the compassion of the old man, and he began to try to comfort me by telling me that during my journey he had heard say that in a desert place not far from the aforesaid town of ARACHI dwelt a very learned and pious man whose name was ABRAMELINO,[24] and he[25] exhorted me that as I had already done so much, not to fail to visit him, that perhaps the Most Merciful God might regard me with pity, and grant me that which I righteously wished for. It seemed to me as though I was listening to a Voice, not human but celestial, and I felt a joy in mine heart such as I could not express; and I had neither rest nor intermission until AARON found me a man who conducted me to the nearest route, by which walking upon fine sand during the space of three days and a half without seeing any human habitation I at length arrived at the foot of a hill of no great height, and which was entirely surrounded by trees. My Guide then said "In this small wood dwelleth the man whom you seek;" and having showed me the direction to take he wished to accompany me no further, and having taken his leave of me he returned home by the same route by which we had come, together with his mule which had served to carry our food. Finding myself in this situation I could think of no other thing to do than to submit myself to the help of the Divine Providence by invoking His very holy Name, Who then granted unto me His most holy Grace, for in turning my eyes in the aforementioned direction, I beheld coining towards me a venerable aged Man, who saluted me in the Chaldean language in a loving manner, inviting me to go with him into his habitation; the which courtesy I accepted with an extreme pleasure, realising in that moment how great is the Providence of the Lord. The good old Man was very courteous to me and treated me very kindly, and during an infinitude of days he never spake unto me of any other matter than of the Fear of God, exhorting me to lead ever a well-regulated life, and from time to time warned me of certain errors which man commits through human frailty, and, further, he made me understand that he detested the acquisition of riches and goods which we were constantly employed in gaining in our towns through so severe usury exacted from, and harm wrought to, our neighbour. He required from me a very solemn and precise promise to change my manner of life, and to live not according to our false dogmas, but in the Way and Law of the Lord. The which promise I having ever after inviolably observed, and being later on again among my relatives and other Jews, I passed among them for a wicked and foolish man; but I said in myself Let the Will of God be done, and let not respect of persons turn us aside from the right path, seeing that man is a deceiver".

The aforesaid ABRAMELIN, knowing the ardent desire which I had to learn, he gave me two manuscript books, very similar in form unto these which I now bequeath unto thee, O Lamech, my son; but very obscure: and he told me to copy them for myself with care, which I did, and carefully examined both the one and the other. And he asked me if I had any money, I answered unto him "Yes". He said unto me that he required ten golden florins, which he must himself, according to

---

24   Thus spelt here.

25   Aaron the Jew.

the order which the Lord had given unto him, distribute by way of alms among seventy-two poor persons, who were obliged to repeat certain Psalms;[26] and having kept the feast of Saturday, which is the day of the Sabbath, he set out to go to ARACHI, because it was requisite that he should himself distribute the money. And he ordered me to fast for three days, that is to say, the Wednesday, Thursday, and Friday following; contenting myself with only a single repast in the day, wherein was to be neither blood nor dead things;[27] also he commanded me to make this commencement with exactness, and not to fail in the least thing, for in order to operate well it is very necessary to begin well, and be instructed me to repeat all the seven[28] psalms of David one single time in these three days; and not to do or practise any servile operation. The day being come he set out, and took with him the money which I had given him. I faithfully obeyed him, executing from point to point that which he had ordered me to do. His return was fifteen days later, and being at last arrived he ordered me the day following (which was a Tuesday), before the rising of the Sun, to make with great humility and devotion a general confession of all my life unto the Lord, with a true and firm proposal and resolution to serve and fear Him otherwise than I had done in the past, and to wish to live and die in His most Holy Law, and in obedience unto Him. I performed my confession with all the attention and exactitude necessary. It lasted until the going down of the Sun; and the day following I presented myself unto ABRAMELIN, who with a smiling countenance said unto me: "It is thus I would ever have you". He then conducted me into his own apartment where I took the two little manuscripts which I had copied; and he asked of me whether truly, and without fear, I wished for the Divine Science and for the True Magic. I answered unto him that it was the only end and unique motive which had induced me to undertake a so long and troublesome voyage, with the view of receiving this special grace from the Lord. "And I," said ABRAMELIN, "trusting in the mercy of the Lord, I grant and accord unto thee this Holy Science, which thou must acquire in the manner which is prescribed unto thee in the two little manuscript books, without omitting the least imaginable thing of their contents; and not in any way to gloss or comment upon that which may be or may not be, seeing that the Artist who hath made that work is the same God Who from Nothingness hath created all things. Thou shalt in no way use this Sacred Science to offend the Great God, and to work ill unto thy neighbour; thou shalt communicate it unto no living person whom thou dost not thoroughly know by long practice and conversation, examining well whether such a person really intendeth to work for the Good or for the Evil.

---

26   The Qabalistical reader will at once remark the symbolism of the numbers "ten" and "seventy-two," the first being the Number of the Sephiroth, and the second that of the Schemahamphorasch. But as many readers may be ignorant of the meaning and reference of these terms, I will briefly explain them. The Ten Sephiroth are the most abstract ideas and conceptions of the ten numbers of the ordinary Decimal Scale, and are employed in the Qabalah as an ideal means of explaining the different Emanations or Attributes of the Deity. It was thus that Pythagoras employed the abstract ideas of Numbers as a means of metaphysical instruction. The Schemahamphorasch or "Divided Name" is a Qabalistical method of investigating the natures of the Name of four letters I H V H (Jehovah), which is considered to contain all the Forces of Nature. There are in the Book of Exodus three verses in the fourteenth chapter, describing the pillars of fire and of cloud forming a defence unto the children of Israel against the Egyptians. Each of these three verses consists in the Hebrew of seventy-two letters, and by writing them in a certain manner one above another, seventy-two columns of three letters each are obtained; each column is then treated as a Name of Three Letters, and the explanation of these is sought for in certain verses of the Psalms which contain these Names; and these latter would be the verses of the Psalms alluded to in the text, which the seventy-two poor persons were told to recite.

27   This would not necessarily exclude eggs or milk.

28   So in the MS.

And if thou shalt wish to grant it unto him, thou shalt well observe and punctually, the same fashion and manner, which I have made use of with thee.

And if thou doest otherwise, he who shall receive it shall draw no fruit therefrom. Keep thyself as thou wouldst from a Serpent from selling this Science, and from making merchandise of it; because the Grace of the Lord is given unto us free and gratis, and we ought in no wise to sell the same.

This Veritable Science shall remain in thee and thy generation for the space of seventy-two[29] years, and will not remain longer in our Sect. Let not thy curiosity push thee on to understand the cause of this, but figure to thyself that we are so good[30] that our Sect hath become insupportable not only to the whole human race, but even to God Himself!" I wished in receiving these two small manuscript books to throw myself on my knees before him, but be rebuked me, saying that we ought only to bend the knee before God.

I avow that these two books[31] were so exactly written, that thou, O Lamech my son, mayest see them after my death, and thou shalt thus recognise how much respect I have for thee.[32]

It is true that before my departure I well read and studied them, and when I found anything difficult or obscure I had recourse unto ABRAMELIN, who with charity and patience explained it unto me. Being thoroughly instructed, I took leave of him, and having received his paternal blessing; a symbol which is not only in use among the Christians, but which was also the custom with our forefathers; I also departed, and I took the route to Constantinople, whither having arrived I fell sick, and my malady lasted for the space of two months; but the Lord in His Mercy delivered me therefrom, so that I soon regained my strength, and finding a vessel ready to depart for Venice I embarked thereon, and I arrived there, and having rested some days I set out to go unto Trieste, where having landed, I took the road through the country of Dalmatia, and arrived at length at my paternal home, where I lived among my relatives and my brothers.

THE FIFTH CHAPTER

IT is not sufficient to travel and journey abroad and see many lands, if one does not draw some useful experience therefrom. Wherefore, in order to show unto thee a good example, I will in this chapter speak of the Mysteries[33] of this Art which I discovered in one way and another while travelling in the world, and also of the measure and understanding of their various sciences; while, in the Sixth Chapter following, I will recount the things which I have learned and seen with some among them, and whether in actual practice I found them true or false. I have already before told you that my first Master had been the RABBIN MOSES at MAYENCE, who was indeed a good man, but entirely ignorant of the True Mystery and of the Veritable Magic. He only devoted himself to certain superstitious secrets which he had collected from various infidels, and which were full of the nonsense and foolishness of Pagans and Idolaters; to such an extent that the Good Angels and Holy Spirits judged him unworthy of their visits and conversation; and the Evil Spirits mocked him to a ridiculous extent. At times, indeed, they spake to him voluntarily and by caprice, and obeyed him in matters vile, profane, and of no account, in order the better to entrap, deceive and hinder him from

---

29   Note again the number of seventy-two.

30   This is evidently said ironically.

31   He probably means the copies he himself had been ordered by Abramelin to make, and not the originals.

32   Et tu connoiteras la deference dont je me sers avec toy."

33   Mistères, evidently a slip for Maistres, Masters.

searching further for the true and certain Foundation of this Great Science.

At ARGENTINE I found a Christian called JAMES, who was reputed as a learned and very skilful man; but his Art was the Art of the Juggler, or Cup and Balls Player; and not that of the Magician.

In the town of PRAGUE I found a wicked man named ANTONY, aged twenty-five years, who in truth showed me wonderful and supernatural things, but may God preserve us from falling into so great an error, for the infamous wretch avowed to me that he had made a Pact with the DEMON, and had given himself over to him in body and in soul, and that he had renounced God and all the Saints; while, on the other hand, the deceitful LEVIATHAN had promised him forty years of life to do his pleasure. He made every effort, as he was obliged to by the Pact, to persuade me and drag me to the precipice of the same error and misery; but at first I kept myself apart from him, and at last I took flight. Unto this day do they sing in the streets of the terrible end which befel him, may the Lord God of His Mercy preserve us from such a misfortune. This should serve us as a mirror of warning to keep far from us all evil undertakings and pernicious curiosity.

In AUSTRIA I found an infinitude, but all were either ignorant, or like unto the Bohemians.

In the Kingdom of HUNGARY I found but persons knowing neither God nor Devil, and who were worse than the beasts.

In GREECE I found many wise and prudent men, but, however, all of them were infidels, among whom there were three who principally dwelt in desert places, who showed unto me great things, such as how to raise tempests in a moment, how to make the Sun appear in the night, how to stop the course of rivers, and how to make night appear at mid-day, the whole by the power of their enchantments, and by applying superstitious ceremonies.

Near CONSTANTINOPLE, in a place called EPHIHA, there was a certain man, who, instead of Enchantments, made use of certain numbers which he wrote upon the earth; and by means of these he caused certain extravagant and terrifying visions to appear; but in all these Arts there was no practical use, but only the loss of soul and of body, because all these only worked by particular Pacts, which, had no true foundation; also all these Arts demanded a very long space of time, and they were very false, and when these men were unsuccessful they had always ready a thousand lies and excuses.

In the same city Of CONSTANTINOPLE I found two men of our Law, namely, SIMON and the RABBIN ABRAHAME, whom we may class with RABBIN MOSES of Mayence.

In EGYPT the first time I found five persons who were esteemed and reputed as wise men, among whom were four, namely, HORAY, ABIMECH, ALCAON, and ORILACH, who performed their operations by the means of the course of the Stars and of the Constellations, adding many Diabolical Conjurations and impious and profane prayers, and performing the whole with great difficulty. The fifth, named ABIMELU, operated by the means and aid of Demons, to whom he prepared statues, and sacrificed, and thus they served him with their abominable arts. In ARABIA they made use of plants, of herbs, and of stones as well precious as common. The Divine Mercy inspired me to return thence, and led me to ABRAMELIN, who was he who declared unto me the Secret, and opened unto me the fountain and true source of the Sacred Mystery, and of the Veritable and Ancient Magic which God had given unto our forefathers.

Also at PARIS I found a wise man called JOSEPH, who, having denied the Christian faith, had made himself a Jew. This man truly practised Magic in the same manner as ABRAMELIN, but he was very far from arriving at perfection therein; because God, Who is just, never granteth the perfect, veritable and fundamental treasure unto those who deny Him; notwithstanding that in the rest of their life they might be the most holy and perfect men in the world. I am astonished when I consider the blindness of many persons who let themselves be led by Evil Masters, who take pleasure in falsehood, and, we may rather say, in the DEMON himself; giving themselves over unto Sorceries and Idolatries, one in one manner, another in another manner, with the result of losing their souls. But the Truth is so great, the Devil is so deceitful and malicious, and the World so frail and so infamous that I must admit that things cannot be otherwise. Let us then open our eyes, and follow that which I shall lay down in the following chapters; and let us not walk

In another Path, whether of the Devil, or of men, or of Books which boast of their Magic; for in truth I declare unto thee that I had so great a quantity of such matters written out with so much Art, that had I not had these of ABRAMELIN, I could herein have given thee those. However, it is true that just as there is only one God, that not one of these Books is worth an obolus.[34] Yet with all this there are men so blind that they buy them at exorbitant prices, and they lose their money, their time, and their pains, and which is worse, very often their souls as well.

THE SIXTH CHAPTER

THE Fear of the Lord is the True Wisdom, and he who hath it not can in no way penetrate the True Secrets of Magic, and he but buildeth upon a foundation of sand, and his building can in no way last. The RABBIN MOSES persuaded me to be wise, while he himself, with words which neither he himself nor any other person understood, and with extravagant symbols made bells to sound, and while with execrable conjurations he made appear in glasses him who had committed a theft, and while he made a water causing an old man to appear young (and that only for the space of two hours and no longer). All the which things he indeed taught me, but the whole was but vanity, low curiosity, and a pure deception of the DEMON, leading to no useful end imaginable, and tending to the loss of the Soul. And when I had the Veritable Knowledge of the Sacred Magic, I both forgot them, and banished them from mine heart.

That impious Bohemian,[35] with the aid and assistance of his Associate, performed astounding feats. He rendered himself invisible, he used to fly in the air, he used to enter through the keyholes into locked-up rooms, he knew our greatest secrets, and once he told me things which God alone could know. But his Art cost him too dear, for the Devil had made him swear in the Pact that he would use all his secrets to the dishonour of God, and to the prejudice of his neighbour. Ultimately his body was found dragged through the streets, and his head without any tongue therein, lying in a drain. And this was all the profit he drew from his Diabolical Science and Magic.

In AUSTRIA I found an infinitude of Magicians who only occupied themselves in killing and maiming men, in putting discord among married people, in causing divorces, in tying witch-knots in osier or willow branches to stop the flow of milk in the breasts of nursing women, and similar infamies. But these miserable wretches had made a Pact with the Devil, and had become his slaves, having sworn unto him that they would work without cessation to destroy all living creatures. Some of these had two years (for their Pact) to run, some three, and after that time they underwent the same fate as the Bohemian.

At LINTZ I worked with a young woman, who one evening invited me to go with her, assuring me that without any risk she would conduct me to a place where I greatly desired to find myself. I allowed myself to be persuaded by her promises. She then gave unto me an unguent, with which I rubbed the principal pulses of my feet and hands; the which she did also; and at first it appeared to me that I was flying in the air in the place which I wished, and which I had in no way mentioned to her. pass over in silence and out of respect, that which I saw, which was admirable, and appearing to myself to have remained there a long while, I felt as if I were just awakening from

---

34   A coin of base money formerly in use, its value being about a halfpenny.

35   I.e. Antony, of whom he makes mention in the preceding chapter.

a profound sleep, and I had great pain in my head and deep melancholy. I turned round and saw that she was seated at my side. She began to recount to me what she had seen, but that which I had seen was entirely different. I was, however, much astonished, because it appeared to me as if I had been really and corporeally in the place, and there in reality to have seen that which had happened. However, I asked her one day to go alone to that same place, and to bring me back news of a friend whom I knew for certain was distant 200 leagues. She promised to do so in the space of an hour. She rubbed herself with the same unguent, and I was very expectant to see her fly away; but she fell to the ground and remained there about three hours as if she were dead, so that I began to think that she really was dead. At last she began to stir like a person who is waking, then she rose to an upright position, and with much pleasure began to give me the account of her expedition, saying that she had been in the place where my friend was, and all that he was doing; the which was entirely contrary to his profession. Whence I concluded that what she had just told me was a simple dream, and that this unguent was a causer of a phantastic sleep; whereon she confessed to me that this unguent had been given to her by the Devil.

All the Arts of the Greeks are Enchantments and Fascinations, and the Demons hold them enchained in these accursed arts so that the Foundation of the True Magic may be unknown to them which would render them more powerful than they; and I was the more Confirmed in this opinion because their operations were of no practical use whatever, and caused injury unto him who put them into practice, as in fact many of them avowed plainly to me, when I had the True and Sacred Magic. There are also many operations which they say are handed down from the Ancient Sibyls. There is an Art called White and Black;[36] another Angelical, TEATIM; in which I avow that I have seen orations so learned and beautiful, that had I not known the venom therein hidden, I would have given them herein. I say all this because it is very easy to him who is not constantly upon his guard to err.

One old scribbler of symbols[37] gave me many enchantments which only tended to work evil. He performed other operations by means of numbers, which were all odd, and of a triple proportion, in no way similar to the other, and for proof of this, he caused by such means in my presence a very fine tree which was near my house to fall to the ground, and all the leaves and fruits were consumed in a very short time. And he told me that in Numbers there was hidden a very Great Mystery, because that by the means of numbers one can perform all the operations for friendships, riches, honours, and all sorts of things, good and evil; and he assured me that he had tried them, but that yet some that he knew to be very true had not yet succeeded with him. With regard to this particular, I found out the reason through the Wise ABRAMELIN, who told me that this came and depended from a Divine Ministry, that Is to say, from the Qabalah, and that without that, one could not succeed. All these things have I beheld, and many others, and those who possessed these secrets gave them to me out of friendship. I burned these recipes afterwards in the house of ABRAMELIN, they being absolutely things very far removed from the Will of God, and contrary to the charity which we owe unto our neighbour. Every learned and prudent man may fall if he be not defended and guided by the Angel of the Lord, who aided me, and prevented me from falling into such a state of wretchedness, and who led me undeserving from the mire of darkness unto the Light of the Truth. I have known and felt the effects of the goodness of the Wise ABRAHA MELIN,[38] who of his own free will, and before I had asked him so to do, accepted me for his disciple. And before that I had declared my wish unto him he would accomplish and fulfil my desire; and all that I wished to obtain from him he knew before I could open my mouth. Also he recounted to me all that I had seen, done, and suffered from the time

36   ? the Book "Ambrosius".

37   Evidently the man mentioned in Chapter V., as living at Ephiha, near Constantinople. The word I have rendered by "scribbler of symbols" is grifas.

38   So written here in the MS.

of my father's death down to this moment; and this in words obscure and as it were prophetic, which I did not then comprehend, but which I understood later. He told me many things touching my good fortune, but, which was the principal thing, he discovered to me the Source of the Veritable Qabalah, the which according to our custom, I have in turn communicated unto thine elder brother JOSEPH, after that he had fulfilled the requisite conditions without the accomplishment of which the Qabalah and this Sacred Magic cannot be exercised, and which I will recount in the two following books. Afterwards he did manifest unto me the Regimen of the Mystery of that Sacred Magic which was exercised and put into practice by our forefathers and progenitors, NOAH, ABRAHAM, JACOB, MOSES, DAVID, and SOLOMON, among whom the last misused it, and he received the punishment thereof during his life.

In the Second Book I will describe the whole faithfully and clearly, in order that if the Lord God should wish to dispose of me before that thou shalt have attained a competent age, thou shalt find these three small manuscript books as forming at the same time both an inestimable treasure and a faithful master and teacher; because there are very many secrets in the Symbols of the Third Book which I have seen made experiment of with mine own eyes by ABRAMELIM,[39] and to be perfectly true, and which afterwards I myself have performed. And after him I found no one who worked these things truly; and although JOSEPH at Paris walked in the same Path, nevertheless God, as a just Judge, did not in any way wish to grant unto him the Sacred Magic in its entirety, because he had despised the Christian Law. For it is an indubitable and evident thing that he who is born Christian, Jew, Pagan, Turk, Infidel, or whatever religion it may be, can arrive at the perfection of this Work or Art and become a Master, but he who hath abandoned his natural Law, and embraced another religion opposed to his own, can never arrive at the summit of this Sacred Science.[40]

THE SEVENTH CHAPTER

GOD the Father of Mercy, having granted unto me the grace to return safe and sound into my country; I paid unto Him according to my small power, some little portion of that which I owed Him; thanking Him for so many benefits which I had received from Him, and in particular for the acquisition of the Qabalah which I had made at the house of ABRAMELIM.[41] It now only remained for me to reduce to Practice this Sacred Magic, but many things of importance and hindrances presented themselves; among the which my marriage was one of the greatest. I therefore judged it fitting to defer putting it in practice, and a principal obstacle was the inconvenience of the place in which I dwelt. I resolved to absent myself suddenly, and go away into the Hercynian Forests, and there remain during the time necessary for this operation, and lead a solitary life. It was not possible for me to do it sooner for many reasons and dangers of which latter I ran a risk in that place, besides which it would be necessary to leave my wife, who was young and now enceinte. Finally, I resolved to follow the example of ABRAMELIN,[42] and I divided my house[43] into two parts; I took

---

39   Thus spelt here.

40   Many Occultists will doubtless not be of this opinion. It is one thing to simply quit one debased and materialised form or sect of religion for another, which is perhaps little if any better; and quite another thing to seek out the true religion which is at the basis of all, and which could not be entirely true, were it not free from Sect.

41   Thus spelt here.

42   D'embrasser le Parti d'Abramelin.

43   Probably meaning "household".

another house at rent, which I in part furnished, and I gave over to one of my uncles the care of providing the necessaries of life and the needs thereof. Meanwhile I with my wife and a servant remained in my own house, and I began to accustom myself to the solitary life, which it was to me extremely difficult to support, because of the melancholic humour which dominated me, and I lived thus till the season of Easter which I celebrated with all the family according to custom. Then first, on the following day, in the Name and to the honour of God Almighty the Creator of Heaven and of Earth, I commenced this holy operation, and I continued it for Six Moons without omitting the slightest detail, as thou wilt understand later. And the period of the Six Moons being expired, the Lord granted unto me His Grace by His Mercy; according to the promise made unto our forefathers, since while I was making my prayer unto Him He deigned to grant unto me the vision and apparition of His holy Angels, together with which I experienced so great joy, consolation and contentment of soul, that I could neither express it nor put it into writing. And during the three days, while I was enjoying this sweet and delightful presence with an indicible contentment, my holy Angel, whom God the Most Merciful had destined from my creation for my Guardian, spake unto me with the greatest goodness and affection; who not only manifested unto me the Veritable Magic, but even made easier for me the means of obtaining it. He confirmed as being true the Symbols of the Qabalah which I had received from ABRAMELIN; and he gave me the fundamental means by which I could have an infinitude of others in my operations according to my pleasure, assuring me that he would instruct me fully thereon. (These Symbols are all like those of the Third Book.) He gave me further very useful advice and admonition, such as an Angel could give; how I should govern myself the following days with the Evil Spirits so as to constrain them to obey me; the which I duly followed out fulfilling always from point to point his instructions very faithfully, and by the Grace of God I constrained them to obey me and to appear in the place destined for this operation; and they obligated themselves to obey me, and to be subject unto me. And since then even until now, without offending God and the Holy Angels I have held them in my power and command, always assisted by the power of God and of His Holy Angels. And this with so great a prosperity of our house, that I confess that I held myself back from the vast riches which I could have accumulated; although I possess enough to be counted among the number of the rich, as thou wilt know when thou shalt be more advanced in age. May the Grace of the Lord, and the defence and protection of His Holy Angels never then depart from me, ABRAHAM, nor from my two sons JOSEPH and LAMECH; nor from all those who by your means and by the Will of God, shall receive this operation! So be it!

THE EIGHTH CHAPTER

IN order to show that Man ought to make use of the good things of the Lord by applying them unto a good end, that is to say, unto His honour and glory, both for his own use and that of his neighbour; I will describe in a few words in this present chapter many and the most considerable operations which I have carried out; and the which, with the aid of the All-Powerful Lord and of the Holy Angels, by the means of this Art I have easily conducted unto the desired end. And I write not this description in any way to vaunt myself, nor out of vain glory, the which would be a great sin against God, because it is He Who hath done the whole, and not I; but only do I write this that it may serve for instruction unto others, so that they may know wherein they ought to avail themselves of this Art, as also that they may use it to the honour of Him Who hath given this wisdom Unto men. and glorify Him; and in order that each one may know how great and inexhaustible are the treasures of the Lord, and render unto Him particular thanks for so precious a gift. And especially (do I thank Him) for having granted unto me, who am but a little worm of Earth, through the means of ABRAMELIN the power to give and communicate unto others this Sacred Science. After my death a book will be found, which I commenced to write at the time when I was beginning to put in practice this Art, which, reckoning the number of the years, was in 1409, until to-day on which I am arrived at the 96th[44] year of mine age, with all honour and augmentation of fortune; and in this book can be read in detail even to the very least thing which I have done. But here, as I have aforesaid, I will describe only the most remarkable.

Up till now I have healed of persons of all conditions, bewitched unto death, no less than 8413, and belonging unto all religions, without making an exception in any case.

I gave unto mine Emperor SIGISMOND,[45] a very clement Prince, a Familiar Spirit of the Second Hierarchy, even as he commanded me, and he availed himself of its services with prudence. He wished also to possess the secret of the whole operation, but as I was warned by the Lord that it was not His Will, he contented himself with what was permitted, not as Emperor, but as a private person; and I even by means of mine Art facilitated his marriage with his wife; and I caused him to overcome the great difficulties which opposed his marriage.

I delivered also the Count FREDERICK[46] by the means of 2000 artificial cavalry (the which I

44   As this MS. bears the date of 1458, Abraham must have been born in 1362, and was consequently 47 years old in 1409.

45   Sigismond, Emperor of Germany, was born the 14th February, 1368, and died at Znaïm on the 9th December, 1437. Son of the Emperor Charles IV. and of Anne of Silesia, he received an excellent education. At ten years of age his father gave him the Margravate of Brandenburg, and two years later he was betrothed to Mary, the daughter of Louis the Great of Hungary, whom he afterwards married. He was nominated by his father-in-law his successor on the throne of Poland. But the nobles preferred Ladislaus, the nephew of Casimir the Great. However, in 1386, he took possession of Hungary, repulsed the Poles, overcame the rebellious nobles; and then marched against the Wallachians and Turks, but he was beaten, and later, notwithstanding the help of France and England, he lost the Battle of Nicopolis in 1396. He escaped on board a vessel in the Black Sea and for eighteen months was a fugitive from his Kingdom; and a; the moment of his re-entering Hungary he was made prisoner by the discontented nobles, and shut up in the citadel of Ziklos. Escaping thence into Bohemia, he, however, reconquered his throne, and in 1410 was raised to the Empire by one party among the Electors, while Josse, Marquis of Moravia, and Wenceslaus were elected by other factions. A remarkable coincidence, seeing that at this moment when three Emperors possessed the Empire, the Papacy had also three Popes, viz.: John XXIII. (Balthazar Cossa), a Neapolitan; Gregory XII. (Ange Conrario), a Venetian; and Benedict XIII. (Pierre de Lune), a Spaniard. The death of Josse, and the resignation of Wenceslaus, left Sigismond sole master of the Empire. After having received the Silver Crown at Aix-la-Chapelle in 1414, he went to preside at the Council of Constance, where John Huss was condemned, notwithstanding the safe conduct which he had obtained from the Emperor. He endeavoured to end the differences between the Roman and Greek Churches, visited France and England under pretext of reconciling Charles VI. and Henry V., but, as some say, in order to form a league with the latter against France, so as to recover the ancient Kingdom of Arles. The death of his brother, Wenceslaus, in 1419, rendered him Master of Bohemia, at the moment when the revolt of the Hussites was at its height. He commenced a war of extermination against them, but was defeated by Ziska in 1420, p. 29 and a war of fifteen years' duration ensued. In 1431, whilst he was being crowned King of Italy at Milan, his troops experienced such severe defeats that he was forced to concede advantageous terms to the rebels. But dissensions arose among them, and Sigismond profited by this to completely crush them at length and make Bohemia submit. He reigned twenty-seven years as Emperor of Germany, eighteen years as King of Bohemia, and fifty-one years as King of Hungary. His second wife, Barbe, has been called by some, the Messalina of Germany.

46   Frederick I., surnamed the Quarreller, Duke and Elector of Saxony, was born at Altenburg in 1369, and died in 1428. He was son of the Landgrave and Margrave Frederick the Severe, and of Catherine, Countess of Henneberg. At only four years of age, Frederick had been betrothed to Anne, daughter of the Emperor Charles IV.; later on he had serious disputes concerning this matter with the Emperor Wenceslaus (the brother of Anne),

by mine Art caused to appear according unto the tenor of the Twenty-ninth Chapter of the Third Book here following), free out of the hands of the Duke Leopold of Saxonia; the which Count Frederick without me would have lost both his own life, and his estate as well (which latter would not have descended) unto his heirs.

Unto the BISHOP OF OUR CITY also, I showed the betrayal of his government at Orembergh, one year before the same occurred; and I say no more concerning this because he is an Ecclesiastic[47] passing over in silence all that I have further done to render unto him service.

The COUNT OF VARVICH[48] was delivered by me from prison in England the night before he was to have been beheaded.

I aided the flight of the DUKE,[49] and of his POPE JOHN,[50] from the Council of Constance, who

---

who had disposed of her hand to another, but who ultimately consented, in 1397, to pay Frederick a considerable sum by way of damages. In 1388 he fought as ally of the Burgrave of Nuremberg in the war of the German towns; and gained his knightly spurs in 1391, in the war which he, in concert with the Teutonic Knights, waged against the Lithuanians. Next, he fought against Wenceslaus. He married Catherine of Brunswick in 1402, and after various wars and quarrels, the University of Leipzig was founded in 1409. The indefatigable activity which this Prince displayed from 1420 against the movements of the Hussites, who were directly menacing his possessions, pointed him out as a valuable auxiliary to the Emperor Sigismond, who was then in a very critical position. In order to assure himself definitely of the alliance of Frederick the Quarreller, the Emperor conferred upon him the Electorate and Duchy of Saxony; but the former could not long enjoy his new found dignities in peace, for the Emperor shifted the whole weight of the war with the Hussites on to his shoulders. As the other German Princes did not respond readily to the Elector's appeal, the latter had the misfortune to lose the greater part of his p. 30 Army near Brux in 1425. But his wife, Catherine, summoned the whole of Catholic Germany to unite in a Crusade against the innovating Hussites; while 20,000 strange and foreign Warriors came unexpectedly to range themselves under the Standard of Frederick. It is to be noted that Abraham the Jew puts the Artificial Cavalry he supplied at 2000 (though this may easily be a slip for 20,000) and rumour would of course soon magnify the number. But the Elector was at length defeated at the disastrous battle of Aussig in 1426, where the élite of the German Warriors fell. The following year again witnessed a fresh defeat of the Elector, and the chagrin which this excited, ultimately led to his death. He was succeeded by his son, Frederick II., called "the Good" born in 1411, who began to reign in 1428, and died in 1464 (see Dict. Larousse).

47   The same ambiguity exists in the French as in the translation, as to whether it is Abraham or the Bishop who passes over the matter in silence. Et je n'en dis pas davantage acause quil est un eclesiastique passant sous silence ceque joy fait deplus pour luy rendre service. (I preserve the orthography of the French original.)

48   By "Count of Varvich," Abraham evidently means "Count of Warwick," as throughout the MS. a w is never used, but always a v, wherever the former occurs in a proper name. This Count of Warwick is probably Henri de Beauchamp, the brother-in-law of Warwick the "King-Maker," and son of that Richard de Beauchamp, so infamous for his instrumentality in bringing about the torture and burning of the heroic Joan of Arc. Henri de Beauchamp was at first deprived of his goods by Henry VI.; but in 1444 that Monarch created him Duke of Warwick, and later, King of the islands of Wight, Jersey, and Guernsey. He did not long survive to enjoy these honours (Dict. Larousse).

49   Probably Albert V. of Austria.

50   Pope John XXIII. (Balthazar Cossa), Pope from 1410 to 1415, was born at Naples. He had been a corsair in his youth, and at first, after his entry into holy orders, was only notable for his debauches, his exactions, and his violence, Pope Boniface IX. nevertheless appointed him Cardinal in 1402, and afterwards Legate of Bologna, where he is said to have given himself up to such excesses that Gregory XII. thought it necessary to excommunicate him. Notwithstanding this Cossa was elected to the Papacy at the time when the Church was shaken by internal

would otherwise have fallen into the hands of the enraged Emperor and the latter having asked me to predict unto him which one of the two Popes, John XXIII. and Martin V., should gain in the end, my prophecy was verified; that fortune befalling which I had predicted unto him at Ratisbon.

At the time when I was lodged at the house of the DUKE OF BAVARIA,[51] my Lord, for matters of the greatest importance; the door of my room was forced, and I had the value of 83,000 Hungarian pieces stolen from me in jewels and money. As soon as I returned, the thief (although he was a Bishop!) was forced to himself bring it back to me in person and to return with his own hands to me the money, jewels, and account books, and to give me the principal reasons which had forced him to commit the theft, rather than any other person.

Six months ago I did write unto the GRECIAN EMPEROR,[52] and I warned him that the affairs of his Empire were in a very bad condition, and that his Empire itself was on the brink of ruin, [53] unless he could appease the Anger of God. As there only remaineth unto me but a little while to live, those who remain after me will receive the news of the result of this prophecy.

The Operation of the thirteenth chapter[54] of the Second Book, I have twice performed; once in the house of Savonia;[55] and another time in the MARQUISATE OF MAGDEBURGH, and I was the cause that their estates were handed down unto their children.

Now when once the faculty of being able to avail oneself of the Sacred Magic hath been

---

dissension. He promised at first to renounce the Pontificate, if on their side Gregory XII. and Benedict XIII. would abandon their claims. However, he mounted the Papal Throne, and declared for the side of Louis d'Anjou in the war between the latter and Ladislaus regarding the Throne of Naples. At length, after the taking of Rome by Ladislaus, he was forced to implore the support of the Emperor Sigismond. The latter consented to grant him his protection, but on the sole condition of the convocation of the Council of Constance. After much hesitation, and after having taken every possible precaution to ensure his personal safety, John XXIII. consented to the assembling of the Council, which he opened 7th November, 1414. Being then summoned to lay aside the Papal Mitre, he judged it prudent to consent; but a few days later, he succeeded in escaping in disguise, during a tournament given by the Duke of Austria. He retired to Lauffembourg, and protested against the abdication, which he declared to have been obtained from him by force. The Council was for a moment struck with fear and consternation, but the firmness of the Emperor Sigismond, coupled with the effect of the declaration of J. Gerson that the General Councils had higher authority than the Papacy, prevailed. John XXIII. was summoned to appear before the Council, but refused; and soon after, being abandoned by the Duke of Austria, who was too weak to resist the power of the Emperor, he was arrested at Fribourg, and conducted to Rudolfcell. On the 29th May, 1415, this Pontiff was solemnly deposed by the Council of Constance as being given to simony, impudent, a secret poisoner, and a spendthrift of the wealth of the Church; and was imprisoned in the Castle of Heidelberg. At the end of four years he recovered his liberty, on payment of 30,000 golden crowns, and went to Rome, where he made his submission to Martin V., and was by him appointed Cardinal-Bishop of Frascati, and Senior of the Sacred College. He died a few months later at Florence, either of anxiety or by poison.

51   Either Ernest or William I. of Bavaria. They were brothers, and reigned conjointly. From his calling the Duke of Bavaria, his Lord, it would appear that he was living under his dominion, but it is curious that up to this point Abraham has never mentioned the name of his own town.

52   Constantine Palæologos, who was the thirteenth and last Greek Emperor. He was killed, and Constantinople taken by the Turks under Mahomet II. The direct descendant of Constantine Palæologos to-day, is the Princess Eugénie di Cristoforo-Palæologæ-Nicephoræ-Comnenæ.

53   A deux doigts de sa perte.

54   This chapter is entitled: "Concerning the Convocation of the Good Spirits".

55   Thus in MS.--? Saxonia.

obtained, it is permissible to demand from the Angel a sum of coined money proportionate unto thy birth, quality and capacity, the which without difficulty will be granted unto thee. Such money is taken from the Hidden Treasures. It is, however, necessary to note that in all Treasures one is allowed to take the fifth part, God permitting the same, although some braggart chatterers[56] do say that there be an infinitude hereof which be destined and reserved unto Anti-Christ, I do not for a moment say that this may not be true; but undoubtedly from the same Treasures one may also take the fifth part. There are yet more which be destined unto others. Mine own particular treasure was assigned unto me at Herbipolis;[57] and I performed the Operation of the eighth chapter[58] of the Third Book; it was not in any way guarded, and was very ancient. It was of gold, which had never been struck into ingots; and which I afterwards caused to be beaten out and converted into its equivalent weight of golden florins, by the Spirits; the which was done in a few hours; (and I did this operation seeing that) mine own possessions were few and of little worth; and so poor was I that in order to marry a person who had a considerable dowry, I was forced to make use of mine Art, and I employed the Fourth Sign of the Third Book and the Third Sign[59] of the nineteenth chapter; and I married my cousin with 40,000 golden florins as a dowry, the which sum served as a cover to my fortune.

All the Signs which are in the Eighteenth Chapter[60] have been made use of by me so many times that I could not count them. However, they are all given in the Book[61] already mentioned.

I made great and wonderful experiments with the Signs of the second[62] and eighth[63] chapters of the Third Book. The First Sign[64] of the first chapter of the Third Book is the most perfect.

It is necessary to be prompt and adroit in all these operations, seeing that in the things which belong unto God we can easily commit still greater errors than those into which SOLOMON fell.

All these Signs have I worked with great ease and pleasure, and with very great utility (unto myself and others). All these operations and others in infinite number have I performed by the Signs which be in the Third Book, and never have I failed in attaining mine end, I have always been obeyed (by the Spirits), and everything hath succeeded with me because I have myself obeyed the Commandments of God. Also I have from point to point followed out that which mine Angel hath counselled and prescribed unto me; following out also exactly that which ABRA-MELIN [65] had taught me, the which is the same that I shall write in the Two following Books, and which I shall exemplify and explain more clearly; because the instructions which I received, although in very obscure words and Hieroglyphics, have caused me to attain mine object, and have never

---

56   Quelques hableurs.

57   Herbipolis is the Latin mediaeval name of the town of Wurtzbourg in Bavaria. It seems from this passage that it was probably the city of Abraham the Jew, and therefore the one intended a few paragraphs before where he speaks of the "Bishop of our town". Wurzbourg and the surrounding district formed a Bishopric, and in the time of Abraham it was the scene of constant struggles between the Bishop and his party, and the burghers. Later, formidable persecutions against the Jews took place there, and many edicts were promulgated against witchcraft.

58   This is evidently an error for either the sixth, the sixteenth, or the twenty-eighth chapter; probably the latter.

59   To make oneself loved by a relation.

60   The Eighteenth Chapter is entitled: "How to heal divers maladies".

61   I.e. the Third Book.

62   The Second Chapter is entitled: "How to obtain information and be enlightened concerning every kind of proposition and all doubtful sciences".

63   The Eighth Chapter is entitled: "How to excite Tempests".

64   "To know all sorts of matters past and to come, which are, however, not opposed to God and to His Holy Will."

65   Thus spelt here.

permitted me to err and fall into pagan, strange, and superstitious idolatries; I being always kept in the Way of the Lord, Who is the True, the Only, the Infallible End, for arriving at the possession of this Sacred Magic.

THE NINTH CHAPTER

THE infamous BELIAL hath no other desire than that of obtaining the power of hiding and obscuring the True Divine Wisdom, so that he may have more means of blinding simple men and of leading them by the nose; so that they may always remain in their simplicity, and in their error, and that they may not discover the Way which leadeth unto the True Wisdom; seeing that otherwise it is certain that both he and his Kingdom would remain bound and that he would lose the title which he giveth himself of "Prince of this World," having become the slave of man. This is wherefore he seeketh to annul and destroy utterly this Sacred Wisdom. I, however, do pray all and singular to be upon their guard, and in no way to despise the Way and Wisdom of the Lord, nor to allow themselves to be seduced by the DEMON and his adherents; for he is a liar and will be so eternally; and may the Truth for ever flourish; for in following out and obeying with fidelity that which I have written in these Three Books, not only shall we arrive at the desired end, but we shall sensibly know and feel the Grace of the Lord, and the actual assistance of His Holy Angels, who take an incredible pleasure in seeing that they are obeyed and that you intend to follow out the Commandments of God, and that their instructions are observed. Such then are the particular points upon which I insist.

This Wisdom hath its foundation in the High and Holy Qabalah[66] which is not granted unto any other than unto the First-Born, even as God hath ordained, and as it was observed by our predecessors. Thence arose the difference, and the truck[67] or exchange between JACOB and ESAU; the primogeniture being the Qabalah, which is much nobler and greater than the Sacred Magic.[68] And by the Qabalah we can arrive at the Sacred Magic, but by the latter we cannot have the Qabalah. Unto the Child of a Servant, or of an Adulterer, the Qabalah is not granted, but only unto a Legitimate Child; as occurred in the case of ISAAC and ISHMAEL; but the Sacred Wisdom through the Mercy of God all can acquire, provided that they walk in the right Path; and each one should content himself with the Gift and Grace of the Lord. And this must not be done out of curiosity, and with extravagant and ridiculous scruples, wishing to know and understand more than is right; seeing that temerity is certainly punished by God, Who then permitteth him who is presumptuous not only to be turned aside out of the True Way by the Second Causes,[69] but also the DEMON hath power over him, and he ruineth and exterminateth him in such a manner, that we can only say that he himself is the sole cause of his own ruin and misery. It is certain that the OLD SERPENT will attempt to contaminate the present Book with his venom, and even to destroy and lose it utterly, but O LAMECH! as a faithful father I entreat thee by the True God Who hath created thee and all things, and I entreat every other person who by thy means shall receive this method of operating, not to be induced or persuaded to have any other sentiment or opinion, or to

---

66   As I have pointed out in my "Kabbalah Unveiled," I consider this a truer orthography than "Cabala," or "Kabbalah".

67   Troque ou change.

68   That is to say the True and Unwritten Qabalah, which is the Ancient Egyptian Magical Wisdom; and not later Hebrew perversions thereof.

69   That is to say the Administrators of the First Cause, i.e. the various Divine Powers, or Gods and Goddesses, who act more directly on matter.

believe the contrary. Pray unto God and ask Him for His assistance, and place all thy confidence in Him alone. And although thou canst not have the understanding of the Qabalah, nevertheless the Holy Guardian Angels at the end of the Six Moons or Months[70] will manifest unto thee that which is sufficient for the possession of this Sacred Magic.

Wherefore all the Signs and Symbols given in the Third Book, are written with Letters of the Fourth Hierarchy;[71] but the Mysterious Words wherein consisteth the Secret[72] have their origin in and are drawn from the Hebrew, Latin, Greek, Chaldean, Persian, and Arabian languages by a singular Mystery and according unto the Will of the Most Wise Architect and Fabricator of the Universe, Who alone dominateth and governeth it by His All-Power; all the Monarchies and Kingdoms of the World are submitted unto His Infinite Power, and unto this Sacred Magic and Divine Wisdom.

THE TENTH CHAPTER

IT being understood that in this operation we have to do with a Great and Powerful Enemy, whom through our own weakness and human strength or science we cannot resist without particular aid and assistance from the Holy Angels, and from the Lord of the Good Spirits; it is necessary that each one should always have God before his eyes, and in no way offend Him. On the other hand, he must always be upon his guard, and abstain as from a mortal sin from flattering, obeying, regarding, or having respect to the DEMON, and to his Viperine Race; neither must he submit himself unto him in the slightest thing, for that would be his ruin and the fatal loss of his soul. As it happened unto all the seed descended from NOAH, LOT, ISHMAEL, and others who did possess the blessed land (before our forefathers) who inherited this Wisdom from father to son, from family to family; but in the course of time having lent an ear unto the Treacherous Enemy, they let themselves be turned away from the Veritable Path, and did lose the True Science which they had received from God by the means of their fathers, and gave themselves over unto Superstitious Sciences, and unto Diabolical Enchantments, and unto Abominable Idolatries, the which was the cause that thereafter God did chastise them, defy[73] them, and chase them from their country; and did introduce in their stead our predecessors; from which same errors again later came the cause of our present misery and servitude, the which will last even unto the end of the world; since they in no way wished to know the Gift which God had given unto them, but instead abandoned it to embrace and follow the deceits of the DEMON.

This is wherefore each one should take care to submit himself unto him[74] neither by acts, nor by words, nor by thoughts, because he is so adroit and prompt that he can seize one unexpectedly; just as a Spider may take a Bird.[75] Let that miserable Bohemian and the others whom I have before mentioned, serve thee for an example to avoid (even as they did unto me).

In the commencement of the Operation there appeareth a Man of Majestic Appearance, who with great affability doth promise unto thee marvellous things. Consider all this as pure vanity,

70   Abraham here alludes to the period of preparation required from the Neophyte, as described later.

71   Regarding the Hierarchies, see end of Third Book.

72   Thus in the Indian "Mantras" the force and mystery of the Words themselves is especially insisted on.

73   Les deffit.

74   I.e., the Demon

75   There is a very large species of Spider, which can even capture and kill small birds, but it is only met with in tropical regions, especially in Central America and Martinique; the zoological name of this species is Mygalé.

for without the permission of God he can give nothing; but he will do it unto the damage and prejudice, ruin and eternal damnation of whomsoever putteth faith in him, and believeth in him; as we may see in the Holy Scripture in the matter Of PHARAOH and his adherents, the which despised the Veritable and certain Wisdom of MOSES and AARON, and were in the beginning backed up by the Devil who showed them by the means of Enchantments that he could both do and put in practice all the works of the aforesaid holy men, whence he ultimately did reduce them to such a condition of obstinacy and blindness, that without perceiving their own error and the deceit of the DEMON, they were cruelly chastised by God with divers plagues, and were at last all drowned in the Red Sea. This is wherefore in conclusion I say unto thee in few words, that we must rely upon God alone, and put all our confidence in Him.

THE ELEVENTH CHAPTER

GOD be my witness that I have not learned this Science out of curiosity, nor in order to avail myself of it for an evil purpose, but rather to use it for the honour and glory of my,[76] for mine own use, and for that of my neighbour; and I have never wished to employ it for vain and vile things, but I have always laboured with all my strength to aid all creatures, friends and enemies, faithful and unfaithful, as well the one as the other, with a perfect will and a good heart, and I have also made use of it for the animals.

I have before cited certain examples in order to show unto thee that God Almighty doth not in any way grant the Art or the Science unto a person in order that he may use it for himself alone, but in order that he may provide for the needs of others, and of those who do not possess this Sacred Science. This is why I pray every one to follow mine example, and if he doeth otherwise the Malediction of the Lord will fall upon him, and as for myself I shall be excusable and innocent before God, and before all men.

In the Third Book there will be found a very beautiful garden,[77] the like of which assuredly no one hath ever made, and which no King nor Emperor hath ever possessed. He who shall wish to be as an industrious Bee therein, can there suck the honey which it containeth in abundance; but if he shall maliciously wish to transform himself into a Spider, he can also draw poison from thence. God, however, accordeth and giveth His Grace, not unto the Evil, but unto the Good; and if it seemeth unto thee that some chapters of the Third Book can be rather applied unto Evil and unto the hurt of our neighbour, than unto a useful end; each one shall know that I have so placed them, in order that we may understand that this Science can be applied alike for Evil or for Good, as I will show thee more fully in the other Books. We must then study to flee the Evil and to obtain all the Forces of Good. He who shall act thus all the days of his life shall have the succour and assistance of the faithful, benign and holy Angels; and he who shall use it for Evil shall be abandoned by the same Angels, and shall be in the power of the Treacherous Enemy, who never faileth to obey the commands of such an one to work Evil, in order to render him his slave. It is necessary to have as a general rule and maxim which never faileth, that whenever thou shalt see a man filled with an extraordinary desire to procure this operation for himself, if thou wishest to give it unto him, it is necessary to test his sincerity and his intentions, and delay him, according to the instructions which I give unto thee in these three Books. And if he seeketh

76   Here a word is evidently omitted in the MS. by a slip. It should probably read "of my God".

77   This is a very usual expression in Qabalistic Books to denote a valuable collection of Occult or Magical information.

to obtain it by indiscreet methods, and sayeth unto thee that this operation may be true or not true, feigning doubts in order to compel thee to give it unto him, or that he maketh use of other stratagems, thou mayest then conclude that such a man walketh not in the Way of the Lord. If any person wisheth it in a way opposed to that which God employeth to grant it, this would be presumptuous.

And if any person seeketh to obtain it not for himself, (but for either) a child or a relative, who is not such as he should be who receiveth so great a treasure; he who shall grant it unto him shall be culpable of a great evil, and shall himself lose the Grace and Wisdom of the Lord, .and shall deprive his heirs of the same eternally.

If a man of evil life, whom one shall feel by means of this Sacred Science will persist in his evil way of life, shall come unto thee to seek this Sacred Science, it is probable that such a man doth not desire to use it for good and in a right intention, but that having received it, he will use it for evil. I have also in such case myself, however, seen and felt that God, Who penetrateth the secret of our hearts, hath put by indirect means obstacles in the way of such an one's success, causing difficulties to arise of one kind and another. So that he who at the first wisheth to possess this Science in order to use it against his neighbour, and to commit all sorts of abominations, manifesteth himself as an unworthy person unto him who had resolved to give it unto him.

Shun Commerce, and the converse of those who actually in the search for this Science shall do and say all things which tend to Evil; seeing that such men can become the Enchanters of the Devil. Thou shalt know the rest hereafter in the other Books. Here I am very prolix upon this point, and I am exaggerating much, because it is certain that once the Operation is given in due form, it is AN IRREVOCABLE ACT.

But if, on the other hand, after an exact examination and inquisition thou shalt find a person tranquil and sincere, thou must aid him, because God Who hath aided thee wisheth also to aid him; unto this end hath He put into thine hands this Sacred Science.

Thou must make every effort to procure peace amongst those who are at discord, and sworn enemies among themselves; and it is imperative to do good unto every one, this being the sole and true means of rendering favourable unto thee, God, the Angels, and Men; and of making the DEMON thy slave, and obedient in all and through all. And such an one shall pass the rest of his life with a good and right conscience, in honour and peace, with contentment, and useful unto all beings. I entreat those who shall be possessors of a so great treasure to employ it in the proper manner, and never to cast it before swine.

Thou shalt use it for thyself, O LAMECH, MY son, but of the fruit which thou shalt draw therefrom, thou shalt make partakers those who have need, and the more thou shalt give, the more shall thy means increase. The same shall happen unto him to whom thou shalt give it.

In these regions and countries we are slaves, and justly afflicted for our sins and those of our fathers; however, we ought to serve the Lord in the best manner which shall be possible unto us.

And by such an one shall the Treasure be kept secret, and shall be given unto his heirs as far as he can, being ware of disinheriting them in order to give it unto others, and of causing it to fall into the hands of the Infidels, or of rendering the Wicked possessors thereof.

THE TWELFTH CHAPTER

MINE intention was in no way to be so prolix in this First Book; but what will not paternal love do? and the importance of the matter permitteth it.

Let each one who will carry out this glorious enterprise rest in peace and surety, because in these Three Books is comprised all that can be necessary for this operation. For I have written it with much care, attention, and exactitude; so that there is no phrase which doth not give thee some instruction or advice. However, I pray such an one for the love of God, Who reigneth and will reign eternally, to commence no operation unless beforehand for the space of Six Months he hath read and re-read this Book with care and attention, considering all points in detail; for I am more than sure that he will not encounter any doubtful matter which he will not be able to solve himself, but further day by day will he assume unto himself a great and ardent desire, pleasure, and will, to undertake this so glorious operation; the which can be effected by any person of any religion soever,[78] provided, however, that during the Six Moons he hath not committed any sin against the Law and Commandments of God.

Now it remaineth unto me, O LAMECH, my son, to show unto thee the marks of my extreme paternal tenderness, by giving thee two principal pieces of advice, by the means of which, and observing all the other particulars which I shall describe, thou (and any person unto whom thou shalt accord this Sacred Science) mayest indubitably arrive at the perfection of this same Wisdom. It is necessary, however, to understand that many have undertaken this operation; and that some have obtained their wish; but that there are others who have not succeeded, and the reason of this hath been because their Good Angel hath not appeared unto them in the day of the Conjuration, their Angel being by its nature Amphiteron,[79] because the Angelic nature differeth to so great an extent from that of men, that no understanding nor science could express or describe it, as regardeth that great purity wherewith they[80] be invested.

I do not wish that thou, LAMECH, my son, and thy successor, and friends, should be deprived of a so great treasure. I in no way wish to abandon thee in so essential a matter. The other point is the Psalm which I will tell thee also; and though thou givest the operation unto another person, although he be a friend, thou shalt in no wise communicate this unto him, because this Psalm is the preservative against all those to whom thou shalt have given the Holy Magic, should they wish to make use of it against thee; and thou shalt be able thyself to make excellent use of it against them. This was granted by the Lord unto DAVID for his own preservation.

For the first point: the day being come when it is necessary to perform the Orations, Prayers, and Convocations of thy Guardian Angel, thou shalt have a little Child[81] of the age of six, seven, or eight years at the most, who shall be clothed in white, the which child thou shalt have washed from head to foot, and thou shalt place upon his forehead a veil of white silk very fine and transparent, which covereth the forehead even unto the eyes; and upon the veil it is necessary to write beforehand in gold with a brush a certain Sign made and marked in the manner and order as it will be shown in the Third Book; the which doth serve to conciliate and to give grace unto the mortal and human creature to behold the face of the Angel. He who operateth shall do the same thing, but upon a veil of black silk, and shall put it on in the same manner as the Child. After this

---

78   It is noticeable how constantly Abraham the Jew insists upon this point.

79   This word in Greek would mean "exhausted in every way," or "hemmed in and hindered on every side."

80   I.e., the Angels.

81   The following instructions recall some of Cagliostro's methods of magical working.

thou shalt make the Child enter into the Oratory and thou shalt cause him to place the fire and the perfume in the censer, then he shall kneel before the Altar; and he who performeth the operation shall be at the door and prostrate upon the ground, making his Oration, and supplicating his Holy Angel that he will deign to appear and show himself unto this innocent being,[82] giving unto him another Sign if it be necessary in order to see him himself[83] on the two following days.

It is requisite that he who shall operate shall take heed to in no wise regard the Altar, but having his face towards the ground let him continue his Orations, and as soon as the child shall have seen the Angel thou shalt command him to tell thee, and to look upon the Altar and take the lamen or plate of silver which thou shalt have placed there for this purpose, in order to bring it unto thee if it be necessary, and whatever other thing the Holy Angel shall have written thereon, wherewith thou oughtest to work on the two following days. The which being done he will disappear. Which being carefully done, the Child will tell thee (for this, it is necessary to have instructed him beforehand), and thou shalt command him to bring unto thee the little plate,[84] by the which when thou hast received it thou shalt know what the Angel hath ordered thee to do. And thou shalt cause it to be replaced upon the Altar, and thou shalt quit the Oratory, thou shalt close it, and thou shalt in no wise enter therein during the first day, and thou shalt be able to send away the Child. And he who shall perform the Operation shall prepare himself during the rest of the day for the morrow following, to enjoy the admirable presence of the Holy Guardian Angel, in order to obtain the end so earnestly desired, and which shall not fail thee if thou followest the Path which He shall show unto thee. And these two Signs are the Key of the whole Operation. Unto the Glory of the Most Holy Name of God and of His Holy Angels!

END OF THE FIRST BOOK.

---

82   I.e., the Child.

83   I.e., the Operator.

84   I.e., the lamen of silver, previously alluded to.

THE SECOND BOOK

OF THE
HOLY MAGIC,
WHICH GOD GAVE UNTO MOSES, AARON, DAVID, SOLOMON, AND OTHER
SAINTS, PATRIARCHS AND PROPHETS; WHICH TEACHETH
THE TRUE DIVINE WISDOM.

———————

BEQUEATHED BY ABRAHAM UNTO LAMECH HIS SON.

———————

TRANSLATED FROM THE HEBREW.

———————

1458

PROLOGUE

THE Wisdom of the Lord is an inexhaustible fountain, neither hath there ever been a man born who could penetrate its veritable origin and foundation. The Sages and Holy Fathers have drunk long draughts thereof, and have been fully satisfied therewith. But with all this, not one among them hath been able to comprehend or know the Radical Principles, because the Creator of all things reserveth that unto Himself; and, like a jealous God, He hath indeed wished that we should enjoy the fruit thereof, but He hath not wished to permit us to touch either the Tree or its Root. It is then not only proper, but further also we are compelled to conform ourselves unto the Will of the Lord, walking in that Path, by the which also our predecessors went, without seeking out through a vain curiosity how it is that God reigneth and governeth in His Divine Wisdom; because such would be a very great presumption and a bestial conceit. Let us then content ourselves with only knowing how many blessings He hath granted unto us Sinners, and what extent of power He hath given unto us mortals over all things, and in what way it is permitted unto us to use them. Let us then content ourselves with this, laying aside all other curiosity, observing without any comment that which shall be set down in this Book with fidelity. And if ye do follow my advice, ye shall be infallibly comforted thereby. [85]

THE FIRST CHAPTER.
WHAT AND HOW MANY BE THE FORMS OF VERITABLE MAGIC

WHOSO should wish to recount all the Arts and Operations which in our times be reputed and preached abroad as Wisdom and Magical Secrets; he should as well undertake to count the waves and the sands of the Sea; seeing that the matter hath come to such a pass that every trick of a buffoon is believed to be Magic, that all the abominations of impious Enchanters, all Diabolical Illusions, all Pagan Idolatries, all Superstitions, Fascinations, Diabolical Pacts, and lastly all that the gross blindness of the World can touch with its hands and feet is reckoned as Wisdom and Magic! The Physician, the Astrologer, the Enchanter,

---

[85]   The style of the writing here is much more quaint and obscure than that of the First Book; and is evidently the translation of Abraham the Jew from a more ancient writer.

the Sorceress, the Idolater, and the Sacrilegious, is called of the common People a Magician! Also he who draweth his Magic whether from the Sun, whether from the Moon, whether from the Evil Spirits, whether from Stones, Herbs, Animals, Brutes, or lastly from thousand divers sources, so that the Heaven itself is astonished thereat. There be certain who draw their Magic from Air, from Earth, from Fire, from Water, from Physiognomy, from the Hand, from Mirrors, from Glasses, from Birds, from Bread, from Wine, and even from the very excrements themselves; and yet, however, all this is reputed as Science!

I exhort you, ye who read, to have the Fear of God, and to study Justice, because infallibly unto you shall be opened the Gate of the True Wisdom which God gave unto NOAH and unto his descendants JAPHET, ABRAHAM, and ISHMAEL; and it was His Wisdom that delivered LOT from the burning of Sodom. MOSES learned the same Wisdom in the desert, from the Burning Bush, and he taught it unto AARON his brother. JOSEPH, SAMUEL, DAVID, SOLOMON, ELIJAH, and the Apostles, and Saint JOHN particularly (from whom we hold a most excellent book of Prophecy[86]) possessed it. Let every one then know that this, this which I teach, is that same Wisdom and Magic, and which is in this same Book, and independent of any other Science, or Wisdom, or Magic, soever. It is, however, certainly true that these miraculous operations have much in common with the Qabalah; it is also true that there be other Arts which have some stamp of Wisdom; the which alone would be nothing worth were they not mingled with the foundation of the Sacred Ministry, whence later arose the Mixed Qabalah. The Arts are principally twelve. Four in number, 3, 5, 7, 9, among the numbers in the Mixed Qabalah. The second is the most perfect one, the which operateth by Sign and Visions. Two of the even numbers, namely 6 and 2, which operate with the Stars and the Celestial Courses which we call Astronomy. Three consisteth in the Metals, and[87] in the Planets. 2 As to all these Arts, the which be conjoined and mingled together with the Sacred Qabalah; both he who maketh use of these same, either alone, or mingled with other things which be in no way from the Qabalah; and he who seeketh to exercise himself in performing operations with these Arts; is alike liable to be deceived by the DEMON; seeing that of themselves they possess no other virtue than a natural property; and they can produce no other thing than probable[88] effects, and they have absolutely no power in spiritual and supernatural things; but if, however, on certain occasions they[89] cause you to behold any extraordinary effect, such is only produced by impious and diabolical Pacts and Conjurations, the which form of Science ought to be called Sorcery.

Finally, let us conclude that from the Divine Mystery are derived these three kinds of Qabalah, viz.: the Mixed Qabalah, and the True Wisdom, and the (True) Magic. We will, therefore, show forth this last, and the manner of becoming its possessors in the Name of God and of His Celestial Court!

---

86   I.e., the Revelation, or Apocalypse.

87   This whole passage about the signification of these numbers is very obscurely worded in the original. I take the meaning to be the following: The Arts or methods of Magical working are twelve, if we class them under the twelve Signs of the Zodiac. The second number mentioned above, 5, is perfect because of its analogy with the Pentagram that potent Symbol of the Spirit and the Four Elements; 6 is the number of the Planets (as known to the Ancients, without the recently discovered Herschel and Neptune). As the Chaldean Oracles of Zoroaster say: "He made them Six, and for the Seventh, He cast into the midst thereof the Fire of the Sun". 2 operates in the Stars and Planets as representing their Good or Evil influence in the Heavens, in other words their dual nature. 3 consists in the Metals because, the ancient Alchemists considered their bases to be found in the three principles which they called Sulphur, Mercury, and Salt; but by which they did not mean the substance which we know under these names.

88   I.e., "probable" as opposed to "certain".

89   I.e., professing Magicians.

THE SECOND CHAPTER.
WHAT WE SHOULD CONSIDER BEFORE UNDERTAKING THIS OPERATION

WE[90] have already said what is the Science which I [91] am to, teach you, that is to say. that it is neither in any way human nor diabolical, but (that it is) the True and Divine Wisdom and Magic, which has been handed down by our predecessors unto their successors as a hereditary treasure. In like manner as I myself at present, so even should ye think, before entering into this matter,[92] and before taking possession of so great a treasure, how much this Gift is sublime and precious, and how vile and base are ye yourselves who be about to receive it. This is wherefore I say unto ye that the beginning of this Wisdom is the Fear of God and of justice. These be the Tables of the Law, the Qabalah, and the Magic; they should serve unto ye for a rule. It is necessary that ye should begin to attach yourselves unto the very beginning, if ye truly do wish to have the Veritable Wisdom; and thus shall ye walk in the right Path, and be able to work; all the which is contained in this Book, and all the which is therein prescribed. For to undertake this Operation with the simple intention of using it unto dishonest, impious, and wicked ends, is neither just nor reasonable; for it is absolutely necessary to perform this Operation unto the praise, honour, and glory of God; unto the use, health, and well-being of your neighbour, whether friend or enemy; and generally for that of the whole earth. Furthermore, it is also necessary to take into consideration other matters, which though less important be still necessary; namely, whether ye be capable, not only of commencing, but also of carrying through the Operation unto its end; this being a necessary point to consider before coming unto a final determination upon the matter; because n this case we are not negotiating with men, but with God, by the intermediation of His Holy Angels, and with all Spirits, both good and evil.

I am not here intending to play the Saint and Hypocrite, but it is necessary to have a true and loyal heart. Ye have here to do with the Lord, Who not only beholdeth the outer man, but Who also penetrateth the inmost recesses of the heart. But having taken a true, firm, and determined resolution, relying upon the Will of the Lord, ye shall arrive at your desired end, and shall encounter no difficulty. Often also man is changeable, and while beginning a thing well, finisheth it badly, being in no way firm and stable in resolution. Ponder the matter then well before commencing, and only begin this Operation with the firm intention of carrying it out unto the end, for no man can make a mock of the Lord with impunity. Furthermore it is likewise necessary to think and consider whether your goods and revenue be sufficient for this matter; and, further, whether if your quality or estate be subject unto others, ye may have time and convenience to undertake it; also whether wife or children may hinder you herein; these being all matters worthy of observation, so as not to commence the matter blindly.

The chief thing that ye should consider is whether ye be in good health, because the body being feeble and unhealthy, it is subject to divers infirmities, whence at length result impatience and want of power to operate and pursue the Operation; and a sick man can neither be clean and pure, nor enjoy solitude; and in such a case it is better to cease. Consider then the safety of your person, commencing this Operation in a place of safety, whence neither enemies nor any disgrace can drive you out before the end because ye must finish where ye begin.

---

90   In the original MS.: "Nous avons deja dit quelle est la science que je dois vous enseigner cest adire quelle nest point humaine," etc.

91   Ibid.

92   In the original: " Comme je suis apresent vous devez donc penser avant que d'entrer dans ce bal." etc.

But the first part of this chapter is the most important, and see that ye keep well in mind the necessity of observing the same, because as regardeth the other disadvantages, they may perhaps be remedied. And be ye sure that God doth aid all those who put their confidence in Him and in His Wisdom, and such as wish to live rightly, making use with honour of the deceitful world, which ye shall hold in abomination, and see that ye make no account of ts opinion when ye shall be arrived at the perfection of the work, and that ye shall be possessors of this Sacred Magic.

THE THIRD CHAPTER.
OF THE AGE AND QUALITY OF THE PERSON WHO WISHETH TO UNDERTAKE THIS OPERATION

IN order to describe the aforesaid and other considerations in the best possible manner; I will here make a general recapitulation; mentioning also first what may bring hindrance unto the matter.

It is, then, necessary that such a man[93] give himself up unto a tranquil life, and that his habits be temperate; that he should love retirement; that he should be given neither unto avarice nor usury (that he should be the legitimate child of his parents is a good thing, but not as necessary as for the Qabalah, unto which no man born of a clandestine marriage[94] can attain); his age ought not to be less than twenty-five years nor more than fifty; he should have no hereditary disease, such as virulent leprosy; whether he be free or married importeth little; a valet, lackey, or other domestic servant, can with difficulty arrive at the end required, being bound unto others and not having the conveniences at disposal which are necessary, and which this Operation demandeth. Among women, there be only Virgins who are suitable; but I[95] , strongly advise that so important a matter should not be communicated to them, because of the accidents that they might cause by their curiosity and love of talk.

THE FOURTH CHAPTER.
THAT THE GREATER NUMBER OF MAGICAL BOOKS ARE FALSE AND VAIN

ALL the Books which treat of Characters, Extravagant Figures, Circles, Convocations, Conjurations, Invocations, and other like matters, even although any one may see some effect thereby, should be rejected, being works full of Diabolical Inventions;[96] and ye should know that the DEMON maketh use of an infinitude of methods to entrap and deceive mankind. This I have myself proved, because when I have

---

93   I.e., he who intends to undertake the Operation.

94   I doubt this assertion very much.

95   Here comes another touch of prejudice. In the present day many of the profoundest students of the Qabalah are women, both married and single.

96   It is necessary that the reader should not misunderstand this passage. What are meant are those Black Magic works containing garbled and perverted words and characters; and which teach nothing but hurtful and selfish practices; the great point in which is generally the forming of a Pact with an Evil Spirit. Because true Characters represent the Formulas of the Currents of the Hidden Forces of Nature and true Ceremonies are the Keys of bringing the same into action.

operated with the Veritable Wisdom, all the other enchantments which I had learned have ceased, and I could no longer operate with them, and I made a very careful trial of those which I had learned with the RABBIN MOSES; the cause of which is that the deceit and fraud of the DEMON can never appear where the Divine Wisdom is.

Furthermore, the most certain mark of their falsity is the election of certain days; since there be those which God hath expressly commanded to sanctify, we can freely operate on all other days, and at all times. And whenever ye shall see tables which do mark the days and their differences, the Celestial Signs, and other like matters,[97] pay no attention thereto, because herein is a very great sin[98] hidden, and a deceit of the DEMON; it being one of his many methods of endeavouring to confound the True Wisdom of the Lord with evil matters. Because this True Wisdom of the Lord can operate and perform its effects every day, and at any moment and second.

The Gates of His Grace are daily open, He wisheth, and it is pleasing unto Him to aid us, as well on this day as on the morrow; and in no way could it be true that He desireth to be subjected to the day and hour which men would wish to prescribe for Him; seeing that He is the Master to elect such days as He Himself wisheth, and also may they be sanctified! Flee also all such Books as those whose Conjurations include extravagant, inexplicable, and unheard-of words,[99] and which be impossible to understand, and which be truly the inventions of the Devil and of wicked men.

It is well also to recall that which I have said in the First Book, viz., that in the greater part of their Conjurations there was not the slightest mention made of God Almighty, but only of Invocations of the Devil, together with very obscure Chaldean words. Surely it would be a rash thing of a man who should deal with God by the intermediary of His Holy Angels, to think that he ought to address Him in a jargon, neither knowing what he saith nor what he demandeth.

Is it not an act of madness to wish to offend God and His Holy Angels! Let us then walk in the right way, let us speak before God with heart and mouth alike opened, in our own maternal language[100] since how can ye pretend to obtain any Grace from the Lord, if ye yourselves know

---

97   It seems again to me here that Abraham the Jew stretches the matter too far. it is perfectly and utterly true without doubt that Angelic Magic is higher than that form of Talismanic Magic which has its basis in the Astrological positions of the Heavenly Bodies; and can therefore do more, and be also independent of Astrological considerations, because the matter is relegated to a higher plane than this, and one wherein the laws of Physical Nature do not obtain. But certainly when working with the rays of the Sun, we shall more easily find his occult force of heat attainable when he himself is producing that effect upon the earth, i.e., when he is in the Sign of the Lion; while when he is in that of the Bull, his force will be rather that of Germination, etc., when in the Northern Hemisphere. And the same with the other Planets. Also if working by the Indian Tatwas, we shall find it necessary to consider the position of the Moon, the time in the day, and the course of the Tatwa in the period of five Gharis. Of course Abraham could not make the experiments of Rabbin Moses succeed if he substituted the laws of another plane for their own

98   So it would be if he applied it to the Angelic working; but equally it would be an error which, though not so great, would still entail failure, to apply laws exclusively of the Angelic plane to those experiments which would mainly depend on the physical rays of the Planets; though undoubtedly the Angels of a Planet govern its rays. But the Angels of Mars do not govern the rays of Jupiter, nor those of the latter the rays of Mars.

99   The Grimoires of Black Magic would usually come under this head. But, nevertheless, the extravagant words therein will be usually found to be corruptions and perversions of Hebrew, Chaldee, and Egyptian titles of Gods and Angels. But it is undoubtedly evil to use caricatures of Holy Names; and these for evil purposes also. Yet it is written in the Oracles of Zoroaster: "Change not barbarous Names of Evocation, for they are Names Divine, having in the Sacred Rites a Power Ineffable!"

100   Yet, notwithstanding, it is well in a Sacred Magical Operation to employ a language which does not to our minds convey so much the commonplace ideas of everyday life, so as the better to exalt our thoughts. But, as

not what ye ask?

Yet, however, the number of those who lose themselves utterly in this vanity is infinite; many say that the Grecian language is more agreeable unto God, it may be true that it was perhaps at one time, but how many among us to-day understand it perfectly, this is the reason why it would be the most senseless thing to employ it.

I repeat then:--Let each one speak his own language, because thus understanding what it is that ye are demanding of the Lord, ye will obtain all Grace. And if ye demand a thing which is unjust, it will be refused unto you, and ye will never obtain it.

THE FIFTH CHAPTER.
THAT IN THIS OPERATION IT IS NOT NECESSARY TO REGARD THE TIME, NOR THE DAY, NOR THE HOURS

THERE be no other days (to be observed) than those which God hath ordained unto our Fathers, viz., All Saturdays, which be the days of the Sabbath Passover; and the Feast of Tabernacles of which the former is the Fifteenth Day of the First of our Months, and the latter (beginneth on) the Fifteenth Day of the Seventh Month.[101] Now for this Operation, any person of whatever Law[102] he may be, provided that he confesseth that there is One God,[103] may observe these feasts. However, the true time of commencing this Operation is the first day after the Celebration of the Feasts of Easter, and this was ordained unto Noah, being the most convenient time, and the end falleth just at the (Feast of) Tabernacles.[104] Our predecessors have thus observed it, and the Angel[105] also hath approved it; and also it is more advisable to follow good counsel and example, than to be obstinate and follow one's own caprice; and also to treat the election of a particular day as a Pagan idea, paying no regard whatever either to Time nor to the Elements; but only (having respect) unto Him Who granteth such a period. Thus then will we be found men in the fittest condition of Grace and reconciled with God, and purer than at another period; and this being an essential point ye ought well to consider the same.

It is, however, quite true that the Elements and the Constellations do perform of themselves certain operations[106] but this is to be understood of natural things, as it happeneth that one day is different unto another; but such a difference hath not operation in things Spiritual and Supernatural, being thus useless for (higher) Magical Operations. The Election of Days is still more useless, the Election of Hours and Minutes whereof the ignorant make so much, is further a very great error.

Wherefore I have resolved to write this particular chapter, in order that this error might appear more plainly evident unto him who readeth it, and that be may draw profit therefrom so as to operate with judgment.

Abraham says, we should before all things understand what we are repeating.

101   The Passover is about the Vernal Equinox and nearly corresponds to our Easter; it begins on the 15th or 16th of the Jewish First Month = Nisan or Abib. The Feast of Tabernacles begins about the middle of their Seventh Month= Tisri.

102   I.e., religious denomination.

103   It is immaterial whether the religious conception be Theistic or Pantheistic.

104   The Initiates of the True Rosicrucian Wisdom, know that there is a certain force in the observance of the Equinoxes.

105   Abraham evidently means his Guardian Angel.

106   Here Abraham admits to an extent what I have urged in my previous notes.

THE SIXTH CHAPTER.
CONCERNING THE PLANETARY HOURS AND OTHER ERRORS OF THE AS-TROLOGERS

IT is true that the Wise in Astrology do write of the Stars and of their movements, and that these attaining thereto do produce divers effects in inferior and elemental things; and such are, as we have already said, natural operations of the Elements; but that they should have power over the Spirits, or force in all supernatural things, that is not, neither can ever be. But it will instead be found that by the permission of the Great God it is the Spirits who govern the firmament. What foolishness then would it be to implore the favour of the Sun, of the Moon, and of the Stars, when the object would be to have converse with Angels and with Spirits. Would it not be an extravagant idea to demand from the wild beasts the permission to go hunting? But what else is it, when they[107] have elected a certain day, when they have divided it up into many false divisions such as hours, minutes, etc. "Here," they say, "we have the Planetary Hours, and the Planet appropriate to each Hour." O what Planets! O what fine order! Tell me, I pray you, what advantage you get by this division. You will reply: "A very great one, because it shows us in all things, either good or bad fortune!" I tell you, and I repeat absolutely, that this is in no way true; that they produce thus a change of the time and of the Air, I in part concede; but do me the grace to tell me how ye do divide the Planetary Hours. I know that ye begin the first hour of the day with the Planet which itself giveth the name unto the day, as Sunday is ascribed to the Sun, Monday to the Moon, Tuesday to Mars, Wednesday to Mercury, Thursday to Jupiter, Friday to Venus, and Saturday to Saturn; then ye divide the length of the Day into twelve equal portions which ye call Hours, and to each Hour ye assign its planet; and ye do the same thing with the Night, according to whether the days be long or short. Thus do the Hours become long or short. As for example, suppose that on a Sunday the Sun riseth at 7 o'clock and setteth at 5 o'clock in the evening, its course will be ten Hours, the which ye divide up into twelve equal parts, so that each Hour is of fifty minutes' length. I say, therefore, that the first Planetary Hour is of the Sun, and is fifty minutes long; that the second is of Venus; the third of Mercury; and so on of the others; at last the eighth Hour returneth unto the Sun; the ninth unto Venus; the tenth unto Mercury; and so the Day finisheth. Then cometh the Night, which is longer, that is to say, fourteen Hours, and each Planetary Hour of this Night will be seventy minutes, and in order to continue the regular succession as we have begun, the first Hour of the Night will be of Jupiter; the second of Mars; the third of the Sun; and so on until Monday, whose first Hour will be (according to this rule) of the Moon. Now tell me, I pray you, doth it always happen that when the Day of Monday commenceth, that is to say, when the Sun riseth in its horizon, that the Moon riseth also together with him, and that she setteth also together with him? They cannot answer this. Wherefore then do they apportion unto the second day of the week and unto its first hour the Moon? They can tell you no reason, except a likeness to the name (of the Day). [108]

O! how gross an error! Hear and tell me when it is that a Planet hath the greatest force in the Elements; whether when it is above or when it is below your Horizon or Hemisphere? We must however avow that it is more powerful when it is above, because being below it hath no power save according unto the Will of God. Why then, even further than this, should we attribute unto a Planet a Day and Hour, if during the whole period of such Day it appeareth not above the Horizon! ABRAMELIN as a most excellent MASTER in natural things taught unto me a very different

---

107   I.e., the Astrologers to whom Abraham refers in the first sentence of the chapter.

108   I.e., the Moon and Monday; Sun and Sunday; Mars and Tuesday (Tuisco is a name of Mars); Venus and Friday (Freya's day, after Freya, the Scandinavian Goddess), etc.

form of classification (which also well examine, and see whether it be not more surely founded than the aforesaid rule of the Astrologers), and made me to comprehend what should be the true Planetary Hours. When the Planet beginneth to appear upon the Horizon then doth its Day begin (whether it be Light or Dark, Black or White), and until it hath passed its elevation[109] its Day lasteth until it riseth anew, and after that it hath set its Night endureth; so that as well in the Days of the Sun as in those of the Moon and of the others, the Days of all the Planets be mingled, only that one commenceth sooner than another, according to which nature they be mingled together in the Celestial Signs. Now it is requisite that I should tell unto you what be the Planetary Hours! Know then that each Planet hath only an hour during the which it is very powerful, being over you and above your head, that is to say when it is in the Meridian. Then, naturally, will sometimes arrive the Hours of two Planets together and beginning at the same moment; they then produce an effect according unto the nature, quality, and complexion of these stars.[110] But all this only hath power in natural things. Here have I declared and proved unto you the errors of the (common) Astrologers; keep yourselves carefully from the insensate follies of their Days and Hours, because if ye make use of these as do the false Magicians and Enchanters, God will chastise you; and in order to chastise you will pay but little attention unto the awaiting of the Hour of Saturn or of Mars.

I therefore now conclude this chapter, having sufficiently treated of the false and useless method employed by the Astrologers in the Election of Days and of Hours.

THE SEVENTH CHAPTER.
REGARDING WHAT IT IS NECESSARY TO ACCOMPLISH DURING THE FIRST TWO MOONS OF THE BEGINNING OF THIS VERITABLE AND SACRED MAGIC

HE who commenceth this Operation should consider with care that which we have before said, and should pay attention unto that which followeth; and the thing being of importance, I shall leave alone for the present all other considerations, so that we may begin with the Operation which we should perform on the first morning after the celebration of the Feast of Easter (or Passover).

Firstly: Having carefully washed one's whole body and having put on fresh clothing: precisely a quarter of an hour before Sunrise ye shall enter into your Oratory, open the window, and place yourselves upon your knees before the Altar, turning your faces towards the window; and devoutly and with boldness ye shall invoke the Name of the Lord, thanking Him for all the grace which He hath given and granted unto you from your infancy until now then with humility shall ye humble yourselves unto Him, and confess unto Him entirely all your sins; supplicating Him to be willing to pardon you and remit them. Ye shall also supplicate Him that in the time to come He may be willing and pleased to regard you with pity and grant you His grace and goodness to send unto you His Holy Angel, who shall serve unto you as a Guide, and lead you ever in His Holy Way and Will; so that ye fall not into sin through inadvertence, through ignorance, or through human frailty.

In this manner shall ye commence your Oration, and continue thus every morning during the first two Moons or Months.

Meseemeth here that now some may say Wherefore dost thou not write down the words or form of prayer the which I should employ, seeing that, as for me, I am neither sufficiently learned, nor devout, nor wise?

Know ye that although in the beginning your prayer be but feeble, it will suffice, provided that

109   " Et jusqua cequil tremonte son jour dure jusqua cequil se leve derechef."

110   This is the initiated Rosicrucian teaching, which is very different to that of the outer and uninitiated World.

ye understand how to demand the Grace of the Lord with love and a true heart, whence it must be that such a prayer cometh forth. Also it serveth nothing to speak without devotion, without attention, and without intelligence; nor yet to pronounce it with the mouth alone, without a true intent; nor yet to read it as do the ignorant and the impious. But it is absolutely necessary that your prayer should issue from the midst of your heart, because simply setting down prayers in writing, the hearing of them will in no way explain unto you how really to pray.[111] This is the reason that I have not wished to give unto you any special form of prayers and orations, so that ye yourselves may learn from and of yourselves how to pray, and how to invoke the Holy Name of God, our Lord; and for that reason I have not been willing that ye should rely uponme in order to pray. Ye have the Holy and Sacred Scripture, the which is filled with very beautiful and potent prayers and actions of grace. Study then herein, and learn herefrom, and ye shall have no lack of instructions how to pray with fruit. And although in the commencement your prayer may be weak, it sufficeth that your heart be true and loyal towards God, Who little by little will kindle in you His Holy Spirit, Who will so teach you and enlighten your Spirit, that ye shall both know and have the power to pray.

When ye shall have performed your orations, close the window, and go forth from the Oratory; so that no one may be able therein to enter; and ye shall not yourselves enter again until the evening when the Sun shall be set. Then shall ye enter therein afresh, and shall perform your prayers in the same manner as in the morning.

For the rest, ye shall govern yourselves each day as I shall tell you in the following instructions.

Concerning the Bed Chamber and the Oratory, and how they should be arranged, I will tell hereafter in the Eleventh Chapter.[112]

It is requisite that ye shall have a Bed Chamber near the Oratory or else your ordinary habitation, which it is necessary first to thoroughly clean out and perfume, and see that the Bed be both new and clean. Your whole attention must be given to purity in all things; because the Lord hath in abomination all that is impure. You shall sleep in this said Chamber, and you shall continue therein during the day, there transacting the matters which belong unto your business; and those which you can dispense with, leave alone. You may sleep with your Wife in the bed when she is pure and clean; but when she hath her monthly courses you shall not allow her to enter the bed, nor even the Chamber. Every Sabbath-eve it is necessary to change the sheets of the bed, and all the linen. Every Saturday you shall perfume the Chamber. And ye shall not allow any dog, cat, or other animal to enter into nor dwell therein; so that they may in no way be able to render it unclean. As regardeth the matrimonial obligation, it is chastity, and the duty that of engendering children; but the whole should be done in the Fear of God, and, above all things, in such case see that your Wife be not impure. But during the following four Moons ye shall flee sexual intercourse as ye would the Plague. Even if ye have children, endeavour to send them away unto another place before (commencing the Operation), so that they may not be an hindrance from being about you; except the eldest-born of the family, and infants at the breast.

As regardeth the regimen of your life and actions, ye shall have regard unto your status and condition. If you be your own Master, as far as lieth in your power, free yourself from all your business, and quit all mundane and vain company and conversation; leading a life tranquil, solitary and honest. If aforetime you have been a wicked, debauched, avaricious, luxurious and proud man, leave and flee from all these Vices. Consider that this was one of the principal reasons why ABRAHAM, MOSES, DAVID, ELIJAH, JOHN, and other holy men retired into desert places, until that they had acquired this Holy Science and Magic; because where there are many people, many scandals do arise; and where scandal is, Sin cometh; the which at length offendeth and driveth

---

111   This is the great point to be studied in all Magical Operations soever, and unless the whole heart and soul and faith go with the ceremony, there can be no reliable result produced.

112   The title of the Eleventh Chapter of the Second Book is "Concerning the Selection of the Place".

away the Angel of God, and the Way which leadeth unto Wisdom becometh closed unto ye. Fly as far as you can the conversation of men, and especially of such as in the past have been the companions of your debauches; or who have led you into sin. Ye shall therefore seek retirement as far as possible; until that ye shall have received that Grace of the Lord which ye ask. But a Domestic Servant[113] who is compelled to serve a Master cannot well have these conveniences (for working and performing the Operation).

Take well heed in treating of business, in selling or buying, that it shall be requisite that you never give way unto anger, but be modest and patient in your actions.

You shall set apart two hours each day after having dined, during the which you shall read with care the Holy Scripture and other Holy Books, because they will teach you to be good at praying, and how to fear the Lord; and thus day by day shall ye better know your Creator. The other exercises which be free and permitted unto you, are hereafter set forth and principally in the Eleventh Chapter.

As for eating, drinking and sleeping, such should be in moderation and never superfluous. It is especially necessary to shun drunkenness, and flee public dinners. Content yourself with eating at your own house, with your family, in the peace and quiet which God hath granted unto you. You should never sleep during the day, but you may in the morning, for after that you have performed your devotions you may if you wish again go to bed to rest yourself. And if it happeneth by chance that you do not rise sufficiently early, that is to say before sunrise, it doth not greatly matter (provided that it be not done of evil intent), and you shall perform your ordinary morning prayer; [114] but you should not accustom yourself to be slothful, it being always better to pray unto God at an early hour.

CONCERNING CLOTHING AND FAMILY.

Your dress should be clean but moderate, and according to custom. Flee all vanity. You shall have two dresses, in order that you may be able to change them; and you shall change them the eve of each Sabbath, wearing the one one week, and the other the next; brushing and perfuming them always beforehand.

As for that which regardeth the family, the fewer in number, the better also act so that the servants may be modest and tranquil. All these pieces of advice be principal points which it is well to observe. As for the rest, you have only to keep before your eyes the Tables of the Law during all this time, and also afterwards; because these Tables should be the rule of your life.

Let your hand be ever ready to give alms and other benefits to your neighbour; and let your heart be ever open unto the poor, whom God so loveth that one cannot express the same.

And in the case that during this period you should be attacked by some illness, which would not permit you to go unto the Oratory, this need not oblige you to abandon your enterprise at once; but you should govern yourself to the best of your ability; and in such case you shall perform your orations in your bed, entreating God to restore you to health, so that you may be enabled to continue your undertaking, and make the sacrifices which be due, and so with the greater strength be able to work to obtain His Wisdom.

And this is all that we should do and observe during these two Moons.

---

113   Meaning in the case where the Aspirant unto the Sacred Magic is a Servant actually then serving a Master.

114   The object of most of these instructions is of course to keep the Astral Sphere of the Aspirant free from evil influences, and accustom him to pure and holy thoughts and to the exercise of Will power and Self-control. The student of the Indian Tatwas will know the value of active meditation at Sunrise because that moment is the Akâsic commencement of the Tatwic course in the day, and of the power of the Swara.

THE EIGHTH CHAPTER.
CONCERNING THE TWO SECOND MOONS

THE two first Moons being finished; the two second Moons follow, during the which ye shall make your prayer, morning and evening at the hour accustomed; but before entering into the Oratory ye shall wash your hands and face thoroughly with pure water. And you shall prolong your prayer with the greatest possible affection, devotion and submission; humbly entreating the Lord God that He would deign to command His Holy Angels to lead you in the True Way, and Wisdom, and Knowledge, by studying the which assiduously in the Sacred Writings there will arise more and more (Wisdom) in your heart.

The use of the rights of Marriage is permitted, but should scarcely if at all be made use of (during this period).

You shall also wash your whole body every Sabbath Eve.

As to what regardeth commerce and manner of living, I have already given unto you sufficient instruction. Only it is absolutely necessary to retire from the world and seek retreat; and ye shall lengthen your prayers to the utmost of your ability.

As for eating, drinking and clothing, ye shall govern yourselves in exactly the same manner as in the two first Moons; except that ye shall fast (the Qabalistical fast) every Sabbath Eve.

NOTE WELL: The Sabbath is for the Jews, who are accustomed to observe the same every Saturday, but for Christians the Sabbath is the Sunday, and they[115] ought to consider the Saturday as its Eve.

THE NINTH CHAPTER.
CONCERNING THE TWO LAST MOONS WHICH MUST BE THUS COMMENCED

MORNING and Noon ye shall wash your hands and your face on entering the Oratory;[116] and firstly ye shall make Confession of all your sins; after this, with a E very ardent prayer, ye shall entreat the Lord to accord unto you this particular grace, which is, that you may enjoy and be able to endure[117] the presence and conversation of His Holy Angels, and that He may deign by their intermission to grant unto you the Secret Wisdom, so that you may be able to have dominion over the Spirits and over all creatures.

Ye shall do this same at midday before dining, and also in the evening; so that during these two last Moons ye shall perform the prayer three times a day, and during this time ye shall ever keep the Perfume upon the Altar. Also towards the end of your Oration, ye shall pray unto the Holy Angels, supplicating them to bear your sacrifice before the Face of God, in order to intercede for you, and that they shall assist you in all your operations during these two Moons.

The man who is his own master[118] shall leave all business alone, except works of charity towards his neighbour. You shall shun all society except that of your Wife and of your Servants.

---

115   I.e., the Christians.

116   This probably means in the bed-chamber before entering the Oratory.

117   Que vous puissiez jouir et resister à la présence, etc.

118   I.e., independent.

Ye shall employ the greatest part of your time in speaking of the Law of God, and in reading such works as treat wisely thereof; so that your eyes may be opened unto that which from past time even unto the present ye have not as yet seen, nor thought of, nor believed.

Every Sabbath Eve shall ye fast, and wash your whole body, and change your garment.

Furthermore, ye shall have a Vest and Tunic of linen, which ye shall put on every time that ye enter into the Oratory, before ye commence to put the Perfume in the Censer, as I shall tell ye more fully hereafter

Also ye shall have a basket or other convenient vessel of copper filled with Charcoal to put inside the Censer when necessary, and which ye can take outside the Oratory, because the Censer itself should never be taken away from the place. Note well that after having performed your prayer, you ought to take it[119] out of the Oratory, especially during the Two last Moons, and ye should inter it in a place which cannot well be made unclean, such as a garden.

THE TENTH CHAPTER.
CONCERNING WHAT THINGS A MAN MAY LEARN AND STUDY DURING THESE TWO MOONS

ALTHOUGH the best counsel which I can give is that a man should go into retirement in some desert or solitude, until the time of the Six Moons destined unto this Operation be fulfilled, and that he shall have obtained that which he wisheth; as the Ancients used to do; nevertheless now this is hardly possible; and we must accommodate ourselves unto the era (in which we live); and being unable to carry it out in one way, we should endeavour to do so in another; and attach ourselves only unto Divine Things.

But there be certain who cannot even do this thoroughly, notwithstanding they may honestly wish the same; and this because of their divers employments and positions which will not permit them to act in accordance with their desires, so that they are compelled to carry on their worldly occupations.

In order then that such may know what occupations and business they can follow out without prejudice to this Operation, I will here state the same in few words.

We may then exercise the profession of Medicine, and all arts connected with the same; and we may perform all operations which tend unto charity and mercy towards our neighbour purely and simply. As for what concerneth the liberal arts ye may interest yourselves in Astronomy, etc., but flee all arts and operations which have the least tincture of Magic and Sorcery, seeing that we must not confound together God and Belial: God wisheth to be alone; unto Him pertain all honour and glory. All the above matters are however permitted during the two first and the two second Moons.

You may walk in a garden for recreation; but you shall do no servile work; and amidst the flowers and the fruits you can also meditate upon the greatness[120] of God. But during the two third and last Moons ye shall quit every other matter only permitting your recreation to consist in things Spiritual and Divine. If ye wish to be participators in the Conversation of the Angels, and in the Divine Wisdom, lay aside all indiscreet[121] things, and regard it as a pleasure when ye can spare two or three hours to study the Holy Scripture, because hencefrom ye shall derive incred-

---

119   I.e., the ashes of the charcoal and incense.

120   In the text evidently by a slip the word grandeur is repeated la grandeur la grandeur de Dieu.

121   " Laissez apart touttes les choses curieuses."

ible profit; and even the less ye are learned, so much the more will ye become wise and clever. It sufficeth that in the performance of your Orisons ye shall not give way unto sleep, and that ye shall fail in nowise in this operation through negligence and voluntarily.

THE ELEVENTH CHAPTER.
CONCERNING THE SELECTION OF THE PLACE

WE should make the Selection of the Place (for the Operation) before commencing it, and prior to the celebration of the Passover, in order that we may decide upon the same without hindrance, and it is necessary that all things should be prepared.

He who commenceth this Operation in solitude can elect a place according unto his pleasure; where there is a small wood, in the midst of which you shall make a small Altar, and you shall cover the same with a hut (or shelter) of fine branches, so that the rain may not fall thereon and extinguish the Lamp and the Censer. Around the Altar at the distance of seven paces you shall prepare a hedge of flowers, plants, and green shrubs, so that it may divide the entrance[122] into two parts; that is to say, the Interior where the Altar and Tabernacle will be placed after the manner of a Temple; and the part Exterior, which with the rest of the place will be as a Portico thereunto.

Now if you commence not this Operation in the Country, but perform it in a Town, or in some dwelling-place, I will show unto ye what shall be necessary herein.[123]

Ye shall choose an Apartment which hath a Window, joined unto the which shall be an uncovered Terrace (or Balcony), and a Lodge (or small room or hut) covered with a roof, but so that there may be on every side windows whence you may be able to see in every direction, and whence you may enter into the Oratory. In the which place[124] the Evil Spirits shall be able to appear, since they cannot appear within the Oratory itself. In the which place, beside the Oratory towards the quarter of the North, you shall have a rooted or covered Lodge, in the which and from whence one may be able to see the Oratory. I myself also had two large windows made in my Oratory, and at the time of the Convocation of the Spirits, I used to open them and remove both the shutters and the door, so that I could easily see on every side and constrain them[125] to obey me.

The Oratory should always be clear and clean swept, and the flooring should be of wood, of white pine; in fine, this place should be so well and carefully prepared, that one may judge it to be a place destined unto prayer.

The Terrace and the contiguous Lodge where we are to invoke the Spirits we should cover with river sand to the depth of two fingers at the least.

The Altar should be erected in the midst of the Oratory; and if any one maketh his Oratory in desert places, he should build it[126] of stones which have never been worked or hewn, or even touched by the hammer.

The Chamber[127] should be boarded with pine wood, and a Lamp full of Oil Olive should be

---

122   " L'avenue"; the modern sense of this word is, of course, a road or path bordered by trees.

123   Compare the following description with that of Sir Philip Derval's so-called Observatory, in the Strange Story, by Bulwer Lytton.

124   I.e., the Terrace or Balcony.

125   I.e., the Spirits.

126   I.e., the Altar.

127   He here evidently means the Oratory, and not the Bedchamber described in Chapter VII.

suspended therein, the which every time that ye shall have burned your perfume and finished your orison, ye shall extinguish. A handsome Censer of bronze, or of silver if one hath the means, must be placed upon the Altar, the which should in no wise be removed from its place until the Operation be finished, if one performeth it in a dwelling-house; for in the open country one cannot do this. Thus in this point as in all the others, we should rule and govern ourselves according unto the means at our disposal.

The Altar, which should be made of wood, ought to be hollow within after the manner of a cupboard, wherein you shall keep all the necessary things, such as the two Robes, the Crown or Mitre, the Wand, the Holy Oils, the Girdle or Belt, the Perfume; and any other things which may be necessary.

[128]The second habiliments will be a Shirt or Tunic of linen, large and white, with well and properly made sleeves. The other Robe will be of Crimson or Scarlet Silk with Gold, and it should not be longer than just unto the knees, with sleeves of similar stuff. As for these vestments, there is no particular rule for them; nor any especial instructions to be followed; but the more resplendent, clean, and brilliant they are the better will it be. You shall also make a Girdle of Silk of the same colour as the Tunic, wherewithal you shall be girded. You shall have upon your head a beautiful Crown or woven Fillet of Silk and Gold. You shall prepare the Sacred Oil in this manner: Take of myrrh[129] in tears, one part; of fine cinnamon, two parts; of galangal[130] half a part; and the half of the total weight of these drugs of the best oil olive. The which aromatics you shall mix together according unto the Art of the Apothecary, and shall make thereof a Balsam, the which you shall keep in a glass vial which you shall put within the cupboard (formed by the interior) of the Altar. The Perfume shall be made thus: Take of Incense in tears[131] one part; of Stacté[132] half a part; of Lign Aloes a quarter of a part; and not being able to get this wood you shall take that of cedar, or of rose, or of citron, or any other odoriferous wood. You shall reduce all these ingredients into a very fine powder, mix them well together and keep the same in a box or other convenient vessel. As you will consume a great deal of this perfume, it will be advisable to mix enough on the eve of the Sabbath to last the whole week.

You shall also have a Wand of Almond-tree wood, smooth and straight, of the length of about from half an ell to six feet.[133] And ye shall keep the aforesaid things in good order in the cupboard [134] of the Altar, ready for use in the proper time and place.

Here followeth the manner of ordering oneself and of operating.

---

128   The Rosicrucian initiate will note the description of these vestments.

129   " Mirrhe en larmes".

130   ? Galanca, or galanga, an Indian root, used for medicinal purposes. See description of Holy Anointing Oil and Perfume in Exodus xxx.

131   Olibanum.

132   Or storax.

133   A "brasse" is a fathom; but here perhaps implies rather an arm's length: "Lune brasse enveron ou demi aulne".

134   I.e., in the hollow interior of the Altar.

THE TWELFTH CHAPTER.
HOW ONE SHOULD KEEP ONESELF IN ORDER TO CARRY OUT THIS OPERATION WELL

THIS Operation being truly Divine, it is necessary once more to treat of and distinguish the present Consecration into different periods of time.

You shall then understand that during the two first and two second Moons, no other Consecration must be performed, than that of which we have already spoken in the Seventh and Eighth foregoing Chapters,[135] unto the which I refer you, so as not to be too prolix. And I only say unto you, that during the course of the two first and two second Moons, every Saturday when ye perform the Orison, ye shall also burn the Perfume as well in the morning as in the evening; and in the two third and last Moons ye shall make the Prayer and the Perfume thrice daily.

Now here hath the last part of the time arrived here therefore open ye your eyes and be attentive, and govern yourselves in everything and every place in the way which I have written unto you. Have confidence in God, because if even until then ye have faithfully observed mine instructions which I have given unto you, and if your Orisons shall have been made with a righteous heart and with devotion, there is no manner of doubt that all things will appear easy unto you, and your own spirit and your understanding will teach you the manner in which you should conduct yourself in all points; because your Guardian Angel is already about you, though Invisible, and conducteth and governeth your heart, so that you shall not err. The two Moons being finished, in the morning ye shall commence all that is commanded in the Ninth Chapter,[136] and further observe this present Chapter.

When first ye shall enter into the Oratory, leave your shoes without,[137] and having opened the window,[138] ye shall place the lighted coals in the Censer which[139] you shall have brought with you, you shall light the Lamp, and take from the Cupboard of the Altar your two Vestments, the Crown, the Girdle and the Wand, placing them upon the Altar. Then take the Sacred Oil in your left hand, cast some of the Perfume upon the Fire, and place yourself upon your knees,[140] praying unto the Lord with fervour.

THE ORISON.

O LORD GOD of Mercy; God, Patient, Most Benign and Liberal; Who grantest Thy Grace in a thousand ways, and unto a thousand generations; Who forgettest the iniquities, the sins, and the transgressions of men; in Whose Presence none is found innocent; Who visitest the transgressions of the father upon the children and nephews unto the third and fourth generation; I know my wretchedness, and that I am not worthy to appear before Thy Divine Majesty, nor even to implore and beseech Thy Goodness and Mercy for the least Grace. But, O Lord of Lords, the Source of Thy Bounty is so great, that of Itself It calleth those who are ashamed by reason of their sins and dare not approach, and inviteth them to drink of Thy Grace. Wherefore, O Lord my

---

135 Which give the instructions for these periods.

136 Concerning the two last Moons.

137 "Put off thy shoes from off thy feet, for the place whereon thou standest is holy ground."

138 It will be remarked how this point is insisted on.

139 "Which," apparently, should refer to the coals, and not to the censer.

140 Preferably I should advise upon the Western side of the Altar, and facing therefore the East; also I would have the cupboard opening upon the Western side, for certain mystical reasons.

God, have pity upon me, and take away from me all iniquity and malice; cleanse my soul from all the uncleanness of sin; renew within me my Spirit, and comfort it, so that it may become strong and able to comprehend the Mystery of Thy Grace, and the Treasures of Thy Divine Wisdom. Sanctify me also with the Oil of Thy Sanctification, wherewith Thou hast sanctified all Thy Prophets; and purify in me therewith all that appertaineth unto me, so that I may become worthy of the Conversation of Thy Holy Angels and of Thy Divine Wisdom, and grant unto me the Power which Thou hast given unto Thy Prophets over all the Evil Spirits. Amen. Amen."

This is the Prayer which I myself made use of in my Consecration; the which I give not here to confine you (to a certain form), nor to oblige you to employ the same, nor to tell it you over as I would to a parrot whom I should wish to teach to talk; but only and solely to give unto you an idea of the manner in which we should pray.

Having finished your Orison, rise from your knees, and anoint the centre[141] of your forehead with a little of the Sacred Oil; after this dip your finger into the same Oil, and anoint therewith the four upper corners of the Altar. Touch also with this Holy Oil the Vestments, the Girdle, the Crown, and the Wand, on both sides. You shall also touch the Doors and the Windows of the Oratory. Then with your finger dipped in the Oil you shall write upon the four sides of the Altar these words, so that they may be perfectly clearly written on each side:--

"In whatever place it may be wherein Commemoration of My Name shall be made, I will come unto you and I will bless you."

This being done the Consecration is finished, and then ye shall put the White Tunic and all the other things into the Cupboard of the Altar. Then kneel down and make your ordinary prayer, as is laid down in the Third Chapter;[142] and be well ware to take no consecrated thing out of the Oratory; and during the whole of the ensuing period ye shall enter the Oratory and celebrate the Office with naked feet.

THE THIRTEENTH CHAPTER.
CONCERNING THE CONVOCATION OF THE GOOD SPIRITS

WE are now arrived at a point at which ye shall be able to see clearly, having duly followed out and observed the instructions which I have given unto you, and having during all this time served God your Creator with a perfect heart. We are now arrived at the term, wherefore the following morning rise betimes, neither wash yourselves at all nor dress yourselves at all in your ordinary clothes; but take a Robe of Mourning; enter the Oratory with bare feet; go unto the side of the Censer, take the ashes therefrom and place them upon your head; light the Lamp; and put the hot coals into the Censer; and having opened the windows, return unto the door. There prostrate yourself with your face against the ground, and order the Child [143]to put the Perfume upon the Censer, after which he is to place himself upon his knees before the Altar; following in all things and throughout the instructions which I have given unto you in the last chapter of the First Book, to which I am here referring.[144] Humiliate yourself before God and His Celestial Court, and commence your Prayer with fervour, for then it is that you will begin to enflame yourself in praying,

---

141   The place of the third eye in the Indian figures of Gods.

142   This is apparently a slip for "the Seventh Chapter"; as the Third Chapter is only a short one regarding those who are fitted to undertake the Operation.

143   See Book I., Chapter XII.

144   Because previously when he has mentioned a foregoing chapter, it has been one of those in this Second Book to which he has referred.

and you will see appear an extraordinary and supernatural Splendour which will fill the whole apartment, and will surround you with an inexpressible odour, and this alone will console you and comfort your heart so that you shall call for ever happy the Day of the Lord. Also the Child[145] will experience an admirable feeling of contentment in the presence of the Angel. And you shall continue always your Prayer redoubling your ardour and fervour, and shall pray the Holy Angel that he may deign to Sign, and write upon a small square plate of silver (which you shall have had made for this purpose and which you shall have placed upon the Altar) another Sign if you shall have need of it in order to see him; and everything which you are to do. As soon as the Angel shall have made the Sign by writing, and that he shall have written down some other counsel which may be necessary unto you, he will disappear, but the splendour will remain. The which the Child having observed, and made the sign thereof unto you, you shall command him to bring you quickly the little plate of silver, and that which you find written thereon you shall at once copy, and order the Child to replace it upon the Altar. Then you shall go forth from the Oratory and leave the Window open, and the Lamp alight, and during this whole day you shall not enter into the Oratory; but shall make preparation for the day following; and during the day you shall speak to none, nor make answer, even were it your own wife or children or servants; except to the Child whom you can send away. Also you shall beforehand have set your affairs in order, and so arranged them that no embarrassment may be caused you thereby, which might distract your attention. In the evening when the Sun shall be set, you shall eat but soberly; and then you shall go to rest alone; and you shall live separated from your wife during these days.

During Seven Days shall you perform the Ceremonies without failing therein in any way; namely, the Day of the Consecration, the Three Days of the Convocation of the Good and Holy Spirits, and the Three other Days of the Convocation of the Evil Spirits.

Now the second morning after, you are to be prepared to follow the counsel which the Angel will have given you. You will go early unto the Oratory, you will place the lighted charcoal and perfumes in the Censer, you are to relight the Lamp if it be (by that time) extinguished; and wearing the same Robe of Mourning as of the day before, prostrate with your face towards the ground, you shall humbly pray unto and supplicate the Lord that He may have pity on you, and that He may deign to fulfil your prayer; that He will grant unto you the vision of His Holy Angels, and that the Elect Spirits may deign to grant unto you their familiar converse. And thus shall ye pray unto the utmost degree that shall be possible unto you, and with the greatest fervour that you can bring into action from your heart, and this during the space of two or three hours. Then quit the Oratory, returning thither at midday for another hour, and equally again in the evening; then you shall eat after the manner aforesaid, and go to rest. Understand also that the odour and the splendour will in nowise quit the Oratory.

The third day being now arrived, you shall act thus. The evening (before) you shall wash your whole body thoroughly; and in the morning, being dressed in your ordinary garments, you shall enter into the Oratory, but with naked feet. Having placed the Fire and the Perfumes in the Censer, and lighted the Lamp, you shall put on the White Vestment, and place yourself on your knees before the Altar, to render thanks to God for all His benefits, and firstly for having granted unto you a Treasure so great and so precious. You shall render thanks also unto the Holy Guardian Angels, praying unto them that henceforward they will have you in their care for the whole period of your life; also that he[146] will never abandon you, that he will lead you in the Way of the Lord, and that he will watch carefully over you to assist you, and consent unto the present Operation of the Sacred Magic, so that you shall have such Force and Virtue that you may be able to constrain the Spirits accursed of God, unto the Honour of your Creator, and for your own good and that of your neighbour.

145   If the Operator himself has developed the clairvoyant faculty; which the training he has subjected himself to for six months ought to have greatly aided, and be pure in mind, I can see no necessity for the employment of a Child as Seer.

146   I.e., your special and particular Guardian Angel.

And then shall you first be able to put to the test whether you shall have well employed the period of your Six Moons, and how well and worthily you shall have laboured in the quest of the Wisdom of the Lord; since you shall see your Guardian Angel appear unto you in unequalled beauty; who also will converse with you, and speak in words so full of affection and of goodness, and with such sweetness, that no human tongue could express the same. He will animate you unto your great content in the fear of God, making you a recital of the blessings which you have received from God; and bringing unto your remembrance the sins by which you have offended Him during the whole period of your life, will instruct you and give unto you the manner in which you shall be able to appease Him by a pure, devout, and regulated life, and by honest and meritorious actions, and such things as God shall ordain unto you. After this he will show unto you the True Wisdom and Holy Magic, and also wherein you have erred in your Operation, and how thenceforward you should proceed in order to overcome the Evil Spirits, and finally arrive at your desired ends. He will promise never to abandon you, but to defend and assist you during the whole period of your life; on condition that you shall obey his commands, and that you shall not voluntarily offend your Creator. In one word, you shall be received by him with such affection that this description which I here give unto you shall appear a mere nothing in comparison.

Now at this point I commence to restrict myself in my writing, seeing that by the Grace of the Lord I have submitted and consigned you unto a MASTER so great that he will never let you err.

Observe that on the third day you should remain in familiar conversation[147] with your Guardian Angel. You should quit the Oratory for a short time in the afternoon, remaining without about an hour; then for the rest of the day you shall remain therein, receiving from the Holy Angel distinct and ample information regarding the Evil Spirits and the manner of bringing them into submission, carefully writing down and taking notes of all these matters. Now, the Sun being set, you shall perform the Evening Orison with the ordinary Perfume, giving thanks unto God in particular for the very great Grace that He hath granted unto you in that day, there also Supplicating Him to be propitious unto you and to aid you during your whole life, so that you shall never be able to offend Him. You shall also render thanks unto your Guardian Angel and beseech him not to abandon you.

The Prayer being finished you will see that the Splendour will disappear. Then shall you quit the Oratory, closing the door, but leaving the windows open and the Lamp alight. You shall return as on the preceding days unto your apartment where you shall modestly recreate yourself, and eat your necessary food, then you shall go to rest until the following morning.

THE FOURTEENTH CHAPTER.
CONCERNING THE CONVOCATION OF THE SPIRITS

THOUGH the following advice may be scarcely necessary for the most part, since I have already explained unto you all things necessary to be done; and also seeing that your Guardian Angel will have sufficiently instructed you in all that you should do; yet nevertheless I will here declare plainly certain matters unto you, with the idea rather of making the account of the Operation complete in this Book, [148]and also to give you every opportunity of possessing the matter thoroughly through reading these things many times; so that having received the Vision of the Angel, you may find yourself thoroughly instructed in all the essential points.

Having then reposed yourself during the night, you shall rise in the morning before dawn, and

147   " En la familiarité et conversation delange."

148   I.e., this Second Book of the three constituting the treatise.

shall enter into the Oratory; and having placed the lighted Charcoal in the Censer, light the Lamp also. You shall then robe yourself, taking first the White Vestment, and over this you shall put on that[149] of Silk and Gold, then the Girdle, and upon your head you shall place the Crown, and you shall lay the Wand upon the Altar. Then, having put the Perfume in the Censer you shall fall upon your knees, and pray unto Almighty God to grant you the Grace to finish your Operation unto the Praise and Glory of His Holy Name, and for your own use and that of your neighbour. Also you shall supplicate your Guardian Angel to aid you, and to govern your heart with his counsel, and all your senses. After this you shall take the Wand in your right hand, and pray unto God to give unto this Wand as much virtue, force, and power as He gave unto those of MOSES, of AARON, of ELIJAH, and of the other Prophets whose number is infinite.

Now place yourself beside the Altar looking towards the Door and the open Terrace; or if you be in the Country place yourself at the Western[150] side, and commence by summoning the Chief Spirits and Princes.

But your Angel will already have instructed you how to convoke them, and will have sufficiently impressed it on your heart.

And as well in this as in the Orison, we should never proceed and act by the mouth only or by written Conjurations alone; but with a free heart and intrepid courage because it is certain that there is more difficulty in convoking the Evil Spirits[151] than the Good, which latter usually appear more readily when they are first called if it be by persons of good intent; while the Evil Spirits flee as much as possible all occasion of submitting themselves to man. This is wherefore he who wisheth to constrain them should be upon his guard, and follow out faithfully from point to point the instructions which his Guardian Angel will have given him, and that he impresseth them well upon his memory following them from point to point; seeing that while no Spirit Good or Evil can know the secrets of your heart. before you yourself bring the same to light, unless God Who alone knoweth all things should manifest them; they (the Spirits) nevertheless can penetrate into and understand that which you are thinking by means of your actions and your words.[152] This is the reason why he who wisheth properly to convoke and conjure the Spirits, should first well consider the following Conjuration; and afterward perform it with feeling and freely by heart; and not by writing, because in using that composed by others, the Spirits thence judge that we ourselves are ignorant, and render themselves straightway more intractable and stubborn.[153] The Evil Spirits be about you, though invisible, and they keenly examine whether he who conjureth them is courageous or timid, whether he is prudent, and whether he hath a true faith in God Who

149   I.e., the Red Robe, or Mantle.

150   " Ou si vous estez en Campagne mettes vous ducosté du ponant." This word " ponant" is almost obsolete in modern French, being only employed in a nautical sense, and even then but rarely. It implies the "West," or rather the part of the "Ocean towards the West". Even in the middle ages this expression was not in wide use. The Occult student will remark here the idea of "turning to the East to pray, and to the West to invoke". But usually in Magic it is advisable to turn towards the quarter sympathetic in nature with that of the Spirit you wish to summon.

151   That is if you convoke them to serve you. But all mediæval tradition implies that they are ready enough to come if you are an evil-minded person wishing to make a pact with them to obtain magical force, i.e. a Göetic Magician as opposed to an Initiate Adept.

152   This is why in religious and magical writings such stress is laid on the importance of controlling the thoughts; which are as it were our prototypical speech and action in all matters of importance. Modern thought-reading would alone suggest this to persons unskilled in Occultism.

153   " Les Esprits jugent parla denostre ignoranse et serendent plus reveches et ostinez." The initiate knows the value of an invocation written by himself, in harmony with and expressing exactly his will and idea. But this does not deny the utility of many of the Conjurations handed down by tradition.

can perform all things with ease. We can constrain them (the Spirits), and force them to appear; but a few words ill pronounced by an ill-Intentioned person only produce an effect against the person himself who ignorantly pronounceth them; and an individual of such a character should in no way undertake this Operation, for such would be the true way to make a mock of God and to tempt Him.

OF THE CONJURATIONS.

I have many times repeated unto you that the Fear of God is the principal subject of the instruction of your Guardian Angel, against which you should never commit any fault, even if it be but slight.

Firstly: You should perform the Conjuration in your mother tongue,[154] or in a language that you well understand, and conjure the Spirits by the authority of and their obedience to the Holy Patriarchs, rehearsing unto them examples of their ruin and fall, of the sentence which God hath pronounced against them, and of their obligation unto servitude; and how on one side and on another they have been vanquished by the Good Angels and by Wise Men; all which points you will have had plenty of opportunity to study in the Sacred Writings during the Six Moons (of preparation). Also you shall menace them, in case they are unwilling to obey, with calling unto your aid the Power of the Holy Angels over them. Your Guardian Angel will also have instructed you to perform this Convocation with modesty, and in no wise to be timid, but courageous, yet in moderation, however, without too overbearing hardiness and bravery. And in case of their being inclined to resist, and unwilling to obey you, you must not on that account give way to anger, because thus you will only do injury to yourself; and they will ask nothing better, it being exactly what they would be endeavouring to do; but (on the contrary) with an intrepid heart, and putting your whole trust in God, with a tranquil heart you shall exhort them to yield, letting them see that you have put all your confidence in the Living and Only God, reminding them how powerful and potent He is; thus, therefore, govern yourself, using prudence towards them.

And communicate unto them also the Form[155] in the which you wish them to appear; the which you can not determine, nor even themselves, but you ought the evening before to have demanded this from your Guardian Angel, who knoweth better than you your nature and constitution, and who understandeth the forms which can terrify you, and those of which you can support the sight. [156]

And you must not think that this can be done otherwise, as certain Accursed Persons write; that is to say, by means of Seals, and Conjurations, and Superstitious Figures, and Pentacles, and other Abominations, written by Diabolical Enchanters;[157] for this would be the coin wherewith the Hideous SATAN would buy you for his slave.

But let your whole trust be in the Arm, the Power, and the Force of God Almighty; then shall you be in all safety, and the Guard of your Angel will defend you from all dangers. This is why you should have good courage, and have confidence that no adversity can happen unto you. Observing then the doctrine that your Angel will have given unto you, and persevering in placing all your trust in God, at length they will appear in the form commanded upon the Terrace, upon the sand; when, according to the advice and doctrine received from your Holy Angel, and as I

---

154   Yet the advantage of its being in a language which you do not immediately associate with the things of every-day life is great, provided always that you understand the words and repeat them and pronounce them correctly.

155   This recalls the phrase so frequent in Conjurations, in which the Spirits are commanded to appear "in human form without any deformity or tortuosity".

156   Because some of the Demonic forms are so terrible that the shock of their sight might cause a person of a nervous temperament to lose his reason.

157   I must again repeat that it is only evil and perverted symbols which come under this denunciation of Abraham the Jew; for nearly all Pentacles and Seals are the Symbols and Sigils of Divine and Angelic Names.

will clearly teach you in the following Chapter, you shall propound your demand, and you shall receive from them their oath.[158]

The Spirits which we should convoke on the first day are the Four Superior Princes,[159] whose Names will be written in the Nineteenth Chapter, and this is the Conjuration of the First Day.

THE CONJURATION OF THE SECOND DAY.

On the following day, having performed the ordinary Orison, and the aforesaid Ceremonies, you shall briefly repeat the aforesaid Conjuration unto the said Spirits, bringing to their remembrance their promises and Oaths made on the preceding day to send unto you the Eight Sub-Princes;[160] and address the Conjuration unto all the Twelve together, and in a little while they will appear visibly, the Eight Sub-Princes in the form which hath been commanded them; and they will promise and swear unto you (allegiance), as will be more fully shown in the following Chapter.

The Names of the Eight Sub-Princes are described hereafter in the Nineteenth[161] Chapter.

THE CONJURATION OF THE THIRD DAY.

The Conjuration of the Third Day is the same as that of the Second Day, seeing that we are then to remind the Eight Sub-Princes of their Promises and Oaths (of Allegiance); and we are to call and convoke them with all their adherents, and then they do appear once more in visible forms, the whole particular cohorts of each will appear also invisibly, surrounding the Eight Sub-Princes. But while invoking God your Lord for strength and surety, and your Holy Angel for counsel and assistance, never forget what the latter will have taught you, for it is a necessary point.

Here followeth the Fifteenth Chapter which teacheth what we should demand from the Spirits, who are divided into three classes.

THE FIFTEENTH CHAPTER.

CONCERNING WHAT YOU SHOULD DEMAND OF THE SPIRITS WHO ARE DIVIDED INTO THREE DIFFERENT TROOPS AND CONVOKED ON THREE SEPARATE DAYS

THE Demands we should make to the Spirits are of three different kinds.

THE FIRST DEMAND.

The Demand of the First Day when the Four Superior Princes shall have visibly appeared, you shall make according unto the Order of the Angel:--

Firstly: The Proposition by what Virtue, Power and Authority you make your demands unto them; that is to say by the Virtue of God our Lord Who hath made them subject unto all His creatures, and brought them to your feet.[162] Secondly:[163] That your object is not at all a malign

---

158   I.e., of allegiance to you.

159   The four Superior Spirits and Princes are: Lucifer, Leviathan, Satan, and Belial.

160   The Eight Sub-Princes are: Astaroth, Magoth, Asmodeus, Beelzebuth; Oriens, Païmon, Ariton, and Amaymon.

161   By a very evident slip, " Chapitre IX." is written in the MS. instead of XIX.

162   " Qui les asoumis atouttes ses Creatures et avos pieds."

163   This whole paragraph is difficult of clear translation by literal rendering, so I give the MS. text: " Secondement

curiosity, but (one tending) unto the Honour and Glory of God, and to your own good and that of all the Human Race. That further, every time that you shall summon them, by whatever Sign or Word, and in whatever Time and Place, and for whatever occasion and service, they shall have to appear immediately without any delay, and obey your commands. And that in case they shall have some legitimate hindrance hereto, they are to send unto you some other Spirits assigning then and there such as shall be capable and potent to accomplish and obey your will and your demand in their place. And that they shall promise and swear to observe this by the most rigorous judgment of God, and by the most severe punishment and chastisement of the Holy Angels, inflicted upon them. And that they will consent to obey, and that the Four Sovereign Princes will name unto you the Eight Sub-Princes, whom they will send in their place to take the Oath as I have already said, to appear at once on the following morning when commanded by you; and that they will duly send the Eight Sub-Princes.

For greater certainty, quit the Altar now, and go towards the Door which openeth on to the Terrace, advancing your right hand beyond.[164] Make each one of them touch the Wand, and take the Oath upon that Wand.

THE DEMAND OF THE SECOND DAY.

THE Eight Sub-Princes being invoked, you shall make unto them the same demand and the same admonition which you have (already) made unto the Four Sovereign Princes. And further you shall request from these four, that is to say, from ORIENS, PAIMON, ARITON, and AMAIMON; that each of them shall assign and consign unto you your Familiar Spirit, which from the day of your birth they are compelled to give unto you. These will be given and furnished unto you with their dependants and will afterwards obey you. It is for you to demand from these the other Spirits which you may wish to have; but seeing that they be infinite in number, and one more skilful in service than another, one for one matter, another for another; you shall make a selection of the Spirits whom you wish, and you shall put outside upon the Terrace a written list of their names for the Eight Sub-Princes (to see), and you shall require from these (latter) the Oath, as you did from the Four Superior Princes, that the following morning they shall have to appear before you together with all the Spirits whose names you shall have given in writing, and also your Familiar Spirits.

THE DEMAND OF THE THIRD DAY.

THE Eight Sub-Princes having presented all the Spirits as you have directed them, you shall command that ASTAROT[165] with all his following shall appear visibly in the Form which the Angel

---

que vostre fin nest point curiosité maligne mais alhonneur et gloire de Dieu et alutililè propre et acelle de tout le genre humain elpourtant toutte ces fois que p. 93 vous les appellerez avec quelquesoit signe ou parole etenquelquesoit temps et Lieu etpourquelle soit occasion etservile dabort sans aucunement retarder ayent aparoitre elobeissent avos commandemens etaucas quils eussent un empechemen Legitime quils ayent avous envoyer dautres esprits enles nommant presentement ceux quiseront capable etpuissan pourobeir etaccomplir vostre volonte el vostre demande en leur place etquils vous promeltent et jurent dobserver cela par le tresrigoureux jugement de Dieu etpar latres grande peine et chatiment dessts anges sur eux ils consentiront dobeir et Les 4 princes souverains vous nommeront les 8 sousprinces quils vous enveront enleurplase aleurfaire preter le serment comme jelay deja dit deparoitre dabort," etc. The writer of this manuscript never uses the slightest punctuation, and paragraphs are infrequent.

164   I.e., beyond the Door, but being careful not to go out on to the Terrace yourself.

165   Written "Atarot" by a slip in the MS.

shall have prescribed unto you; and immediately you shall see a Great Army, and all under the same Form. You shall propound unto them the same demand, which you have already made unto the Princes, and you shall cause them to take Oath to observe the same; that is to say, that every time that you shall call one of them by his name, that he shall at once appear in such Form and Place as shall please you, and that he shall punctually execute that which you shall have commanded him. All having sworn, you shall put outside the entry[166] of the Door, all the Signs of the Third Book which belong unto ASTAROT[167] alone, and make him swear thereon, also ordaining unto them[168] , that in cases when it may not seem fit unto you to command them verbally, that as soon as you shall take one of these Signs in your hand and move it from its place that the Spirit marked in the Sign shall do and execute that which the Sign beareth, and that which your intimation[169] joined thereto shall indicate; also that in the case that in the Sign[170] none of them shall be specially named, that all in general shall be obliged promptly and readily to perform the Operation commanded; and that if also in the time to come, other (Signs or) Symbols be made by you which be not here[171] included, that then also they (the Spirits under Astarot) shall be equally bound to observe and execute them also. And when the Oath hath been taken, cause the Prince in the Name of the rest to touch the Wand.

After this, remove those Symbols from the Doorway; and call MAGOT, and after him ASMODEE, and lastly BELZEBUD; and act with all these as you have done with ASTAROT; and all their Symbols having been sworn unto, put them aside in order in a certain place, so arranged that you can easily distinguish one from another, as regards the subject, operation, or effect, for which they have been made, and unto which they belong.

This being done, you shall call ASTAROT and ASMODEE together, with their common Servitors,[172] and shall propound unto them their Symbols; and having made them swear in the forementioned manner, you shall call in similar fashion ASMODEE and MAGOT, with their Servitors, and shall make them take oath upon their Signs in the aforesaid manner.

And thus shall you observe this method with the Four other Sub-Princes;[173] but first of all convoke them with their common Servitors, and make them swear upon the common Signs, then AMAIMON and ARITON together, and finally each one apart, as in the first case.[174]

And when you have put back all the Symbols into their proper place, request from each of these last Four[175] your Familiar Spirit, and make them repeat its Name, which you shall at once write down, together with the time during which they shall be obliged to serve you. Then you shall propound unto them the Signs of the Fifth Chapter of the Third Book;[176] and shall make them not only swear upon these Symbols (collectively), but also each one (separately), that from this time

---

166   I.e., upon the sand on the Terrace.

167   Again erroneously " Atarot".

168   I.e., unto the subservient Spirits of Astaroth.

169   I.e., whether Verbal, or Mental, or by Gesture.

170   Again note that the whole of the operations of this Magic of Abra-Melin and of Abraham the Jew depends on these Symbols, so that it is not the true and sacred pentacles and symbols which he condemns; but erroneous and corrupted ones made use of ignorantly.

171   I.e., in those which the Operator has written down from the Third Book, and placed at the entry of the Door for Astaroth to take oath upon.

172   I.e., Servitors belonging equally to these two Sub-Princes together.

173   I.e., Oriens, Paimon, Ariton, and Amaimon. Ariton is often called Egin or Egyn in other works on Magic.

174   I.e., following the order of the classification in the Nineteenth Chapter of this Second Book.

175   I.e., Oriens, Paimon, Ariton, and Amaimon; one Spirit from each for a Familiar.

176   Entitled: "How one may retain the Familiar Spirits, bound or free, in whatsoever form".

forward he will observe duly and with diligence the six hours destined;[177] and you shall cause them to promise to serve you with fidelity, performing all which they are obliged to do, and that you shall command their (services); and that they shall not in the slightest degree be false and lying as regardeth you; also, that if by chance you should assign over one of them unto another person, that he shall act as faithfully by him as by yourself; and, lastly, that they are to fulfil, perform, and execute, that which God for their Chastisement hath destined unto them for Sentence (of judgment).

You shall then observe this form with all the Princes, and until all the Symbols shall be sworn to, with the Four Familiar Spirits and the others dominating (them).

THE SIXTEENTH CHAPTER.
CONCERNING THE SENDING THEM AWAY

CONCERNING the sending away of the Spirits as well during the Three Days, as hereafter:-- It is not necessary to observe many Ceremonies in order to send away the Spirits, [178] because they themselves are only too glad to be far away from you. This is wherefore you need not otherwise I cense them to depart; that is to say that during the Three Days, having finished speaking with the Four Sovereign Princes, and afterwards with the Eight Sub-Princes, and received their Oath (of allegiance), you shall say unto them that for the present they can go unto their destined place; and that every time that they shall be summoned, let them remember their Oath made upon the Symbols.

(And you shall send away) the Familiar Spirits and all other Spirits with the aforesaid words.

It is true, however, that as regardeth the Familiar Spirits you shall tell them that at the time when they are on guard-duty they shall remain near you visible or invisible, in whatever form shall please you, in order to serve you during the destined Six Hours.

---

177   I.e., so that each of the four Familiars shall serve a fourth part of the twenty-four hours of the day, that is six hours.

178   However in all Magical Works great stress is laid on the importance of licensing a Spirit invoked in the Operation to depart, and if he be unwilling, of even compelling him against his will to return to his place. It must be remembered here, in this Operation of Abraham the Jew, that not only his Oratory but his Bed-chamber also is kept pure and consecrated, and therefore- it would be next to impossible for an Evil Spirit to break through to attack him. But in all Magical Evocations by the Circle, the Magician should never quit the same, without having licensed and even forced the Evil Spirits to depart; as cases are on record of the Operator experiencing sudden p. 98 death. I myself was present on an occasion when in the Evocation by the Circle, the Magician incautiously having stooped forward and outward just over the limit of the Circle, received a shock like that from a powerful electric battery, which nearly threw him down, struck the Magical Sword from his hand, and sent him staggering back to the centre of the Circle. Compare also with this incident Allan Fenwick's experience in the Strange Story, when his hand accidentally went beyond the limits of the Circle when he was replenishing the Lamps during the Evocation.

THE SEVENTEENTH CHAPTER.

WHAT WE SHOULD ANSWER UNTO THE INTERROGATIONS OF THE SPIRITS, AND HOW WE SHOULD RESIST THEIR DEMANDS

THE Wicked Devil knoweth full well that you are in no way obliged unto him, and that you have commenced this Operation under the Grace and Mercy of God, and under the protection and defence of the Holy Angels; nevertheless, he will not fail to try his fortune, and he will seek to turn you aside from the Veritable Path; but be you constant and courageous, and swerve not in any way, either to the right hand or to the left. If he showeth himself proud with you, render unto him the like, and in your turn show him your pride. If he be humble, be in no wise too rude and severe toward him, but be moderate in all things. If he asketh you some matter, you shall make answer unto him according to the instruction which the Guardian Angel shall have given you; and understand that the Four Princes,[179] more than all the rest, will powerfully tempt you, saying unto you "Who is he who hath given thee so great authority?" They will reproach you with your hardihood and presumption in summoning them, knowing how powerful they are, and contrariwise, how weak and sinful you yourself are. They will reproach you with your sins, and will especially seek to dispute with you concerning your religion and your faith in God: if you be a Jew they will tell you that your faith and your religion have been refuted by God Himself, and that you observe not the True Law as it should be (observed): also if you be a Pagan they will say, What hath God to do with you or His Creatures either, seeing that you know not God? if you be a Christian they will say unto you, What business is it of yours to have to do with Hebrew Ceremonies which are tainted with idolatry, and the like? But let none of this disquiet you in the least; answer them in few words, and laughingly, that it is none of their business to discuss these matters with you, and to deliver their opinions concerning them; and that although you may be a worthless wretch and a great sinner, you will yet hope that the True and Only God, Who hath created the Heaven and the Earth, and Who hath condemned them[180] and brought them into submission under your feet, will forgive you your sins, both now and in future, whatever may be the religion which you profess. (Further that) you wish to know, understand, confess, and honour no other than the Great and Only God, the Lord of Light, by Whose Power, Virtue, and Authority you command them to obey you.

When you shall have spoken unto them thus, then will they sing another song, telling you that if you wish them to serve and to be obedient unto you, that you must first come to terms with them. Then shall you answer them on this wise:--

"God our Lord hath condemned and sentenced you[181] to serve me, and I do not treat as an equal with those who are accustomed to obey".

Then will they demand of you some sacrifice or courtesy if you wish to be served and obeyed promptly. You shall reply that sacrifice is not to be made unto them, but rather unto the only God.

They will then entreat you not to hinder or bring to shame by means of this Wisdom any of their Devotees and Enchanters in their operations and enchantments. You shall then make answer that you are obliged to pursue the Enemies of God and the Lord, and to repress their malice, and also to save and defend your neighbour, and any who are offended and hurt by them.

Then with much verbiage, and an infinitude of different ways will they make severe attacks upon you, and even the Familiar Spirits will rise up against you in their turn. These latter will demand

---

179   Viz.: Lucifer, Leviathan, Satan, and Belial.

180   I.e., the Demons and Evil Spirits generally.

181   The Demons generally.

and beseech of you that you will in no way give them over unto others (to serve them). Hold firm, however, and promise nothing either to one class (of Spirits) or another; but reply to them that every true and brave man is obliged to aid and serve his friends to the best of his ability, and with all his possessions, among the which they must assuredly also be comprised.

When at length they see that they have lost all hope of making you prevaricate, and that they can obtain nothing notwithstanding all their requests; they will definitely surrender, and will ask nothing else of you unless it be that you shall not be too rude and insulting in commanding them. You shall make answer to this, that if they prove themselves to be obedient and prompt in serving you, that it may be that your Angel, by whose instruction and command you are governing yourself, may instruct you not to be so rigid and severe with them if they shall obey, and that in such case you will act as may be right.

THE EIGHTEENTH CHAPTER.

HOW HE WHO OPERATETH SHOULD BEHAVE AS REGARDETH THE SPIRITS

WE have already seen how one should constrain the Spirits, and what one should ask of them; also how to dismiss them without hurt, and how we should make answer loll unto their demands and presentments. [182]

All that I am about to say unto you now is superfluous, because it is certain that any one who shall have observed with a true heart and firm resolution the advice which I have given regarding the Six Moons, will be instructed with so much thoroughness and clearness by his Guardian Angel, that no doubtful point will present itself which he will not be able easily to clear up of himself.

We have also already sufficiently shown how on every or any occasion, he who operateth should comport himself as regardeth the Spirits; that is to say as their Lord, and not as their Servitor. Yet in all matters there should be a reasonable mean, seeing that we are not treating with men, but with Spirits, of whom each one knoweth more than the whole Universe together.

Now if you shall make some demand unto a Spirit, and he shall refuse to execute it; first well and carefully examine and consider whether it be in the power and nature of the Spirit to whom you make such demand, to fulfil the same. For one Spirit knoweth not all things, and that which appertaineth unto the one, another knoweth not. For this reason, see that ye well take heed before endeavouring to force them to perform a matter. Yet if, however, the Inferior Spirits be disobedient, you shall call their Superiors, and remind them of the oaths which they have taken unto you, and of the chastisement which awaiteth the breaking of such vows. And immediately, on beholding your steadfastness, they will obey you; but should they not, you ought then to Invoke your Guardian Angel, whose chastisement they will quickly feel.

Yet, notwithstanding, we should never employ harsh means, in order to have that which we can obtain by gentleness and courtesy. [183] If during the Invocation they should appear with tumult and insolence, fear nothing; neither give way to anger; but appear to make no account thereof. Only show them the Consecrated Wand, and if they continue to make a disturbance, smite upon

---

182   In the original: " demandes etapparitions".

183   Let me here once again insist on the absolute necessity in Occult working of being courteous, even to the Evil Spirits; for the Operator who is insolent and overbearing will speedily lay himself open to obsession by a Spirit of like nature, the which will bring about his ultimate downfall.

the Altar twice or thrice therewith, and all will be still.

It should be noted, that after you shall have licensed them to depart, and they shall have disappeared, you shall take the Censer from the top of the Altar, and having put perfume therein, take it out of the Oratory on to the Terrace whereon the Spirits shall have appeared, and you shall perfume the place all round; for otherwise the Spirits might work some evil unto persons entering by chance therein. Now should you be willing to content yourself with the Symbols which be in the Third Book here following; you shall the day after take away all the Sand from the Terrace and cast it into a secret place; but above all things take care not to throw it either into a river or into the navigable sea.

But should you desire to procure for yourself various other Symbols and Secrets, leave the Sand and all things in place, as we shall also describe more particularly in the last chapter.

Also, should you wish it, you can retain your arrangements in place, and keep the Apartment of the Oratory proper and clean, as well as the Altar; which latter you may place in a corner, should it incommode you in the centre of the room. For in this Apartment, if it be not contaminated nor profaned, you may every Saturday enjoy the presence of your Guardian Angel; the which is one of the most sublime things which you can desire in this Sacred Art.

THE NINETEENTH CHAPTER.

A DESCRIPTIVE LIST OF THE NAMES OF THE SPIRITS WHOM WE MAY SUMMON TO OBTAIN THAT WHICH WE DESIRE

I will here give a very exact description of many spirits, the which (names) either altogether or in part, or else as many of them as you may wish, you should give written upon paper unto the eight sub-princes, on the second day of the conjuration. Now all these (spirits) be those who will appear on the third day, together with their princes. And these (spirits) be not vile, base, and common, but of rank, industrious, and very prompt unto an infinitude of things. Now their names have been manifested and discovered by the angels, and if you should wish for more the angel will augment them for you as far as you shall wish; seeing that their number is infinite.

The four princes and superior spirits be:

LUCIFER. LEVIATAN. SATAN. BELIAL.

The eight sub-princes be:

ASTAROT. MAGOT. ASMODEE. BELZEBUD. ORIENS. PAIMON. ARITON. AMAIMON.[184]

1. D: Astaroth, Magoth, Asmodi, Beelzebub, Oriens, Paymon, Arito, Amaymon.
The spirits common unto these four sub-princes, namely ORIENS, PAIMON, ARITON, and AMAIMON, be:

Hosen. Saraph. Proxosos. Habhi. Acuar. Tirana. Alluph. Nercamay. Nilen. Morel. Traci. Enaia. Mulach. Malutens. Iparkas. Nuditon. Melna. Melhaer. Ruach. Apolhun. Schabuach. Mermo.

---

184   A similar name, "Buriol," is given under the Spirits subservient to Amaymon.

Melamud. Poter. Sched. Ekdulon. Mantiens. Obedama. Sachiel. Moschel. Pereuch. Deccal. Asperim. Katini. Torfora. Badad. Coelen. Chuschi. Tasma. Pachid. Parek. Rachiar. Nogar. Adon. Trapis. Nagid. Ethanim. Patid. Pareht. Emphastison. Paraseh. Gerevil. Elmis. Asmiel. Irminon. Asturel. Nuthon. Lomiol. Imink. Plirok. Tagnon. Parmatus. Iaresin. Gorilon. Lirion. Plegit. Ogilen. Tarados. Losimon. Ragaras. Igilon. Gosegas. Astrega. Parusur. Igis. Aherom. Igarak. Geloma. Kilik. Remoron. Ekalike. Isekel. Elzegan. Ipakol. Haril. Kadolon. Iogion. Zaragil. Irroron. Ilagas. Balalos. Oroia. Lagasuf. Alagas. Alpas. Soterion. Romages. Promakos. Metafel. Darascon. Kelen. Erenutes. Najin. Tulot. Platien. Atloton. Afarorp. Morilen. Ramaratz. Nogen. Molin. (= 111 spirits servient.)[185]

2. D: Moreh, Saraph, Proxonos, Nabhi, Kosem, Peresch, Thirama, Alluph, Neschamah, Milon, Frasis, Chaya, Malach, Malabed, Yparchos, Nudeton, Mebhaer, Bruach, Apollyon, Schaluah, Myrmo, Melamod, Pother, Sched, Eckdulon, Manties, Obedamah, Jachiel, Iuar, Moschel, Pechach, Hasperim, Katsin, Phosphora, Badad, Cohen, Cuschi, Fasma, Pakid, Helel, Marah, Raschear, Nogah, Adon, Erimites, Trapis, Nagid, Ethanim. Patid, Nasi, Parelit, Emfatison, Parasch, Girmil, Tolet, Helmis, Asmiel, Irminon, Asturel, Flabison, Nascelon, Lomiol, Ysmiriek, Pliroky, Afloton, Hagrion, Permases, Sarasim, Gorilon, Afolop, Liriel, Alogil, Ogologon, Laralos, Morilon, Losimon, Ragaras, Igilon, Gesegas, Ugesor, Asorega, Parusur, Sigis, Aherom, Ramoras, Igarag, Geloma, Kilik, Romoron, Negen, Ekalak, Ilekel, Elzegar, Ipakol, Nolom, Holop, Aril, Kokolon, Osogyon, Ibulon, Haragil, Izozon, Isagas, Balabos, Nagar, Oroya, Lagasaf, Alpas, Soterion, Amillis, Romages, Promachos, Metoseph, Paraschon.

These be the spirits common unto ASTAROT and ASMODEE, viz.:

Amaniel. Orinel. Timira. Dramas. Amalin. Kirik. Bubana. Buk. Raner. Semlin. Ambolin. Abutes. Exteron, Laboux. Corcaron. Ethan. Taret. Dablat. Buriul.[186] Oman. Carasch. Dimurgos. Roggiol. Loriol. Isigi. Tioron. Darokin. Horanar. Abahin. Goleg. Guagamon. Laginx. Etaliz. Agei. Lemel. Udaman. Bialot. Gagalos. Ragalim. Finaxos. Akanef. Omages. Agrax. Sagares. Afray. Ugales. Hermiala. Haligax. Gugonix. Opilm. Daguler. Pachei. Nimalon.4 (= 53 spirits servient.)

3. A similar name, "Buriol", is given under the spirits subservient to Amaymon.

4. D: Amamil, Orinel, Tinira, Dramas, Anamalon, Kirik, Bubanabub, Ranar, Namalon, Ampholion, Abusis, Exenteron, Taborix, Corcavion, Oholem, Tareto, Tabbat, Buriub, Oman, Carasch, Dimurgos, Kogiel, Pemfodram, Liriol, Igigi, Dosom, Darochim, Horamar, Ahabhon, Yragamon, Lagiros, Eralyz, Golog, Leniel, Hageyr, Udaman, Bialod, Galagos, Bagalon, Tinakos, Akanef, Omagos, Argax, Afray, Sagares, Ugalis, Ermihala, Hahyax, Gagonix, Opilon, Dagulez, Pachahy, Nimalon.

These be the spirits common unto AMAIMON and ARITON, viz.:

Hauges. Agibol. Rigolen. Grasemin. Elafon. Trisaga. Gagalin. Cleraca. Elaton. Pafesla.5 (= 10 spirits servient.)

5. D: Harog, Agebol, Rigolen, Irasomin, Elafon, Trisacha, Gagolchon, Klorecha, Yritron, Pafesla.

These be the spirits in common between ASMODEE and MAGOT, viz.:

185   See same Name under Oriens.

186   See same Name under Belzebud.

Toun. Magog. Diopos. Disolel. Biriel. Sifon. Kele. Magiros. Sartabakim. Lundo. Sobe. Inokos. Mabakiel. Apot. Opun.6 (= 15 spirits servient.)

6. D: Magog, Sochen, Diopos, Lamargos, Disolel, Siphon, Kelef, Magyros, Mebaschel, Sartabakim, Sobhe, Inokos, Biriel.
The following be those of ASTAROT, viz.:

Aman. Camal. Toxai. Kataron. Rax. Gonogin. Schelagon. Ginar. Isiamon. Bahal. Darek. Ischigas. Golen. Gromenis. Rigios. Nimerix. Herg. Argilon. Okiri. Fagani. Hipolos. Ileson. Camonix. Bafamal. Alan. Apormenos. Ombalat. Quartas. Ugirpen. Araex. Lepaca. Kolofe.7 (= 32 spirits servient.)

7. D: Aman, Camal, Texai, Kataron, Rax, Schelegon, Giriar, Asianon, Bahal, Barak, Golog, Iromenis, Kigios, Nimirix, Hirih, Okirgi, Faguni, Hipolepos, Iloson, Camonix, Alafy, Apormanos, Ombalafa, Garsas, Ugirpon, Gomogin, Argilon, Earaoe, Lepacha, Kalotes, Ychigas, Bafamal.
These be those of MAGOT and KORE,8 viz.:

Nacheran. Katolin. Luesaf. Masaub. Urigo. Faturab, Fersebus. Baruel. Ubarin. Butarab. Ischiron. Odax. Roler. Arotor. Hemis. Arpiron. Arrabin. Supipas. Forteson. Dulid. Sorriolenen. Megalak. Anagotos. Sikastin. Petunof Mantan. Meklboc. Tigrafon. Tagora. Debam. Tiraim. Irix. Madail. Abagiron. Pandoli. Nenisem. Cobel. Sobel. Laboneton. Arioth. Marag. Kamusil. Kaitar. Scharak. Maisadul. Agilas. Kolam. Kiligil. Corodon. Hepogon. Daglas. Hagion. Egakireh. Paramor. Olisermon. Rimog. Horminos. Hagog. Mimosa. Amchison. Ilarax. Makalos. Locater. Colvam. Batternis.9 (65 spirits servient.)

8. D: "Magoth's" (alone)

9. D: Nacheran, Natolico, Mesaf, Masadul, Sapipas, Faturab, Fernebus, Baruel, Ubarin, Urgido, Ysquiron, Odax, Rotor, Arator, Butharuth, Harpinon, Arrabim, Kore, Forteson, Serupulon, Megalleh, Anagnostos, Sikastir, Mechebber, Tigraphon, Matatam, Tagora, Petanop, Dulid, Somis, Lotaym, Hyrys, Madail, Debam, Obagiron, Nesisen, Lobel, Arioth, Pandoli, Laboneton, Kamusel, Cayfar, Nearach, Masadul, Marag, Kolan, Kiligil, Corocon, Hipogon, Agilas, Nagan, Egachir, Parachmon, Olosirmon, Daglus, Ormonas, Hagoch, Mimosa, Aracuson, Rimog, Ilarak, Mokaschef, Kobhan, Batirmiss, Lachatyl.
Those of ASMODEE be:

Onei. Ormion. Preches. Maggid. Sclavak. Mebbesser. Bacaron. Holba. Hifarion. Gilarion. Eniuri. Abadir. Sbarionat. Utifa. Omet. Sarra.10 (= 16 spirits servient.)

10. D: Iemuri, Mebhasser, Bacaron, Hyla, Enei, Maggid, Abhadir, Presfees, Ormion, Schaluach, Gillamon, Ybarion.
These be those of BELZEBUD, viz.:

Alcanor. Amatia. Bilifares. Lamarion. Diralisen. Licanen. Dimirag. Elponen. Ergamen. Gotifan.

Nimorup. Carelena. Lamalon. Igurim. Akium. Dorak. Tachan. Ikonok. Kemal. Bilico. Tromes. Balfori. Arolen, Lirochi. Nominon. Iamai. Arogor. Holastri. Hacamuli. Samalo. Plison. Raderaf. Borol. Sorosma.11 Corilon. Gramon. Magalast. Zagalo. Pellipis. Natalis. Namiros. Adirael. Kabada. Kipokis. Orgosil. Arcon. Ambolon. Lamolon. Bilifor.12 (= 49 spirits servient.)

11. See same name under Oriens.

12. D: Altanor, Armasia, Belifares, Camarion, Corilon, Diralisin, Eralicarison, Elpinon, Garinirag, Sipillipis, Ergonion, Iotifar, Mynymarup, Karelesa, Natalis, Camalon, Igarim, Akahim, Golog, Namiros, Haraoth, Tedeam, Ikon, Kemal, Adisak, Bilek, Iromas, Baalsori, Arolen, Kobada, Liroki, Nominon, Iamai, Arogor, Ipokys, Olaßky, Hayamen, Samalo, Aloson, Ergosil, Borob, Ugobog, Haokub, Amolom, Bilifot, Granon, Pagalust, Xirmys, Lemalon, Radarap.
    These be of ORIENS, viz.:

Sarisel. Gasarons. Sorosma.13 Turitel. Balaken. Gagison. Mafalac. Agab.14 (= 8 spirits servient.)

13. See same name under Belzebud.

14. D: Gazaron, Sarisel, Sorosma, Turitel, Balachem, Gagison, Mafalac, Zagal.
    These be of PAIMON, viz.:

Aglafos. Agafali. Dison. Achaniel. Sudoron. Kabersa. Ebaron. Zalanes. Ugola. Came. Roffles. Menolik. Tacaros. Astolit. Rukum.15 (= 15 spirits servient.)

15. D: Ichdison, Sumuran, Aglafys, Hachamel, Agasaly, Kalgosa, Ebaron, Zalanes, Zugola, Carah, Kafles, Memnolik, Tacaros, Astolit, Marku.
    These be of ARITON, viz.:

Anader. Ekorok. Sibolas. Saris. Sekabin. Caromos. Rosaran. Sapason. Notiser. Flaxon. Harombrub. Megalosin. Miliom. Ilemlis. Galak. Androcos. Maranton. Caron. Reginon. Elerion. Sermeot. Irmenos.16 (= 22 spirits servient.)

16. Anadir, Ekorok, Rosaran, Nagani, Ligilos, Secabim, Calamosi, Sibolas, Forfaron, Andrachos, Notiser, Filaxon, Harosul, Saris, Elonim, Nilion, Ilemlis, Calach, Sarason, Semeot, Maranton, Caron, Regerion, Megalogim, Irmenos, Elamyr.
    These be those of AMAIMON, viz.:

Romeroc. Ramison. Scrilis. Buriol. Taralim. Burasen. Akesoli. Erekia. Illirikim. Labisi. Akoros. Mames. Glesi. Vision. Effrigis. Apelki. Dalep. Dresop. Hergotis. Nilima.17 (= 20 spirits servient.)

17. D: Ramiuson, Sirgilis, Bariol, Tarahim, Bumahan, Akefeli, Erkaya, Bemerot, Kilikimil, Abisi, Akorok, Maraos, Glysy, Quision, Efrigis.
    UNDER WHAT RULERS.   TOTAL OF SPIRITS SERVIENT.

Oriens, Paimon, Ariton, Amaymon   111
Ashtaroth and Asmodeus   53
Amaymon and Ariton   10
Asmodeus and Magoth 15
Ashtaroth 32
Magoth and Koré   65
Asmodeus   16
Beelzebub   49
Oriens   8
Paymon   15
Ariton   22
Amaymon   20
Total of names of servient spirits   316

Infinite be the spirits which I could have here set down, but in order not to make any confusion, I have thought fit to put only those whom I have myself employed, and whom I have found good and faithful in all the operations wherein I have availed myself of them.

Also it is true that he who shall perform this operation will be able thereafter, according to his need, to obtain (the names of) more.

NOTES TO THE FOREGOING LISTS OF NAMES OF SPIRITS by S. L. Mac Gregor-Mathers.

I have thought it advisable to give as far as possible some idea of the significations of these names of spirits, which are for the most part derived from the Hebrew or Chaldee, and also from Greek and Latin and Coptic, etc.

THE CHIEF SPIRITS.
LUCIFER:
From Latin, Lux, Light, and Fero, to bear, = A Light Bearer. There is a name "Lucifuge" also employed occasionally, from Lux, Light, and Fugio, to fly from, = He who shuns the Light.
LEVIATAN:
From Hebrew, LVIThN (usually written Leviathan instead of Leviatan), = the Crooked or Piercing Serpent or Dragon.
SATAN:
From Hebrew, ShTN, = an Adversary.
BELIAL:
From Hebrew, BLIOL, = a Wicked One.
THE EIGHT SUB-PRINCES.
ASTAROT:
From Hebrew, OShThRVTh, = flocks, crowds, or assemblies. Usually written "Ashtaroth". Also a name of the Goddess Astarté; Esther is derived from the same root.
MAGOT:
May be from Hebrew, MOVTh, = small stones or pebbles; or from MG, = a changing of camp or place; or from Greek, Magos, a magician. Usually written Maguth. Compare the French word "Magot," meaning "a sort of baboon," and also "a hideous dwarfish man"; this expression is often

used in fairy-tales to denote a spiteful dwarf or elf. This spirit has also been credited with presiding over hidden treasure. Larousse derives the name either from ancient French or German.

ASMODEE:

Usually written "Asmodeus," and sometimes "Chashmodai". Derived by some from the Hebrew word "Asamod," = to destroy or exterminate; and by others from the Persian verb "Azmonden," = to tempt, to try or prove. Some Rabbins say that Asmodeus was the child of the incest of Tubal-Cain and his sister Naamah. Others say that he was the Demon of impurity. Others again relate that he was employed by Solomon in the building of the Temple at Jerusalem; that he then attempted to dethrone Solomon, to put himself in his place; but that the King vanquished him, and the angel Gabriel chased him into Egypt, and there bound him in a grotto. The Rabbins say that when Asmodeus was working at the building of the Temple, he made use of no metal tool; but instead of a certain stone which cut ordinary stone as a diamond will glass.

BELZEBUD:

Also written frequently "Beelzebub", "Baalzebub", "Beelzebuth", and "Beelzeboul". From Hebrew, BOL, = Lord, and ZBVB,= Fly or Flies; Lord of Flies. Some derive the name from the Syriac "Beel d'Bobo," = Master of calumny, or nearly the same signification as the Greek word Diabolos, whence are derived the modern French and English "Diable" and "Devil".

ORIENS:

These four names of Oriens, Païmon, Ariton, and Amaymon, are usually allotted to the evil kings of the four quarters of the World. Oriens, from Latin, Oriens, = rising or Eastern. This name is also written Uriens, from Latin, URO, = to burn, or devour with flame. It is probably from Uriens that a mediaeval title of the Devil, viz., "Sir Urien", is derived. The Name is also sometimes written "Urieus," from Latin, "URIOS", a title given to Jupiter as presiding over the wind. Urieus is also derivable from the Greek Adj. "EURUS, EUREIA, EURU," meaning vast or extensive. By the Rabbins he is also called SMAL, Samael, which is derived from the Hebrew root SML, which means "a figure, image, or idol". It is a name given in the Qabalah to one of the chief evil spirits.

PAIMON:

Is also frequently written "Paymon", and sometimes "Paimonia". Probably from Hebrew, POMN, = a tinkling sound or small bell. This is again derived from the Hebrew root POM, = to agitate, impel, or strike forward. The word POMN is employed in Exodus 28.34, 28.33, and 39.25. Paimon is also called by the Rabbins by the title of OZAZL, Azazel, which is a name used in Leviticus with reference to the scape-goat. Its derivation is from OZ, = a goat; and AZL, = to go away. It has frequently been warmly discussed whether the word in question means simply the scape-goat, or whether it signifies a demon to whom that animal was dedicated. But in Rabbinic demonology it is always used to mean one of the chief demons.

ARITON:

It is also often called "Egyn," or "Egin". This name may be derived from the Hebrew root ORH, = to lay bare, to make naked. It may also be derived from the Greek word ARHRETON, = secret, or mysterious, in any sense good or bad. Egin may be derivable from Hebrew OGN = to delay, hinder, or retard. There may also be a connection with the Greek AIX, AIGOS, = a goat. This spirit is also called by the Rabbins OZAL, Azael, from the root OZ, which means both a goat, and also vigour, vehemence of force; thus having partly the same root as "Azazel".

AMAIMON:

Also written frequently "Amaymon"; perhaps from the Greek word MAIMON, present participle of MAIMAO; and A as an enforcing particle; hence Amaimon would mean "terrible violence and vehemence". This spirit is also called by the Rabbins MHZAL, Mahazael, perhaps from the root MZ, = to consume, or devour. Amaymon is spoken of in the various mediaeval Magical works as being a very potent spirit, and the use of a ring, with magical characters to hold before the mouth while conversing with him, is recommended as a protection against his deadly, fiery, and poisonous breath.

THE SERVITORS OF ORIENS, PAYMON, ARITON, AND AMAYMON.

Hosen:

From Chaldaic, ChVSN, chosen, = strong, vigorous, powerful.

Saraph:

From Hebrew, ShRP, = to burn, or devour with fire.

Proxosos:

Perhaps from Greek, PROX, PROXOKOS, = a kid.

Habhi:

From Chaldee, ChBA, or Hebrew, ChBH, = hidden.

Acuar:

From Hebrew, AKR, = a tiller of the earth.

Tirana:

Perhaps from Hebrew, ThRN, = the mast of a ship, also an apple tree.

Alluph:

From Hebrew, ALVP, = a leader, a duke; also a bull, from his leading the herd.

Nercamay:

Perhaps from Hebrew, NOR, = a boy, and ChMH = a companion.

Nilen:

Perhaps from NILUS, Latin, or NEILOS, Greek, = the River Nile.

Morel:

Perhaps from Hebrew, MRH, = to rebel.

Traci:

From Greek, TRACHUS, etc., = harsh, rude.

Enaia:

Perhaps from Hebrew, ONIH, = poor, afflicted.

Mulach:

Probably the same as "Moloch," from Hebrew, MLK, = to rule.

Malutens:

Perhaps from Hebrew, MOL, = to lie, or deceive, or prevaricate.

Iparkas:

Probably from Greek, HIPPARCHES, = a commander of cavalry, or leader of horse.

Nuditon:

Apparently from the Latin, NUDITAS, = nakedness, derived in its turn from NUDATUS.

Melna:

Perhaps from Hebrew, LN, to abide or rest.

Melhaer:

Perhaps from Hebrew, ML, to cut off, or divide, and ChR, whiteness, purity.

Ruach:

From Hebrew, RVCh = spirit.

Apolhun:

From Greek, APOLLUON, Apollyon, = the destroyer.

Schabuach:

From Arabic = to calm or assuage.

Mermo:

From Coptic, MER, across, and MOOU, water, = across water.

Melamud:

From Hebrew, MLMD, = stimulus to exertion.

Poter:

From Greek, POTER, = a drinking cup, or vase.

Sched:

From Hebrew, ShDD, the Hebrew name for a devastating demon. But the Hebrew root ShD implies the same idea as the English words "to shed" ; and signifies a female breast.

Ekdulon:

Probably from Greek, EKDUO, = to despoil.

Mantiens:

From Latin, MANTIENS, and Greek, MANTEIA, = prophesying, divining.

Obedama:

From Hebrew, OBD, = a servant. AMA = mother. But AMH = a maid-servant, whence Obe-dama should signify a woman-servant.

Sachiel:

Is a name frequently given in magical works to an angel of the planet Jupiter. SKK = to cover or protect, but SChH = to trample down.

Moschel:

From Hebrew, MVSh, = to move oneself about.

Pereuch:

Perhaps from Greek, PER and EUCHE, = concerning prayer, or given unto prayer.

Deccal:

From Hebrew, DChL, = to fear.

Asperim:

Perhaps from Latin, ASPERA, = rude, rigorous, perilous, dangerous.

Katini:

From Hebrew, KThN, = a tunic, whence the Greek word CHITON.

Torfora:

From Hebrew, ThOR,= a small knife, or lancet.

Badad:

From Hebrew, BDD, = solitary.

I have thus far given the probable derivations at length; but I shall, for the sake of brevity, here continue them without giving their roots and remarks thereon:

Coelen. - Latin. Heavens.

Chuschi. - Hebrew. Silent.

Tasma. - Hebrew and Chaldaic. Weak.

Pachid. - Hebrew. Fear.

Parek. - Hebrew. Roughness, Savage.

Rachiar. - Greek. Sea breaking on rocks.

Nogar. - Hebrew. Flowing.

Adon. - Hebrew. Lord.

Trapis. - Greek. Turning.

Nagid. - Hebrew. A Leader.

Ethanim. - Hebrew. An ass; a furnace.

Patid. - Hebrew. Topaz.

Pareht. - Hebrew. Fruit.

Emphastison. - Greek. Image, representation.

Paraseh. - Chaldaic. Divided.

Gerevil. - Hebrew. Divining lot, sortilege.

Elmis. - Coptic. Flying.

Asmiel. - Hebrew. Storing up.

Irminon. - Greek. Supporting.

Asturel. - Hebrew. Bearing authority.

Nuthon. - Perhaps Coptic, Godlike; or Greek, piercing.

Lomiol. - Perhaps Hebrew. Binding, bitter.

Imink. - Perhaps Coptic. Devouring.

Plirok. - Perhaps Coptic. Burning up.

Tagnon. - Perhaps Greek. Heating.

Parmatus. - Greek and Latin. Shield-bearing.

Iaresin. - Hebrew. Possessing.

Gorilon. - Coptic. Axe; cleaving either to, or asunder; bones.

Lirion. - Greek. A lily.

Plegit. - Perhaps Greek. Smiting, smitten.

Ogilen. - Hebrew. Round, wheel. Tarados. - Perhaps Coptic. Dispersion.

Losimon. - Perhaps Coptic. Understanding of restriction.

Ragaras. - Perhaps Coptic. To incline, or bow the head.

Igilon. - Perhaps Greek. After the fashion of EIKELOS.

Gosegas. - Probably Hebrew or Chaldaic. Shaking strongly.

Astrega. - Perhaps Coptic. Expeditious.

Parusur. - Perhaps Greek. Present to assist.

Igis. - Perhaps from Greek HIKO, root of HIKNEOMAL. Coming.

Aherom. - Hebrew. Separation, from ChRM.

Igarak. - Perhaps Celtic, from CARAC. Terrible.

Geloma. - Hebrew, GLM, and Latin, GLOMUS. Wrapped, or wound together.

Kilik. - Hebrew. Wrinkled with age.

Remoron. - Latin. Hindering, staying.

Ekalike. - Perhaps Greek. At rest, or quiet.

Isekel. - Hebrew. Anointing, or Anointed.

Elzegan. - Perhaps Hebrew = Turning aside.

Ipakol. - Hebrew. Breathing forth.

Haril. - Hebrew. Thorny.

Kadolon. - Perhaps Greek. A small vase, or urn.

Iogion. - Perhaps Greek. Noise of battle.

Zaragil. - Perhaps Hebrew. Scattering.

Irroron. - Latin. Sprinkling with dew.

Ilagas. - Greek. Obtaining; having obtained.

Balalos. - Perhaps Greek, BALLO, to throw.

Oroia. - Probably Greek. Returning in due season.

Lagasuf. - Perhaps Hebrew. In paleness, pining away.

Alagas. - Perhaps Greek. Wandering.

Alpas. - Probably Greek. Yielding.

Soterion. - Greek. Saving, delivering.

Romages. - Perhaps Hebrew. To throw and to touch.

Promakos. - Greek. A fighter in the front of a conflict.

Metafel. - Hebrew. To fasten.

Darascon. - Perhaps Celtic. Turbulent.

Kelen. - Greek. Going swiftly, as in a race.

Erenutes. - Perhaps Greek. Receiving.

Najin. - Hebrew. Propagating.

Tulot. - Chaldaic. Triple.

Platien. - Greek. Flat, broad.

Atloton. - Greek. Insufferable.

Afarorp. - Perhaps Hebrew. Breaking, rending.

Morilen. - Perhaps Greek. Foolish speaking.

Ramaratz. - Hebrew. Raised ground, or earth.

Nogen. - Hebrew. To strike a musical instrument.

Molin. - Hebrew. Abiding in a place.

THE SERVITORS OF ASHTAROTH AND ASMODEUS.

Amaniel. - Hebrew. Nourishment of God. (Frequently in Qabalistic magic "El," the name of God, is joined to the names even of evil spirits, to intimate that even these have no power except by his permission.)

Orinel. - Hebrew. Ornament of God; also tree of God; also elm tree.

Timira. - Hebrew. Palm.

Dramas. - Greek. Action.

Amalin. - Chaldaic. Languidness.

Kirik. - Hebrew. A stole or mantle.

Bubana. - Perhaps Hebrew. Emptiness.

Buk. - Hebrew. Perplexity.

Raner. - Perhaps Hebrew, singing; or Greek, watering.

Semlin. - Hebrew. Simulacra; appearances.

Ambolin. - Perhaps Hebrew. Tending unto nothingness.

Abutes. - Perhaps Greek. Bottomless, measureless.

Exteron. - Latin. Without, foreign, distant.

Laboux. - Perhaps Latin, and conveying the sense of "laborious".

Corcaron. - Perhaps Greek. Tumultuous, noisy.

Ethan. - Hebrew. An ass.

Taret. - Perhaps Hebrew. Dampness, tending to corruption.

Tablat. - Perhaps Hebrew. Immersions.

Buriul. - Hebrew. In terror and trembling.

Oman. - Perhaps Chaldaic. To cover, or obscure.

Carasch. - Hebrew. Voracity.

Dimurgos. - Greek. A fabricator, artisan, or workman.

Roggiol. - Perhaps Hebrew. To drag down; the feet.

Loriol. - Perhaps Hebrew. Unto horror.

Isigi. - Perhaps from Hebrew, and implying "error," or "to err".

Dioron. - Greek. Delay.

Darokin. - Probably Chaldaic. Paths or ways.

Horanar. - ? ?

Abahin. - Perhaps Hebrew, and signifying "terrible".

Goleg. - Probably Hebrew. Whirling.

Guagamon. - Greek. A net.

Laginx. - ? ?

Etaliz. - Hebrew. The furrow of a plough. Hence agriculture.

Agei. - Probably Hebrew. Meditation.

Lemel. - Perhaps Hebrew. For speech --?.

Udaman. - Perhaps a corruption of Greek, EUDAIMON, = fortunate.

Bialot. - Perhaps Hebrew. Absorption.

Gagalos. - Perhaps Greek. A tumour. (See somewhat similar name, "Gagalin," in the spirits under Amaimon and Ariton.)

Ragalim. - Hebrew. Feet.

Finaxos. - Perhaps Greek. Worthy in appearance --?.

Akanef. - Hebrew. A wing.

Omages. - Greek --? for HO MAGOS, = the magician.

Agrax. - Perhaps Hebrew. Bone.

Sagares. - Greek. A double-headed battle-axe, especially that used by the Amazons.

Afray. - Perhaps Hebrew. Dust.

Ugales. - Probably Greek. Calm.

Hermiala. - ? ? Perhaps traceable to Celtic roots.

Haligax. - ? ? Perhaps traceable to Celtic roots.

Gugonix. - ? ? Perhaps traceable to Celtic roots.

Opilm. - Hebrew. Citadels; eminences.

Daguler. - ? ?

Pachei. - Probably Greek. Thick, coarse.

Nimalon. - Perhaps from Hebrew, relating to "circumcision".

THE SERVITORS OF AMAIMON AND ARITON.

Hauges. - Apparently from thr Greek "AUGE". Brilliance.

Agibol. - Hebrew. Forcible love.

Rigolen. - Perhaps from Hebrew, = to drag down. The same root also is that of the word "Regel," = "foot".

Grasemin. - Perhaps from Hebrew, GRS, = a bone.

Elafon. - Probably from the Greek ELAPHOS, = a stag.

Trisaga. - Greek. Directing by triads.

Gagalin. - Perhaps Greek. Tumour, swelling, ganglion.

CLERACA. - Perhaps from Greek and Latin, " KLERIKOS," and "CLERICUS," = clerical.

ELATON. - Probably Latin. Sublime; borne away.

PAFESLA. - Perhaps from Hebrew-? a sculptured image.

THE SERVITORS OF ASMODEUS AND MAGOTH.

TOUN. - Perhaps from Hebrew. THNH, = Hire, Price.

MAGOG. - Hebrew. The well-known Biblical name for a powerful Gentile nation.

DIOPOS. - Greek. An overseer.

DISOLEL. - ? ?

BIRIEL. - Hebrew. Stronghold of God.

SIFON. - Greek. A Siphon or Tube for raising fluids. or Hebrew. To cover over.

KELE. - Hebrew. To consume.

MAGIROS. - Greek. A cook.

SARTABAKIM.-? ? SRTN in Hebrew = the sign Cancer.

LUNDO. - ? ?

SOBE. - Greek. The tail of a horse; also a fly-flap.

INOKOS. - Perhaps from Latin, "INOCCO," = to rake the earth over the newly sown seed.

MABAKIEL. - Hebrew. Weeping, Lamentation.

APOT. - Hebrew = A Treasure; a tribute.

OPUN. - Perhaps from Hebrew. A wheel.

THE SERVITORS OF ASHTAROTH.
AMAN. - Hebrew. To nourish.
CAMAL. - Hebrew. To desire God; the name of one of the archangels in the Qabalah.
TOXAI. - From Greek, TOXEIA, = Archery; or Latin, TOXICUM, = Poison.
KATARON. - Greek. Casting down.
RAX. - Greek. A grape-seed.
GONOGIN. - Hebrew. Pleasures, delights.
SCHELAGON. - Hebrew. Like snow.
GINAR. - ? ? Perhaps Chaldaic - ? To perfect, or finish.
ISIAMON. - Hebrew = Solitude, desolation.
BAHAL. - Hebrew = To disturb.
DAREK. - Hebrew = a way, or path.
ISCHIGAS. - Perhaps from Hebrew, IShO, = To save, or aid.
GOLEN. - Greek. A cavern.
GROMENIS. - Perhaps Latin or Greek - ? to mark out.
RIGIOS. - Greek. Horrible, terrible.
NIMERIX. - ? ? Perhaps Celtic.
HERG. - Hebrew. To slay.
ARGILON. - Greek. Clay.
OKIRI. - Perhaps Greek - ? To cause to sink or fail.
FAGANI. - Perhaps Greek - ? Devourers.
HIPOLOS. - Greek. A Goat herd.
ILESON. - Greek. Enveloping.
CAMONIX. - ? Greek - ? Perseverance in combat.
BAFAMAL. - ? ?
ALAN. - Chaldaic. A Tree.
APORMENOS. - Greek. Uncertain.
OMBALAT. - ? ?
QUARTAS. - Latin. Fourth.
UGIRPEN. - ? ?
ARAEX. - ? Greek. ? Shock.
LEPACA. - Hebrew. For opening or disclosing.
KOLOFE. - Greek. Summit, or height of achievement.

THE SERVITORS OF MAGOTH AND KORE.
NACHERAN. - Probably Hebrew. Nostrils.
KATOLIN. - Hebrew. Walls.
LUESAF. - Perhaps Hebrew. Unto loss or destruction.
MASAUB. - Hebrew. Circuit.
URIGO. - Latin. Spoiled; unfit for food.
FATURAB. - Perhaps Hebrew - ? Interpretation.
FERSEBUS. - Perhaps Greek - ? A bringer of veneration.
BARUEL. - Hebrew. Food or nourishment from God.
UBARIN. - Greek. Insult, outrage.
BUTARAB. - ? ?
ISCHIRON. - Greek. Strong, mighty.

ODAX. - Greek. Biting.

ROLER. - ? ?

AROTOR. - Greek and Latin. A ploughman or husbandman.

HEMIS. - Greek. Half, half-way.

ARPIRON. - Perhaps Greek - ? Attempting straightway.

ARRABIN. - Greek. Pledge, caution money.

SUPIPAS. - Perhaps Greek - ? relating to swine.

FORTESON. - Greek. Burdened.

DULID. - ? ?

SORRIOLENEN. - ? ?

MEGALAK. - Hebrew. Cutting off.

ANAGOTOS. - Perhaps Greek - ? Conducting.

SIKASTIN. - ? ?

PETUNOF. - Coptic. Exciting.

MANTAN. - Hebrew. A gift.

MEKLBOC. - Perhaps Hebrew - ? Like a dog.

TIGRAFON. - Perhaps Greek - ? Capable of writing any matter.

TAGORA. - Coptic. Assembly.

DEBAM. - Perhaps Hebrew. Strength.

TIRAIM. - Hebrew. Filling up.

IRIX. - Greek. A hawk or falcon.

MADAIL. - Perhaps Hebrew. Drawing out from, consuming.

ABAGIRON. - Perhaps Greek - ? Gathering together.

PANDOLI. - Greek. Altogether a slave; or perhaps from Greek and Latin -- possessing all wiles.

NENISEM. - Perhaps Hebrew - ? Wavings, displayings.

COBEL. - Hebrew. A Chain.

SOBEL. - Hebrew. A Burden.

LABONETON. - Perhaps from Greek, LAMBANO, = to grasp, or seize.

ARIOTH. - Hebrew. Lioness.

MARAG. - Hebrew. To drive forward.

KAMUSIL. - Hebrew. Like a rising or elevation.

KAITAR. - Perhaps from Hebrew, KThR, = a crown or summit.

SCHARAK. - Hebrew. To wind or twine about.

MAISADUL. - ? ?

AGILAS. - Perhaps Greek - ? Sullen.

KOLAM. - Hebrew. Shame; to be ashamed.

KILIGIL. - ? ?

CORODON. - Perhaps Greek - ? a lark.

HEPOGON. - Perhaps Greek - ? a saddle-cloth.

DAGLAS. - ? ?

HAGION. - Greek. Sacred.

EGAKIREH. - ? ?

PARAMOR. - Perhaps the same as the modern word paramour:- a lover.

OLISERMON. - Perhaps Greek and Latin - ? Of short speech.

RIMOG. - Perhaps from Hebrew, RMK, = a mare.

HORMINOS. - Greek. A stirrer up.

HAGOG. - Hebrew. The name of Gog, with the definite prefix "Ha".

MIMOSA. - Perhaps Greek. Meaning imitator. "Mimosa" is also the name of a shrub.

AMCHISON. - ? ?

ILARAX. - Perhaps Greek - ? Cheerful; gay.
MAKALOS. - Perhaps Chaldaic - ? Attenuated, wasted.
LOCATER. - ? ?
COLVAM. - Perhaps from a Hebrew root, signifying "shame".
BATTERNIS. - ? ? Perhaps derived from Greek, BATTARIZO, = to use vain repetitions, to babble.

THE SERVITORS OF ASMODEUS.
ONEI.- Greek, ONE. Purchase; buying.
ORMION.- Perhaps Greek - ? Moored, fastened securely.
PRECHES.- Perhaps Greek, from PRETHO, "to swell out".
MAGGID.- Hebrew. Precious things.
SCLAVAK.- Perhaps from Coptic, SzLAK, = Torture, pain.
MEBBESSER.- Either from Hebrew, BShR, = flesh, or Chaldee, BSR, = to reject.
BACARON.- Hebrew. Firstborn.
HOLBA.- Hebrew. Fatness.
HIFARION.- Greek. A Pony or little horse.
GILARION.- ? ?
ENIURI.- Perhaps Greek. Found in.
ABADIR.- Hebrew. Scattered.
SBARIONAT.- Perhaps Coptic - ? a little friend.
UTIFA.- ? ?
OMET.- Hebrew. A neighbour.
SARRA.- Coptic. To strike.

THE SERVITORS OF BEELZEBUB.
ALCANOR.- Probably Hebrew and Arabic - ? a harp.
AMATIA.- Greek. Ignorance.
BILIFARES.- Hebrew. Lord of Division.
LAMARION.- ? ?
DIRALISEN.- Greek. The ridge of a rock.
LICANEN.- Perhaps from Greek, LIKNON, = a winnowing fan.
DIMIRAG.- Chaldaic. Impulsion, driving forward.
ELPONEN.- Perhaps Greek - ? Force of hope.
ERGAMEN.- Greek. Busy.
GOTIFAN.- Probably Hebrew, expressing the idea of crushing, and turning over.
NIMORUP.- ? ?
CARELENA.- Perhaps Greek, from KAR, = Hair, and LAMBANO, = to seize.
LAMALON.- Perhaps Hebrew. Declining, turning aside.
IGURIM.- Hebrew. Fears.
AKIUM.- Hebrew. Sure.
DORAK.- Hebrew. Proceeding, walking forward.
TACHAN.- Hebrew. Grinding to powder.
IKONOK.- Greek. Phantasmal.
KEMAL.- Hebrew. Desire of God.
BILICO.- Perhaps Hebrew - ? Lord of manifestation.
TROMES.- Greek. Wound or disaster.

BALFORI.- Hebrew. Lord of producing.
AROLEN.- Perhaps Hebrew - ? Strongly agitated.
LIROCHI.- Hebrew. In tenderness.
NOMINON.- Greek. Conventional.
IAMAI.- Hebrew - ? Days, periods.
AROGOR.- Probably Greek - ? a helper.
HOLASTRI.- Perhaps from Coptic, HOLSz, = to surround.
HACAMULI.- Hebrew. Withering, fading.
SAMALO.- Probably Hebrew. His image.
PLISON.- Perhaps Greek, from PLEO, to swim.
RADERAF.- Perhaps Greek - ? a rose-bearer.
BOROL.- Probably from Hebrew, BVR, = a pit, to bury.
SOROSMA.- Perhaps Greek. A funeral urn.
CORILON.- ? ?
GRAMON.- Greek, from GRAMMA, = Writing.
MAGALAST.- Greek. Greatly, hugely.
ZAGALO.- Perhaps Greek, from ZAGKLON, = a reaping-hook.
PELLIPIS.- Perhaps Greek - ? Oppressing.
NATALIS.- Latin. A birthday, nativity, natal.
NAMIROS.- Perhaps Coptico-Greek - ? Naval, Nautical.
ADIRAEL.- Hebrew. Magnificence of God.
KABADA.- Hebrew. Dulness, heaviness.
KIPOKIS.- Hebrew. Like overflowing.
ORGOSIL.- Hebrew. Tumultuous.
ARCON.- Greek. A Ruler.
AMBOLON.- Greek. Earth thrown up, or fresh turned.
LAMPLON.- Hebrew. With detestation.
BILIFOR.- Perhaps Hebrew - ? Lord of Glory.

THE SERVITORS OF ORIENS.
SARISEL. - Hebrew. Minister of God.
GASARONS. - ? ?
SOROSMA. (See same name under Beelzebub.)
TURITEL. - Hebrew. Mountain cast down.
BALAKEN. - Chaldaic. Ravagers.
GAGISON.- Hebrew. Spread out flat.
MAFALAC.- Hebrew. A fragment.
AGAB.- Hebrew. Beloved.

THE SERVITORS OF PAYMON.
AGLAFOS.- Greek. Bright light.
AGAFALI.- Perhaps from Greek, AGE, reverence.
DISON.- Greek. Divided.
ACHANIEL.- Hebrew. Truth of God.
SUDORON.- Greek. Probably a false gift.
KABERSA.- Hebrew. Wide measure.
EBARON.- Greek. Not burdensome.

ZALANES.- Greek. Trouble-bringer.

UGOLA.- ? Greek. Perhaps = Fluent in speech.

CAME.- Greek. Tired.

ROFFLES.- Hebrew. The Lion trembling.

MENOLIK.- Perhaps Greek - ? Winnowing with fury.

TACAROS.- Greek. Soft or tender.

ASTOLIT.- Probably Greek - ? Without garment.

RUKUM.- Hebrew. Diversified.

THE SERVITORS OF ARITON.

ANADER.- Greek. A flayer.

EKOROK.- Hebrew. Thy breaking, thy barrenness.

SIBOLAS.- Hebrew. A rushing lion.

SARIS.- Greek. A pike or spear.

SEKABIN.- Chaldee. Casters down.

CAROMOS.- Perhaps from Greek, CHARMA, = joy.

ROSARAN.- ? Hebrew - ? Evil and wicked.

SAPASON.- Perhaps from Greek, SEPO, to putrefy.

NOTISER.- Perhaps Greek, = Putter to flight.

FLAXON.- Greek. About to rend, or to be rent asunder.

HAROMBRUB.- Hebrew. Exalted in greatness.

MEGALOSIN.- Greek. In great things.

MILIOM.- Hebrew. The ender or destroyer of day.

ILEMLIS.- Hebrew. The silent lion.

GALAK.- Greek. Milky.

ANDROCOS.- Perhaps Greek - ? Arranger or orderer of men.

MARANTON.- Greek. Quenched, having extinguished.

CARON.- Greek. The name of Charon, the ferryman of the souls of the dead in Hades.

REGINON.- Hebrew. Vigorous ones.

ELERION.- Perhaps Greek. A laugher or mocker.

SERMEOT.- Hebrew. Death of the flesh.

IRMENOS.- Perhaps from Greek, HERMENEUS, = an expounder.

THE SERVITORS OF AMAYMON.

ROMERAC.- Hebrew. Violent thunder.

RAMISON.- Hebrew. The movers with a particular creeping motion.

SCRILIS.- Probably Latin, from Sacrilegium, = a sacrilegious offence.

BURIOL.- Hebrew. Devouring fire of God.

TARALIM.- Hebrew. Mighty strongholds.

BURASEN.- Hebrew. Destroyers by stifling smoky breath.

AKESOLI.- Greek - ? the distressful, or pain-bringing ones.

EREKIA.- Greek probably. One who tears asunder.

ILLIRIKIM.- Hebrew. They who shriek with a long drawn cry.

LABISI.- Hebrew. The flesh inclothed.

AKOROS.- Greek. Overthrowers of authority.

MAMES.- Hebrew. They who move by backward motion.

GLESI.- Hebrew. One who glistens horribly, like an insect.

VISION.- Latin. An apparition.

EFFRIGIS.- Greek. One who quivers in a horrible manner.

APELKI.- Greek. The misleaders or turners aside.

DALEP.- Hebrew. Decaying in liquid putrefaction.

DRESOP.- Hebrew. They who attack their prey by tremulous motion.

HERGOTIS.- Greek. A labourer.

NILIMA.- Hebrew. The evil questioners.

(End of Notes on Names of Spirits.)

NOTES TO THE FOREGOING LISTS OF NAMES OF SPIRITS
BY
S. L. MAC GREGOR-MATHERS.

I have thought it advisable to give as far as possible some idea of the Significations of these names of Spirits, which are for the most part derived from the Hebrew or Chaldee, and also from Greek and Latin and Coptic, etc.

THE CHIEF SPIRITS.

LUCIFER:--From Latin, Lux, Light, and Fero, to bear, = A Light Bearer. There is a name "Lucifuge" also employed occasionally, from Lux, Light, and Fugio, to fly from, = He who shuns the Light.

LEVIATAN:--From Hebrew, LVIThN (usually written Leviathan instead of Leviatan), = the Crooked or Piercing Serpent or Dragon.

SATAN:--From Hebrew, ShTN, = an Adversary.

BELIAL:--From Hebrew, BLIOL, = a Wicked One.

THE EIGHT SUB-PRINCES.

ASTAROT:--From Hebrew, OShThRVTh, = flocks, crowds or assemblies. Usually written "Ashtaroth". Also a name of the Goddess Astarté; Esther is derived from the same root.

MAGOT:--May be from Hebrew, MOVTh, = small stones or pebbles; or from MG, = a changing of camp or place; or from Greek, MAGOS, a magician. Usually written Maguth. Compare the French word "Magot," meaning "a sort of baboon," and also "a hideous dwarfish man"; this expression is often used in fairy-tales to denote a spiteful dwarf or elf. This Spirit has also been credited with presiding over hidden treasure. Larousse derives the name either from ancient French or German.

ASMODEE:--Usually written "Asmodeus," and sometimes "Chashmodai". Derived by some from the Hebrew word "ASAMOD," to destroy or exterminate; and by others from the Persian verb "AZMONDEN," = to tempt, to try or prove. Some Rabbins say that Asmodeus was the child of the incest of Tubal-Cain and his sister Naamah. Others say that he was the Demon of impurity. Others again relate that he was employed by Solomon in the building of the Temple at Jerusalem; that he then attempted to dethrone Solomon, to put himself in his place; but that the King vanquished him, and the Angel Gabriel chased him into Egypt, and there bound him in a Grotto. The Rabbins say that when Asmodeus was working at the building of the Temple, he made use of no metal tool; but instead of a certain stone which cut ordinary stone as a diamond will glass.

BELZEBUD:--Also written frequently "Beelzebub," "Baalzebub," "Beelzebuth," and "Beelzeboul". From Hebrew, BOL, = Lord, and ZBVB, = Fly or Flies; Lord of Flies. Some derive the name from the Syriac "BEEL D'BOBO," = Master of Calumny, or nearly the same signification as the Greek word DIABOLOS, whence are derived the modern French and English "Diable" and "Devil".

ORIENS:--These four names of Oriens, Paymon, Ariton and Amaymon, are usually allotted to the Evil Kings of the four quarters of the World. Oriens, from Latin, ORIENS, = rising or Eastern. This name is also written Uriens, from Latin, URO, = to burn, or devour with flame. It is probably from Uriens that a mediæval title of the Devil, viz., "Sir Urien," is derived. The Name is also sometimes written "Urieus," from Latin, "URIOS," a title given to Jupiter as presiding over the Wind. Urieus is also derivable from the Greek Adj. "EURUS, EUREIA, EURU," meaning vast or extensive. By the Rabbins he is also called SMAL, Samael, which is derived from the Hebrew root SML, which means "a figure, image, or idol". It is a name given in the Qabalah to one of the Chief Evil Spirits.

PAIMON:--Is also frequently written "Paymon," and sometimes "Paimonia". Probably from Hebrew, POMN, = a tinkling sound or small bell. This is again derived from the Hebrew root POM, = to agitate, impel, or strike forward. The word POMN is employed in Exodus 28, 34; 28, 33; and 39, 25. Paimon is also called by the Rabbins by the title of OZAZL, Azazel, which is a name used in Leviticus with reference to the Scape-Goat. Its derivation is from OZ, = a Goat; and AZL, = to go away. It has frequently been warmly discussed whether the word in question means simply the Scape-Goat, or whether it signifies a Demon to whom that animal was dedicated. But in Rabbinic Demonology it is always used to mean one of the Chief Demons.

ARITON:--It is also often called "Egyn," or "Egin". This name may be derived from the Hebrew root ORH, = to lay bare, to make naked. It may also be derived from the Greek word ARHRETON, = secret, or mysterious, in any sense good or bad. Egin, may be derivable from Hebrew, OGN, = to delay, hinder, or retard. There may also be a connection with the Greek AIX, AIGOS, = a Goat. This Spirit is also called by the Rabbins OZAL, Azael, from the root OZ, which means both a Goat, and also vigour, vehemence of force; thus having partly the same root as "Azazel".

AMAIMON:--Also written frequently "Amaymon"; perhaps from the Greek word MAIMON, present participle of MAIMAO; and A as an enforcing particle; hence AMAIMON would mean "terrible violence and vehemence". This Spirit is also called by the Rabbins MHZAL, Mahazael, perhaps from the root MZ, = to consume, or devour. Amaymon is spoken of in the various mediæval Magical works as being a very potent Spirit, and the use of a ring, with Magical characters to hold before the mouth while conversing with him, is recommended as a protection against his deadly, fiery, and poisonous breath.

THE SERVITORS OF ORIENS, PAYMON, ARITON AND AMAYMON.

HOSEN:--From Chaldaic, ChVSN, chosen, = Strong, Vigorous, Powerful.

SARAPH:--From Hebrew, ShRP, = to burn, or devour with fire. PROXOSOS:--Perhaps from Greek, PROX, PROXOKOS, = a Kid.

HABHI:--From Chaldee, ChBA, or Hebrew, ChBH, = Hidden.

ACUAR:--From Hebrew, AKR, = a tiller of the earth.

TIRANA:--Perhaps from Hebrew, ThRN, = the Mast of a Ship, also an Apple Tree.

ALLUPH:--From Hebrew, ALVP, = a Leader, a Duke; also a Bull, from his leading the herd.

NERCAMAY:--Perhaps from Hebrew, NOR, = a boy, and ChMH a companion.

NILEN:--Perhaps from NILUS, Latin, or NEILOS, Greek, = the River Nile.

MOREL:--Perhaps from Hebrew, MRH, == to rebel.

TRACI:--From Greek, TRACHUS, etc., = harsh, rude.

ENAIA:--Perhaps from Hebrew, ONIH, = Poor, afflicted.

MULACH:--Probably the same as "Moloch," from Hebrew, MLK, to rule.

MALUTENS:--Perhaps from Hebrew, MOL, = to lie, or deceive, or prevaricate.

IPARKAS:--Probably from Greek, HIPPARCHES, = a commander of cavalry, or leader of horse.

NUDITON:--Apparently from the Latin, NUDITAS, = nakedness, derived in its turn from NUDATUS.

MELNA:--Perhaps from Hebrew, LN, to abide or rest.

MELHAER:--Perhaps from Hebrew, ML, to cut off, or divide, and ChR, whiteness, purity.

RUACH:--From Hebrew, RVCh = Spirit.

APOLHUN:--From Greek, APOLLUON, Apollyon, = the Destroyer.

SCHABUACH:--From Arabic = to calm or assuage.

MERMO:--From Coptic, MER, Across, and MOOU, Water, = Across Water.

MELAMUD:--From Hebrew, MLMD, = stimulus to exertion.

POTER:--From Greek, POTER, = a drinking cup, or vase.

SCHED:--From Hebrew, ShDD, the Hebrew name for a devastating demon. But the Hebrew root ShD implies the same idea as the English words "To Shed"; and signifies a female breast.

EKDULON:--Probably from Greek, EKDUO, = to despoil.

MANTIENS.--From Latin, MANTIENS, and Greek, MANTEIA, = Prophesying, Divining.

OBEDAMA:--From Hebrew, OBD, =a servant. AMA=mother. But AMH = a maid-servant, whence Obedama should signify a woman-servant.

SACHIEL:--Is a name frequently given in Magical works to an Angel of the Planet Jupiter. SKK = to cover or protect, but SChH = to trample down.

MOSCHEL:--From Hebrew, MVSH, = to move oneself about.

PEREUCH:--Perhaps from Greek, PER and EUCHE, = concerning prayer, or given unto prayer.

DECCAL:--From Hebrew, DChL, = to fear.

ASPERIM:--Perhaps from Latin, "ASPERA," = Rude, Rigorous, Perilous, Dangerous.

KATINI:--From Hebrew, KThN, = a tunic, whence the Greek word CHITON.

TORFORA:--From Hebrew, ThOR, = a small knife, or lancet.

BADAD:--From Hebrew, BDD, = solitary.

I have thus far given the probable derivations at length; but I shall, for the sake of brevity, here continue them without giving their roots and remarks thereon:

COELEN.--Latin. Heavens.

CHUSCHI.--Hebrew. Silent.

TASMA.--Hebrew and Chaldaic. Weak.

PACHID.--Hebrew. Fear.

PAREK.--Hebrew. Roughness, Savage.

RACHIAR.--Greek. Sea breaking on rocks.

NOGAR.--Hebrew. Flowing.

ADON.--Hebrew. Lord.

TRAPIS.--Greek. Turning.

NAGID.--Hebrew. A Leader.

ETHANIM.--Hebrew. An Ass; a furnace.

PATID.--Hebrew. Topaz.

PAREHT.--Hebrew. Fruit.

EMPHASTISON.--Greek. Image, Representation.

PARASEH.--Chaldaic. Divided.

GEREVIL.--Hebrew. Divining Lot, Sortilege.

ELMIS.--Coptic. Flying.

ASMIEL.--Hebrew. Storing up.

IRMINON.--Greek. Supporting.

ASTUREL.--Hebrew. Bearing authority,

NUTHON.--Perhaps Coptic, Godlike; or Greek, piercing.

LOMIOL.--Perhaps Hebrew. Binding, Bitter.

IMINK.--Perhaps Coptic. Devouring.

PLIROK.--Perhaps Coptic. Burning up.

TAGNON.--Perhaps Greek. Heating.

PARMATUS.--Greek and Latin. Shield-bearing.

IARESIN.--Hebrew. Possessing.

GORILON.--Coptic. Axe; Cleaving either to, or asunder; Bones.

LIRION.--Greek. A lily.

PLEGIT.--Perhaps Greek. Smiting, Smitten.

OGILEN.--Hebrew. Round, Wheel.

TARADOS.-- Perhaps Coptic. Dispersion.

LOSIMON.--Perhaps Coptic. Understanding of restriction.

RAGARAS.--Perhaps Coptic. To incline, or bow the head,

IGILON.--Perhaps Greek. After the fashion of EIKELOS.

GOSEGAS.-- Probably Hebrew and Chaldaic. Shaking strongly.

ASTREGA.--Perhaps Coptic. Expeditious.

PARUSUR.--Perhaps Greek. Present to assist.

IGIS.--Perhaps from Greek HIKO, root of HIKNEOMAI. Coming.

AHEROM.--Hebrew. Separation, from ChRM.

IGARAK.--Perhaps Celtic, from CARAC. Terrible.

GELOMA.--Hebrew, GLM, and Latin, GLOMUS, Wrapped, or wound together.

KILIK.--Hebrew. Wrinkled with age.

REMORON.--Latin. Hindering, staying.

EKALIKE.--Perhaps Greek. At rest, or quiet.

ISEKEL.--Hebrew. Anointing, or Anointed.

ELZEGAN.--Perhaps Hebrew = Turning aside.

IPAKOL.--Hebrew. Breathing forth.

HARIL.--Hebrew. Thorny.

KADOLON.--Perhaps Greek. A small vase, or urn.

IOGION.--Perhaps Greek. Noise of battle.

ZARAGIL.--Perhaps Hebrew. Scattering.

IRRORON.--Latin. Sprinkling with dew.

ILAGAS.--Greek. Obtaining; having obtained.

BALALOS.--Perhaps Greek, from BALLO, to throw.

OROIA.--Probably Greek. Returning in due season.

LAGASUF.--Perhaps Hebrew. In paleness, pining away.

ALAGAS.--Perhaps Greek. Wandering.

ALPAS.--Probably Greek. Yielding.

SOTERION.--Greek. Saving, Delivering.

ROMAGES.--Perhaps Hebrew. To throw and to touch.

PROMAKOS.--Greek. A fighter in the front of a conflict.

METAFEL.--Hebrew. To fasten.

DARASCON.--Perhaps Celtic. Turbulent.

KELEN.--Greek. Going swiftly, as in a race.

ERENUTES.--Perhaps Greek. Receiving.

NAJIN.--Hebrew. Propagating.

TULOT.--Chaldaic. Triple.

PLATIEN.--Greek. Flat, broad.

ATLOTON.--Greek. Insufferable.

AFARORP.--Perhaps Hebrew. Breaking, rending.

MORILEN.--Perhaps Greek. Foolish speaking.

RAMARATZ.-- Hebrew. Raised ground, or earth.
NOGEN.--Hebrew. To strike a musical instrument.
MOLIN.--Hebrew. Abiding in a place.

THE SERVITORS OF ASHTAROTH AND ASMODEUS.
AMANIEL.--Hebrew. Nourishment of God.[187]
ORINEL.--Hebrew. Ornament of God; also Tree of God; also Elm Tree.
TIMIRA.--Hebrew. Palm.
DRAMAS.--Greek. Action.
AMALIN.--Chaldaic. Languidness.
KIRIK.--Hebrew. A Stole, or Mantle.
BUBANA.--Perhaps Hebrew. Emptiness.
BUK.--Hebrew. Perplexity.
RANER.--Perhaps Hebrew, Singing; or Greek, Watering.
SEMLIN.--Hebrew. Simulacra; Appearances.
AMBOLIN.--Perhaps Hebrew. Tending unto nothingness.
ABUTES.--Perhaps Greek. Bottomless, Measureless.
EXTERON.--Latin. Without, Foreign, Distant.
LABOUX.--Perhaps Latin, and conveying the sense of "Laborious".
CORCARON.--Perhaps Greek. Tumultuous, noisy.
ETHAN.--Hebrew. An Ass.
TARET.--Perhaps Hebrew. Dampness, tending to corruption.
TABLAT.--Perhaps Hebrew. Immersions.
BURIUL.--Hebrew. In terror and trembling.
OMAN.--Perhaps Chaldaic. To cover, or obscure.
CARASCH.--Hebrew. Voracity.
DIMURGOS.--Greek. A fabricator, Artisan, or Workman.
ROGGIOL.--Perhaps Hebrew. To drag down; the feet.
LORIOL.--Perhaps Hebrew. Unto horror.
ISIGI.--Perhaps from Hebrew, and implying "Error," or "to err".
DIORON.--Greek. Delay.
DAROKIN.--Probably Chaldaic. Paths or Ways.
HORANAR.--??
ABAHIN.--Perhaps Hebrew, and signifying "terrible".
GOLEG.--Probably Hebrew. Whirling.
GUAGAMON.--G reek. A net.
LAGINX.--??
ETALIZ.--Hebrew. The furrow of a plough. Hence agriculture.
AGEI.--Probably Hebrew. Meditation.
LEMEL.--Perhaps Hebrew. For speech--?.
UDAMAN.--Perhaps a corruption of Greek, EUDAIMON, Fortunate.
BIALOT.--Perhaps Hebrew. Absorption.
GAGALOS.[188] --Perhaps Greek. A tumour.
RAGALIM.--Hebrew. Feet.
FINAXOS.--Perhaps Greek. Worthy in appearance--?.
AKANEF.--Hebrew. A Wing.

187　　Frequently in Qabalistic Magic "El," the Name of God, is joined to the Names even of Evil Spirits, to intimate that even these have no power except by His permission.

188　　See somewhat similar name, "Gagalin," in the Spirits under Amaimon and Ariton.

OMAGES.--Greek--? for HO MAGOS, = the Magician.

AGRAX.--Perhaps Hebrew. Bone.

SAGARES.--Greek. A double-headed battle-axe, especially that used by the Amazons.

AFRAY.--Perhaps Hebrew. Dust.

UGALES.--Probably Greek. Calm.

HERMIALA.--?? Perhaps traceable to Celtic roots.

HALIGAX.--?? Perhaps traceable to Celtic roots.

GUGONIX.--?? Perhaps traceable to Celtic roots.

OPILM.--Hebrew. Citadels; eminences.

DAGULER.--??

PACHEI.--Probably Greek. Thick, coarse.

NIMALON.--Perhaps from Hebrew, relating to "circumcision".

THE SERVITORS OF AMAIMON AND ARITON.

HAUGES.--Apparently from the Greek "AUGE". Brilliance.

AGIBOL.--Hebrew. Forcible Love.

RIGOLEN.--Perhaps from Hebrew, = to drag down. The same root also is that of the word "Regel," = "foot".

GRASEMIN.--Perhaps from Hebrew, GRS, = a bone.

ELAFON.--Probably from the Greek ELAPHOS, = a stag.

TRISAGA.--Greek. Directing by Triads.

GAGALIN.--Perhaps Greek. Tumour, Swelling, Ganglion.

CLERACA.--Perhaps from Greek and Latin, "KLERIKOS," and "CLERICUS," = clerical.

ELATON.--Probably Latin. Sublime; borne away.

PAFESLA.--Perhaps from Hebrew--? a sculptured Image.

THE SERVITORS OF ASMODEUS AND MAGOTH.

TOUN.--Perhaps from Hebrew. ThNH, = Hire, Price.

MAGOG.--Hebrew. The well-known Biblical name for a powerful Gentile nation.

DIOPOS.--Greek. An overseer.

DISOLEL.--??

BIRIEL.--Hebrew. Stronghold of God.

SIFON.--Greek. A Siphon or Tube for raising fluids. or Hebrew. To cover over.

KELE.--Hebrew. To consume.

MAGIROS.--Greek. A cook.

SARTABAKIM.--?? SRTN in Hebrew = the Sign Cancer.

LUNDO.--??

SOBE.--Greek. The tail of a horse; also a fly-flap.

INOKOS.--Perhaps from Latin, "INOCCO," = to rake the earth over the newly sown seed.

MABAKIEL.--Hebrew. Weeping, Lamentation.

APOT.--Hebrew = A Treasure; a Tribute.

OPUN.--Perhaps from Hebrew. A Wheel.

THE SERVITORS OF ASHTAROTH.

AMAN.--Hebrew. To nourish.

CAMAL.--Hebrew. To desire God; the name of one of the Archangels in the Qabalah.

TOXAI.--From Greek, TOXEIA, = Archery; or Latin, TOXICUM, Poison.

KATARON.--Greek. Casting down.

RAX.--Greek. A grape-seed.

GONOGIN.--Hebrew. Pleasures, Delights.
SCHELAGON.--Hebrew. Like Snow.
GINAR.--?? Perhaps Chaldaic--? To perfect, or finish.
ISIAMON.--Hebrew = Solitude, Desolation.
BAHAL.--Hebrew = To disturb.
DAREK.--Hebrew = a way, or path.
ISCHIGAS.--Perhaps from Hebrew, IShO, = To save, or aid.
GOLEN.--Greek. A cavern.
GROMENIS.--Perhaps Latin or Greek--? to mark out.
RIGIOS.--Greek. Horrible, Terrible.
NIMERIX.--?? Perhaps Celtic.
HERG.--Hebrew. To slay.
ARGILON.--Greek. Clay.
OKIRI.--Perhaps Greek--? To cause to sink or fail.
FAGANI.--Perhaps Greek--? Devourers.
HIPOLOS.--Greek. A Goat herd.
ILESON.--Greek. Enveloping.
CAMONIX.--? Greek--? Perseverance in combat.
BAFAMAL.--??
ALAN.--Chaldaic. A Tree.
APORMENOS.--Greek. Uncertain.
OMBALAT.--??
QUARTAS.--Latin. Fourth.
UGIRPEN.--??
ARAEX.--? Greek.? Shock.
LEPACA.--Hebrew. For opening or disclosing.
KOLOFE.--Greek. Summit, or height of achievement.

THE SERVITORS OF MAGOTH AND KORE.
NACHERAN.--Probably Hebrew. Nostrils.
KATOLIN.--Hebrew. Walls.
LUESAF.--Perhaps Hebrew. Unto Loss or Destruction.
MASAUB.--Hebrew. Circuit.
URIGO.--Latin. Spoiled; unfit for food.
FATURAB.--Perhaps Hebrew--? Interpretation.
FERSEBUS.--Perhaps Greek--? A bringer of veneration.
BARUEL.--Hebrew. Food or nourishment from God.
UBARIN.--Greek. Insult, Outrage.
BUTARAB.--??
ISCHIRON.--Greek. Strong, Mighty.
ODAX.--Greek. Biting.
ROLER.--??
AROTOR.--Greek and Latin. A ploughman or husbandman.
HEMIS.--Greek. Half, half-way.
ARPIRON.--Perhaps Greek--? Attempting straightway.
ARRABIN.--Greek. Pledge, caution money.
SUPIPAS.--Perhaps Greek--? relating to swine.
FORTESON.--Greek. Burdened.
DULID.--??

SORRIOLENEN.--??

MEGALAK.--Hebrew. Cutting off.

ANAGOTOS.--Perhaps Greek--? Conducting.

SIKASTIN.--??

PETUNOF.--Coptic. Exciting.

MANTAN.--Hebrew. A gift.

MEKLBOC.--Perhaps Hebrew--? Like a dog.

TIGRAFON.--Perhaps Greek--? Capable of writing any matter.

TAGORA.--Coptic. Assembly.

DEBAM.--Perhaps Hebrew. Strength.

TIRAIM.--Hebrew. Filling up.

IRIX.--Greek. A hawk or falcon.

MADAIL.--Perhaps Hebrew. Drawing out from, consuming.

ABAGIRON.--Perhaps Greek--? Gathering together.

PANDOLI.--Greek. Altogether a slave; or perhaps from Greek and Latin-Possessing all wiles.

NENISEM.--Perhaps Hebrew--? Wavings, Displayings.

COBEL.--Hebrew. A Chain.

SOBEL.--Hebrew. A Burden.

LABONETON.--Perhaps from Greek, LAMBANO, = to grasp, or seize.

ARIOTH.--Hebrew. Lioness.

MARAG.--Hebrew. To drive forward.

KAMUSIL.--Hebrew. Like a rising or elevation.

KAITAR.--Perhaps from Hebrew, KThR, = a crown or summit.

SCHARAK.--Hebrew. To wind or twine about.

MAISADUL.--??

AGILAS.--Perhaps Greek--? Sullen.

KOLAM.--Hebrew. Shame; to be ashamed.

KILIGIL.--??

CORODON.--Perhaps Greek--? a lark.

HEPOGON.--Perhaps Greek--? a saddle-cloth.

DAGLAS.--??

HAGION.--Greek. Sacred.

EGAKIREH.--??

PARAMOR.--Perhaps the same as the modern word Paramour: a Lover.

OLISERMON.--Perhaps Greek and Latin--? Of short speech.

RIMOG.--Perhaps from Hebrew, RMK, = a Mare.

HORMINOS.--Greek. A stirrer up.

HAGOG.--Hebrew. The name of Gog with the definite prefix "Ha".

MIMOSA.--Perhaps Greek. Meaning Imitator. "Mimosa" is also the name of a Shrub.

AMCHISON.--??

ILARAX.--Perhaps Greek--? Cheerful; gay.

MAKALOS.--Perhaps Chaldaic--? Attenuated, Wasted.

LOCATER.--??

COLVAM.--Perhaps from a Hebrew root, signifying "shame".

BATTERNIS.--?? Perhaps derived from Greek, BATTARIZO,= to use vain repetitions, to babble.

THE SERVITORS OF ASMODEUS.

ONEI.--Greek, ONE. Purchase; buying.

ORATION.--Perhaps Greek--? Moored, fastened securely.
PRECHES.--Perhaps Greek, from PRETHO, to swell out
MAGGID.--Hebrew. Precious things.
SCLAVAK.--Perhaps from Coptic, SzLAK, Torture, Pain.
MEBBESSER.--Either from Hebrew, BShR, flesh, or Chaldee, BSR, = to reject.
BACARON.--Hebrew. Firstborn.
HOLBA.--Hebrew. Fatness.
HIFARION.--Greek. A Pony or little horse.
GILARION.--??
ENIURI.--Perhaps Greek. Found in.
ABADIR.--Hebrew. Scattered.
SBARIONAT.--Perhaps Coptic--? a little friend.
UTIFA.--??
OMET.--Hebrew. A neighbour.
SARRA.--Coptic. To strike.

THE SERVITORS OF BEELZEBUB.
ALCANOR.--Probably Hebrew and Arabic--? a harp.
AMATIA.--Greek. Ignorance.
BILIFARES.--Hebrew. Lord of Division.
LAMARION.--??
DIRALISEN.--Greek. The ridge of a rock.
LICANEN.--Perhaps from Greek, LIKNON, = a winnowing fan.
DIMIRAG.--Chaldaic. Impulsion, Driving forward.
ELPONEN.--Perhaps Greek--? Force of hope.
ERGAMEN.--Greek. Busy.
GOTIFAN.--Probably Hebrew, expressing the idea of crushing, and turning over.
NIMORUP.--??
CARELENA.--Perhaps Greek, from KAR, = Hair, and LAMBANO, = to seize.
LAMALON.--Perhaps Hebrew. Declining, turning aside.
IGURIM.--Hebrew., Fears.
AKIUM.--Hebrew. Sure.
DORAK.--Hebrew. Proceeding, Walking forward.
TACHAN.--Hebrew. Grinding to powder.
IKONOK.--Greek. Phantasmal.
KEMAL.--Hebrew. Desire of God.
BILICO.--Perhaps Hebrew--? Lord of manifestation.
TROMES.--Greek. Wound or disaster.
BALFORI.--Hebrew. Lord of producing.
AROLEN.--Perhaps Hebrew--? Strongly agitated.
LIROCHI.-- Hebrew. In tenderness.
NOMINON.--Greek. Conventional.
IAMAI.--Hebrew--? Days, periods.
AROGOR.--Probably Greek--? a helper.
HOLASTRI.--Perhaps from Coptic, HOLSz, = to surround.
HACAMULI.--Hebrew. Withering, fading.
SAMALO.--Probably Hebrew. His image.
PLISON.--Perhaps Greek, from PLEO, to swim.
RADERAF.--Perhaps Greek--? a rose-bearer.

BOROL.--Probably from Hebrew, BVR, = a pit, to bury.
SOROSMA.--Perhaps Greek. A funeral urn.
CORILON.--??
GRAMON.--Greek, from GRAMMA, = Writing.
MAGALAST.--Greek. Greatly, hugely.
ZAGALO.--Perhaps Greek, from ZAGKLON, = a reaping-hook.
PELLIPIS.--Perhaps Greek--? Oppressing.
NATALIS.--Latin. A birthday, nativity, natal.
NAMIROS.--Perhaps Coptico-Greek--? Naval, Nautical.
ADIRAEL.--Hebrew. Magnificence of God.
KABADA.--Hebrew. Dulness, heaviness.
KIPOKIS.--Hebrew. Like Overflowing.
ORGOSIL.--Hebrew. Tumultuous.
ARCON.--Greek. A Ruler.
AMBOLON.--Greek. Earth thrown up, or fresh turned.
LAMOLON.--Hebrew. With detestation.
BILIFOR.--Perhaps Hebrew--? Lord of Glory.

THE SERVITORS OF ORIENS.
SARISEL.--Hebrew. Minister of God. GASARONS.--?? SOROSMA[189] .
TURITEL.--Hebrew. Mountain cast down.
BALAKEN.--Chaldaic. Ravagers.
GAGISON.--Hebrew. Spread out flat.
MAFALAC.--Hebrew. A fragment.
AGAB.--Hebrew. Beloved.
THE SERVITORS OF PAYMON.
AGLAFOS.--Greek. Bright light.
AGAFALI.--Perhaps from Greek, AGE, reverence.
DISON.--Greek. Divided.
ACHANIEL.--Hebrew. Truth of God.
SUDORON.--Greek. Probably a false gift.
KABERSA.--Hebrew. Wide measure.
EBARON.--Greek. Not burdensome.
ZALANES.--Greek. Trouble-bringer.
UGOLA.--? Greek. Perhaps = Fluent in speech.
CAME.--Greek. Tired.
ROFFLES.--Hebrew. The Lion trembling.
MENOLIK.--Perhaps Greek--? Winnowing with fury.
TACAROS.--Greek. Soft or tender.
ASTOLIT.--Probably Greek--? Without Garment.
RUKUM.--Hebrew. Diversified.

THE SERVITORS OF ARITON.
ANADER.--Greek. A flayer.
EKOROK.--Hebrew. Thy breaking, Thy barrenness.
SIBOLAS.--Hebrew. A rushing Lion.
SARIS.--Greek. A pike or spear.
SEKABIN.--Chaldee. Casters down.

---

189   See same name under Beelzebub.

CAROMOS.--Perhaps from Greek, CHARMA, = joy.
ROSARAN.--? Hebrew--? Evil and wicked.
SAPASON.--Perhaps from Greek, SEPO, to putrefy.
NOTISER.--Perhaps Greek, = Putter to flight.
FLAXON.--Greek. About to rend, or to be rent asunder.
HAROMBRUB.--Hebrew. Exalted in greatness.
MEGALOSIN.--Greek. In great things.
MILIOM.--Hebrew. The ender or destroyer of day.
ILEMLIS.--Hebrew. The silent Lion.
GALAK.--Greek. Milky.
ANDROCOS.--Perhaps Greek--? Arranger or orderer of men.
MARANTON.--Greek. Quenched, having extinguished.
CARON.--Greek. The name of Charon, the ferryman of the souls of the dead in Hades.
REGINON.--Hebrew. Vigorous ones.
ELERION.--Perhaps Greek. A Laugher or Mocker.
SERMEOT.--Hebrew. Death of the flesh.
IRMENOS.--Perhaps from Greek, HERMENEUS, = an Expounder.

THE SERVITORS OF AMAYMON.
ROMERAC.--Hebrew. Violent thunder.
RAMISON.--Hebrew. The movers with a particular creeping motion.
SCRILIS.--Probably Latin, from Sacrilegium, = a sacrilegious offence.
BURIOL.--Hebrew. Devouring fire of God.
TARALIM.--Hebrew. Mighty strongholds.
BURASEN.--Hebrew. Destroyers by stifling smoky breath.
AKESOLI.--Greek--? the distressful, or pain-bringing ones.
EREKIA.--Greek probably. One who tears asunder.
ILLIRIKIM.--Hebrew. They who shriek with a long drawn cry.
LABISI.--Hebrew. The flesh inclothed.
AKOROS.--Greek. Overthrowers of authority.
MAMES.--Hebrew. They who move by backward motion.
GLESI.--Hebrew. One who glistens horribly, like an insect.
VISION.--Latin. An apparition.
EFFRIGIS.--Greek. One who quivers in a horrible manner.
APELKI.--Greek. The misleaders or turners aside.
DALEP.--Hebrew. Decaying in liquid putrefaction.
DRESOP.--Hebrew. They who attack their prey by tremulous motion.
HERGOTIS.--Greek. A labourer.
NILIMA.--Hebrew. The evil questioners.
(End of Notes on Names of Spirits.)

THE TWENTIETH CHAPTER.
HOW THE OPERATIONS SHOULD BE PERFORMED

THE aforesaid Operation being finished, it is necessary, in order to render this instruction complete, to say how we should manage the Operations which he who operateth wisheth to put into practice.

Firstly, then, having come unto the end, and having obtained all that is necessary; you cannot sufficiently praise and honour God, and His Most Holy Name, even although you had a thousand tongues; neither also can you sufficiently magnify and thank your Holy Angel Guardian as he meriteth. However, you ought to render thanks proportionate to your estate and to the Great Treasure which you have received. It is necessary also that you should fully understand how you ought to enjoy these immense riches, so that they may not be in your hands unfruitful, or even harmful. Because this Art is like a Sword in your hand, capable of serving for all kinds of evil and for hurt unto your neighbour. But in putting it into practice for that sole end for which it hath been made, namely for vanquishing therewith the DEMON and Enemies, then shall you be making a good use hereof. I wish also further to give you some instruction upon certain necessary and principal points.

The Operation of the Spirits being finished, you shall continue a whole week to praise God; and as regardeth yourself personally, you shall do no servile work during the Seven Days, neither shall you make any Convocation of the Spirits in general, nor of the Familiars; and afterwards, when the Seven Days be passed, you shall commence to exercise your power, as. shall be hereafter said:--

(1) Take heed before all things to perform no Magical Operation soever, or Invocations of the Spirits on the Sabbath Day, during the whole period of your life, seeing that that day is consecrated unto God, and is the day on which you should repose and sanctify yourself, and you should solemnise it by prayers.

(2) Keep yourself as you would from the Eternal Fire, from manifesting unto any living being that which your Guardian Angel shall have confided unto you; excepting unto him who hath given unto you the Operation, unto whom you have as it were a greater obligation than unto your own father.

(3) As far as lieth in your power take heed in no way to make use of this Art against your neighbour; except for a just Vengeance; although I counsel you even in this particular to imitate God, who pardoneth even you yourself, and there is not in the world a more meritorious action than to pardon.

(4) In the case of your Angel dissuading you from some Operation, and forbidding you to do the same, keep well from becoming obstinate therein, for you would in such a case ever repent it.

(5) Fly all kinds of (Evil) Science, Magic, and Enchantments, because they be all Diabolical Inventions; also put no trust in books which teach them, though in appearance they may seem reliable to you, for these be nets which the perfidious BELIAL stretcheth out to take you.

(6) In conversing with Spirits Good or Evil, never employ words which you do not understand, because even so will you have shame and hurt.

(7) You shall never demand of your Guardian Angel any Symbol wherewith to operate for an Evil end, seeing that you would grieve him. You will find only too many persons who will beseech you to do thus; see that you do it not!

(8) Accustom yourself as much as possible to purity of body and cleanliness of raiment, seeing that this is very necessary; for the Spirits, both Good and Evil alike, love purity.

(9) As far as possible shun the employment of your Wisdom for others in evil things; but first

well consider him to whom you would render a service; because it often happeneth, that in doing service unto another one worketh evil for oneself.

(10) In no way attempt to procure the Operation of the Holy Angels unless you have extreme need thereof, seeing that these Holy Angels be so far above you that it is useless for you to wish to compare yourself unto Them, you being nothing in comparison of Them Who are the Angels of God.

(11) If the Operations can be performed by the Familiar Spirits, it is not necessary to employ others therein.

(12) Though it should be an easy matter for you to employ your Familiars to annoy your neighbour, seek to abstain therefrom, unless it were to repress the insolence of such as might attempt aught against you personally. Never keep the Familiar Spirits in idleness, and should you wish to give one over unto any person, see that such person be distinguished and meritorious, for they love not to serve those of base and common condition. But should such person unto i whom you give them have made some express Pact (with Spirits) in such case the Familiar Spirits will fly in haste to serve him.

(13) These three Books of this present Operation ought to be read and re-read an infinitude of times; so that in the space of Six Months before commencing, he who operateth should be fully instructed and informed therein; and if he be not a Jew, he should further be conversant with many of the customs and ceremonies which this Operation demandeth, so as to become accustomed unto that retirement which is so necessary and useful.

(14.) Should he who performeth this Operation during the Six Months or Moons commit voluntarily any mortal sin prohibited by the Tables of the Law, be certain that he will never receive this Wisdom.

(15) Sleep in the day-time is entirely forbidden, unless absolutely requisite, owing to some infirmity, or to old age, or to debility of constitution; for God is always willing to employ mercy [190] towards mankind, because of their infirmities.

(16) If you have not the fixed intention of continuing the Operation, I counsel you on no account to commence it; because the Lord doth not care to be mocked, and He chastiseth with corporal maladies those who make a mock of Him. Howbeit, he who is hindered from continuing through some unforeseen accident, sinneth in no way.

(17) It is impossible for him who hath passed fifty years of age to undertake this Operation. Thus also was it the custom in the true and ancient Jewish Law concerning the Priesthood. Also, he should not be less than twenty-five years of age.

(18) You shall not permit the Familiar Spirits to familiarise themselves too much with you, through your disputing and arguing with them; because they will propound so many affairs and things at once as to confound and trouble the mind.

(19) With the Familiar Spirits you should not make use of the Symbols of the Third Book, unless it be those of the Fifth Chapter thereof;[191] but if you desire anything, command them aloud to perform it. Never commence many Operations at once and in the same time, but when you have finished one then begin another, until you are perfect in the practice; for an Apprentice Artist doth not become a Master suddenly, but little by little.

(20) Without reasons of the very last importance, the Four Princes[192] or the Eight Sub-Princes [193] , should never be summoned, because we must make a great distinction between these and the others (who are inferior to them).

---

190   In MS., " User d'humanitè".

191   Entitled: "How we may retain the Familiar Spirits bond or free, in whatsoever form".

192   Viz. Lucifer, Leviathan, Satan, and Belial.

193   Viz. Ashtaroth, Maguth, Asmodeus, and Beelzebub; Oriens, Paymon, Ariton or Egyn, and Amaymon.

(21) In operating, as rarely as possible insist upon the Spirits appearing visibly;[194] and thus you will work all the better, for it should suffice you for them to say and do what you wish.

(22) All Prayers, Orations, Invocations, and Conjurations, and in fact everything you have to say, should be pronounced aloud and clearly, without however shouting like a madman[195] but speaking clearly and naturally, and pronouncing distinctly.

(23) During the Six Moons, you shall sweep the Oratory every Sabbath Eve, and keep it strictly clean, for it is a place dedicated unto the Holy and Pure Angels.

(24) Take heed that you commence no Operation at night if it be important, unless the need be very pressing.

(25) Your only object during your whole life should be to shun as far as possible an ill-regulated life, and especially the vices of debauchery, gluttony, and drunkenness.[196]

(26) Having completed the Operation, and being now the Possessor of the True Wisdom, you shall fast three days before commencing to put it in practice.

(27) Every year you should make a commemoration of the Signal benefit which the Lord hath conferred upon you; at such time feasting, praying, and honouring your Guardian Angel that day with your whole strength.

(28) During the Three Days on which you constrain the Spirits you shall fast, for this is essential, so that when you are working you may find yourself freer and more tranquil both in body and mind.

(29) Note that the fasts are to be understood as commencing always from the first nocturnal Star, and not otherwise.

(30) Keep as an indubitable precept never to give this Operation unto a Monarch,[197] because Solomon was the first who abused it; and if you should do the contrary, both you and your successors would alike lose the Grace hereof. With regard to this command, I myself having been sought by the Emperor Sigismond, gave him willingly the best Familiar Spirit which I had; but I steadily refused to give him the Operation; and it should not be given unto Emperors, Kings, or other Sovereigns.

(31) You may assuredly give, but it is not permissible to sell, this (Operation), for this would be to abuse the Grace of the Lord who hath given it unto you, and should you act contrariwise unto this, you would lose its control.

(32) Should you perform this Operation in a town, you should take a house which is not at all overlooked by any one; seeing that in this present day.[198] Curiosity is so strong that you ought to be upon your guard; and there ought to be a garden (adjoining the house) wherein you can take exercise.

(33) Take well heed during the Six Moons or Months to lose no blood from your body, except that which the expulsive Virtue in you may expel naturally of its own accord.

(34) Finally, during that whole time, you shall touch no dead body of any description soever.

(35) You shall eat during this whole period neither the flesh nor the blood of any dead animal; and this you shall do for a certain particular reason.[199]

(36) You shall bind by an Oath him unto whom you shall give this Operation, neither to give

---

194   For not only does constraining them to visible appearance require reiterated conjurations, but also they must be in some way provided with the necessary elements wherefrom to build up a body to manifest in.

195   In the Original: " Sanspourtant crier comme unfou".

196   I have by this phrase translated the expression in the Original " Le vice de crapule".

197   This also seems like mere prejudice on the part of Abraham.

198   Remember that "this present day" means of course the period when Abraham was writing this work, i.e., 1458. In this particular of curiosity the world has doubtless changed little since.

199   Probably implying that the Evil Spirits could easily obsess such animal, so as to act upon the Operator through whatever he might eat of it.

nor sell it unto any avowed Atheist or Blasphemer of God.

(37) You shall fast for three days before giving the Operation unto any; and he who shall receive it shall do likewise; and he also shall hand over unto you at the same time the sum of Ten Golden Florins, or their value, the which you should with your own hand distribute unto poor persons whom you shall charge to repeat the Psalms, Miserere Mei Deus, etc., "Have mercy upon me, O God and the De Profundis, etc., "Out of the Depths".

(38) It will be a good thing, and one which will facilitate the Operation, for you to repeat all the Psalms of David, seeing that they contain great power and virtue; and to say them at least twice in the week.

Also you shall shun gaming as you would the plague; because it ever is an occasion of Blasphemy. Also during this time prayer, and the study of the Sacred Books, should take the place of gaming with you.[200]

All this advice, and much more which you would be certain to receive from your Angel Guardian, I have here set down, so that by observing the same perfectly, without failing in the slightest particular, you shall at the end of the Operation find the value thereof. I am now, therefore, about to give you distinct and sufficient information how to employ the Symbols[201] and how to proceed if you wish to acquire others.

You are then to understand that once he who operateth hath the power, it is not necessary (in all cases[202]) to use written Symbols, but it may suffice to name aloud the Name of the Spirit, and the form in which you wish him to appear visibly; because once they[203] have taken Oath, this sufficeth. These Symbols, then, be made for you to avail yourself of them when you be in the company of other persons; also you must have them upon you, so that in touching or handling them simply, they may represent your wish. Immediately then he[204] unto whom the Symbol appertaineth will serve you punctually; but if you should desire something special which is in no way connected with or named in the Symbol, it will be

By "jeu," here is evidently meant gaming or gambling, and not simple recreation and amusement, which latter would be almost a necessity during this period, to prevent the brain giving way from the intense nervous strain necessary to signify the same at least by showing your desire by two or three words. And here it is well to observe, that if you use prudence, you can often reason with those persons who be with you in such a manner that the Spirits, having however been beforehand invoked by you, will understand what they are to do; but it is necessary to discover your intent unto them by words. For they be of such great intelligence, that from a single word or a single motive, they can draw the construction of the whole matter; and although they cannot penetrate into the inmost parts of the human mind, yet nevertheless by their astuteness and subtlety they be so adroit that they comprehend by perceptible signs the wish of the person in question.

But when it is a grave and important matter, you should retire into a secret place apart, provided it be appropriate, for any place is good to invoke the Spirits proper unto the Operation. There give them their commission regarding that which you wish them to perform, the which they will either execute then or in the days following. But always give them the signal by word of mouth, or in any other manner that may be pleasing unto you, whenever you wish them to begin to operate. Thus did ABRAMELIN in Egypt, JOSEPH in Paris, and as for myself, I have always acted in the

---

200   In the Original MS.: " Vous fuirez lejeu comme la peste parcequiloccasionne toujours du blaspheme outreque dans ce temps la leveritable jeu est loraison et la lecture des livres sacrez".

201   I.e., those of the Third Book.

202   I have here interpolated "in all cases," as otherwise this passage would clash with remarks elsewhere.

203   I.e., the Spirits, who have sworn allegiance to the Operator at his convocations of them.

204   I.e., that Spirit.

same manner. I have also made myself a very great man, and especially one who hath been of service unto Princes and great Lords.

I will hereafter tell clearly what Operations belong unto this or unto that Spirit, and how it is necessary to act.

Now will I teach you how all those (Symbols) which be in this Book, as well as those which you will (hereafter) receive from the Spirits (themselves), ought to be written down and acquired. For the number of Operations is infinite, and it would be an impossibility to set them all down in this work. If therefore you should wish to perform certain fresh Operations by the use of a Symbol not set down in any way in the Third Book [I am speaking of good and permissible Operations], [205]you shall make the demand thereof from your Guardian Angel in this manner:--

Fast the day before, and on the following morning you, being well washed, shall enter into the Oratory, put on the White Tunic, illumine the Lamp, and put the Perfume in the Censer. Then lay the Lamen of Silver upon the Altar, whereof the two Angles shall be touched with the Holy Anointing Oil; fall upon your knees and make your Orison unto the Lord, rendering unto Him grace for the benefits which you have received in general.

Then shall you supplicate Him to be willing to send unto you your Holy Angel, that he may instruct you in your ignorance, and that he may deign to grant your demand. After this, invoke your Holy Guardian Angel, and pray him to favour you with his vision, and to instruct you how you should design and prepare the Symbol of the Operation desired. Also you shall remain in prayer until you shall see appear in the room the Splendour of your Angel. Then wait to see if he shall expound or command anything touching the form of the Symbol demanded. And when you have finished your supplication, arise and go to the Plate of Silver, whereon you shall find written as it were in drops of dew, like a sweat exuding therefrom, the Symbol as you ought to make it, together with the Name of the Spirit who should serve you for this Operation, or else that of his Prince. And without touching or moving the Lamen, copy at once the Symbol just as it appeareth, and leave the Plate of Metal upon the Altar until the even; at the which time, after having made your ordinary Orison, and returned your thanks, you shall put it away in a piece of clean silk.

The most convenient Day for procuring these Symbols is the Sabbath; because by such an Operation, we do not in any way violate (its sanctity), neither do we injure the same at all. Also we can prepare all things necessary the day before. But if the Angel should not appear, and should not in any way manifest unto you the Symbol, then may you be certain that the pretended Operation, although it may appear good in your eyes, is not so considered by God and by your Guardian Angel and in such case you shall change your demands.

Now, as regardeth the Symbols for Evil Operations, these shall you obtain more easily; seeing that after (putting on) the Perfume, there is nothing else to do but to make your Orisons. Then being clad in your White Tunic, you shall put on over it the Silken Vestment and the Girdle, and after that the Crown, taking the Wand in your hand, and placing yourself at the side of the Altar towards the Terrace. Then, holding the Wand, conjure in the same manner as you did on the Second Day. And when the Spirits shall have appeared, you shall command them in no way to quit the place, until they shall have manifested unto you the Symbol of the Operation which you desire, together with the Names of the Spirits capable of putting the same into execution, together with their Symbols. And then you shall see the Prince unto whom the Operation appertaineth avow, write, and sign upon the Sand the Symbol, together with the Name of the Spirit who is to serve for this Operation. Then shall you take the Surety and Oath of the Prince upon the Symbol, and also of his Ministers, as you will have previously done in accordance with the (directions given in the) Fourteenth Chapter.[206] And should several Symbols be given, make them take Oath upon them all. This being done, you can dismiss them in the manner we have already described, taking

---

205   This Parenthesis is Abraham's.

206   I.e., of this Second Book. The Chapter is entitled: "Concerning the Convocation of the Spirits".

heed before this to copy the Symbols which they shall have traced upon the Sand, because in departing they will destroy the same. And when they have gone, take the Censer and perfume the place, as before said.

I do not however write this, so that you may hereby, as well as by the use of certain of the Symbols described in the Third Book, work Evil; I have in no way written them down for such an end; but only that you may understand the full perfection of this Art, and what we can herewith perform. For the Evil Spirits be exceeding prompt and exceeding obedient in the working of Evil; it is to be wished that they were as much so for the Good. However, take heed that you be upon your guard.

And remember, that as there is a God to write these aforesaid Symbols, there is no particular preparation necessary of Pens, of Ink, and of Paper; nor yet of elections of particular Days, nor other things to be observed, which the False Magicians and Enchanters of the Devil would have you believe. It sufficeth that the Symbols should be clearly written with any kind of Ink and Pen, provided that we may easily discern unto what Operation each Sign appertaineth, the which also you can easily do by means of a properly arranged and drawn up Register of them. But the greatest part of the Symbols of the Third Book I counsel you to make before commencing the Operation, keeping them until that time in the interior of the Altar. And after that the Spirits shall have taken Oath thereupon, you shall carefully keep (the Symbols) in a safe place, where they can neither be seen nor touched by any other person, because thus great harm might befal such person.

Now will we declare unto you what Symbols be manifested by the Good Angels and what by the Evil, and unto what Prince each Operation is subject, and lastly, what should be observed as regardeth each Symbol.

BY WHOM THE SYMBOLS OF THE CHAPTERS OF THE THIRD BOOK BE MANIFESTED[207]

The Symbols of the Chapters of the Third Book, which be manifested only by the Angels, or by the Guardian Angel, be these, namely:--

Chapter I. (To know all manner of things Past and Future, which be not however directly opposed to God, and to His Most Holy Will.)

Chapter III. (To cause any Spirit to appear, and take any form, such as of man, animal, bird, etc.)

Chapter IV. (For divers Visions.)

Chapter V. (How we may retain the Familiar Spirits bond or free in whatsoever form.)

Chapter VI. (To cause Mines to be pointed out, and to help forward all kinds of work connected therewith.)

Chapter VII. (To cause the Spirits to perform with facility and promptitude all necessary chemical labours and Operations, as regardeth Metals especially.)

Chapter X. (To hinder any Necromantic or Magical Operations from taking effect, except those of the Qabalah, or of this Sacred Magic.)

Chapter XI. (To cause all kinds of Books to be brought to one, and whether lost or stolen.)

Chapter XVI. (To find and take possession of all kinds of Treasures, provided that they be not at all magically guarded.)

Chapter XVIII. (To heal divers Maladies.)

Chapter XXV. (To walk upon, and operate under, Water.)

Chapter XXVIII. (To have as much gold and silver as one may wish, both to provide for one's necessities, and to live in opulence.)

---

207   I have thought it advisable to add here the headings of these chapters at length.

The following (Symbols) be manifested in part by the Angels and in part by the Evil Spirits, which is why we must not avail ourselves hereof without the permission of the Holy Angel. They are those of:--

Chapter II. (To obtain information concerning, and to be enlightened upon, all sorts of Propositions, and all doubtful Sciences.)

Chapter VIII. (To excite Tempests.)

Chapter XII. (To know the Secrets of any person.)

Chapter XIII. (To cause a Dead Body to revive, and perform all the functions which a Living Person would do, and this during a space of Seven Years by means of the Spirits.)

Chapter XIV. (The Twelve Symbols for the Twelve Hours of the Day and of the Night, to render oneself Invisible unto every person.)

Chapter XV. (For the Spirits to bring us anything we may wish to eat or to drink, and even all (kinds of food) that we can imagine.)

Chapter XVII. (To fly in the Air, and travel any whither.)

Chapter XIX. (For every description of Affection and Love.)

Chapter XX. (To excite every description of Hatred and Enmity, Discords, Quarrels, Contentions, Combats, Battles, Loss, and Damage.)

Chapter XXIV. (To discover any Theft that hath occurred.)

Chapter XXVI. (To open every kind of Lock without a Key, and without making any noise.)

Chapter XXIX. (To cause Armed Men to appear.)

The following (Symbols) be only manifested by the Evil Spirits, namely:--

Chapter IX. (To transform Animals into Men, and Men into Animals, etc.)

Chapter XXI. (To transform oneself, and take different Faces and Forms.)

Chapter XXII. (This Chapter is only for Evil, for with the Symbols herein we can cast Spells, and work every kind of Evil; we should not avail ourselves hereof.)

Chapter XXIII. (To demolish Buildings and Strongholds.)

Chapter XXVII. (To cause Visions to appear.)

Chapter XXX. (To cause Comedies, Operas, and every kind of Music and Dances to appear.)

UNTO WHAT PRINCE THE OPERATIONS OF EACH CHAPTER ARE SUBMITTED

ASTAROT and ASMODEE do together execute the Symbols and Operations of:--

Chapter VI. (To cause Mines to be pointed out, and to help forward all kinds of work connected therewith.)

Chapter VII. (To cause the Spirits to perform with facility and promptitude all necessary Chemical labours and operations, as regardeth Metals especially.)

Chapter IX. (To transform Animals into Men, and Men into Animals, etc.)

ASMODEE and MAGOT together do execute the Operations of:--

Chapter XV. (For the Spirits to bring us anything we may wish to eat or to drink, and even all (kinds of food) that we can imagine.)

ASTAROT and ARITON both do execute the following Chapter by their Ministers, yet not together', but each separately:--

Chapter XVI. (To find and take possession of all kinds of Treasures, provided that they be not at all magically guarded.)

ORIENS, PAIMON, ARITON, and AMAIMON will execute by means of the Ministering Spirits common unto them, the following, namely:--

Chapter I. (To know all manner of things Past and Future, which be not however directly opposed to God, and to His Most Holy Will.)

Chapter II. (To obtain information concerning, and to be enlightened upon all sorts of Propositions, and all doubtful Sciences.)

Chapter III. (To cause any Spirit to appear, and take any form, such as of Man, Animal, Bird, etc.)

Chapter IV. (For divers Visions.)

Chapters V. (How we may retain the Familiar Spirits bond or free, in whatsoever form.)

Chapter XIII. (To cause a Dead Body to revive, and perform all the functions which a Living Person would do, and this during a space of Seven Years, by means of the Spirits.)

Chapter XVII. (To fly in the Air, and travel any whither.)

Chapter XXVII. (To cause Visions to appear.)

Chapter XXIX. (To cause Armed Men to appear.)

AMAIMON and ARITON together perform:--
Chapter XXVI. (To open every kind of Lock without Key, and without making any noise.)

ORIENS alone performeth:--
Chapter XXVIII. (To have as much Gold and Silver as one may wish, both to provide for one's necessities, and to live in Opulence.)

PAIMON (alone) performeth:--
Chapter XXIX. (To cause Armed Men to appear.) (It is to be noted that this chapter has already been classed under those performed by Oriens, Paimon, Ariton, and Amaimon, together.)

ARITON performeth:--
Chapter XXIV. (To discover any Theft that hath occurred.)

AMAIMON (performeth):--
Chapter XVIII. (To heal divers Maladies.)

ASTAROT (performeth):--
Chapter VIII. (To excite Tempests.)
Chapter XXIII. (To demolish Buildings and Strongholds.)

MAGOT (performeth):-- [208]
Chapter X. (To hinder any Necromantic or Magical Operations from taking effect, except those of the Qabalah, or of this Sacred Magic.)

Chapter XI. (To cause all kinds of Books to be brought to one, and whether lost or stolen.)

Chapter XXI. (To transform oneself, and take different Faces and Forms.)

Chapter XXIV. (To discover any Theft that hath occurred.)

Chapter XXX. (To cause Comedies, Operas, and every kind of Music and Dances to appear.)

ASMODEE (performeth):--
Chapter XII. (To know the Secrets of any person.)
BELZEBUD (performeth):--

---

208   in addition to the chapters here given, Magoth is said to rule the operations of Chapter XIV. (Invisibility), in the special instructions of Abraham, the Jew, concerning that chapter.

Chapter IX. (To transform Animals into Men, and Men into Animals, etc.)

Chapter XX. (To excite every description of Hatred and Enmity, Discords, Quarrels, Contentions, Combats, Battles, Loss, and Damage.)

Chapter XXII. (This Chapter is only for Evil, for with the Symbols herein we can cast Spells, and work every kind of Evil; we should not avail ourselves hereof.)

The Operations of the following Chapters can also (to a great extent) be administered by the Familiar Spirits, namely:--

Chapter II. (Scientific Information.)

Chapter IV. (Visions.)

Chapter XII. (Secrets of other persons.)

Chapter XVIII. (Healing of Maladies.)

Chapter XIX. (Affection and Love.)

Chapter XXIII. (Demolishing Buildings.)

Chapter XXIV. (Discovery of Theft.

Chapter XXVII. (Causing Visions to appear.)

Chapter XXVIII. (Obtaining Money.)

Chapter XXX. (Visions of Operas, Comedies, etc.)

If at the beginning they excuse themselves from the performance, there is probably some hindering cause, and in this case you should make use of other Spirits; but otherwise they must obey you in and throughout everything that you shall command them.

INSTRUCTIONS AND EXPLANATIONS CONCERNING WHAT POINTS WE SHOULD PARTICULARLY OBSERVE

Chapter I. (To know all manner of things Past and Future, which be not however directly opposed to God, and to His Most Holy Will.)

First take the Symbol in your hand, place it (upon the top of your head) under your hat, and either you will be secretly warned by the Spirit, or he will execute that which you have the intention of commanding him to do.

(This next instruction is given in the MS. as relating to Chapter II., but it evidently is more appropriate to:--)

Chapter III. (To cause any Spirit to appear, and take any form, such as of Man, Animal, Bird, etc.)

Take in your hand the Symbol, and name the Spirit, who will appear in the form commanded.

(The next following information evidently has reference to the Symbols of the Fifth Chapter, but there is no number subjoined as in the other cases in the original MS.:--)

Chapter V. (How we may retain the Familiar Spirits bond or free, in whatsoever form.)

We must understand that every man may have Four Familiar or Domestic Spirits, and no more. These Spirits can serve you in many ways, and they are granted unto you by the Sub-Princes.

The First hath his period of power from Sunrise until Noon.

The Second, from Noon until the Setting of the Sun.

The Third, from the Setting of the Sun until Midnight.

And the Fourth, from Midnight even unto the Sun-rising of the following Day.

He who possesseth them is free to avail himself of their services under whatever form may be pleasing unto him.

Of this kind of Spirits there s an infinite number, who at the time of their fall were condemned to serve man; and to each man there be four of them destined and each one is obliged to serve during a period of Six Hours, and in the case of your giving one over unto some other person, you can no longer avail yourself of his services, but in order to replace him during his time of service, you may call upon some other Spirit. And should you wish to send away one of the said Spirits before the Six Hours during which he is on Guard be expired, it sufficeth for you to make him some sign that he can go, and at once he will obey. But when the Six Hours of their Guard be expired, the aforesaid Spirits will depart of their own accord without demanding your permission, and the next in rotation will successively take the place (of his predecessor). But if you have given one away (unto another person), you will employ one of the common kind in his place. [209]

Chapter VIII. (To excite Tempests.)

If you should wish to excite Tempests, give the Signal above your head (and touch the Symbol on the top); and when you wish to make them cease, you shall touch it on the underneath side.

Chapter IX. (To transform Animals into Men, and Men into Animals, etc.)

Let the being, whether Man or Animal, see the Symbol, and then touch them suddenly with it, when they will appear transformed; but this will be only a species of Fascination. When you wish to make it cease, you shall put the Symbol upon the head (of the being) and strike it with the Wand, and the Spirit will then restore matters to their former condition.

Chapter XI. (To cause all kinds of Books to be brought to one, and whether lost or stolen.)

Our predecessors, from the commencement of the World, have written many and divers excellent Books of the Qabalah, whose value surpasseth that of all the riches of the World. These Books have been for the most part lost by the Providence or Command of God, who hath not been willing that His High Mysteries should be made public by such means; seeing that hereby through such Books the Worthy and Unworthy can equally arrive at the enjoyment and possession of the Secret things of the Lord. Some also have been burned in fires, or swept away by the Waters, and other similar accidents (have occurred) through the Evil Spirits, who are jealous of Man's possessing such great treasures, and of being obliged to obey him. But this Third Part (of this Book), that is to say the Sacred Magic, is that which hath not been entirely lost, but the greater part hath been hidden and built up within a wall, and this hath happened by order of the Good Spirits, who have not permitted this Art to altogether perish, being willing that he who should (desire the same) should employ honourable means to obtain the same from the True and only God, and not from that Perfidious One and Deceiver, the Devil, and his following.

This Operation being completed in the proper manner, you will be able to see and to read these Books; but it is not permitted unto you to copy them, nor to keep them in your memory more than once. As for myself I have made every effort to copy them, but as fast as I wrote, the writing used to disappear from the page; whence you may conclude that the Lord knowing our nature, which is inclined unto Evil, doth not wish that such great Treasures should be employed to serve unto that end, [210] and unto the destruction of the Human Race.

Chapter XII. (To know the Secrets of any person.)

For this Operation it sufficeth to touch the Symbol, for at once the Spirit doth whisper the reply in your ear; but should you comprehend by such a means anything vile, whatever it may be, as you love the Grace of the Lord, see that you keep yourself from making manifest that which (you have obtained by the use of) the Symbol, seeing that by so doing you might work harm unto your neighbour. Every time that you touch the Symbol you should mention by name the person whose Secrets you desire to know.

Chapter XIII. (To cause a dead body to revive, and perform all the functions which a living

209   It is of course evident that the number Four of the Familiar Spirits = one for each of the Four Elements of which Man is composed, ruled by the Holy Name of Four Letters, IHVH, Tetragrammaton.

210   I.e., the Evil.

person would do, and this during a space of Seven Years, by means of the Spirits.)

I can in truth both say and affirm that a man who hath just died is divided into Three Parts, viz.: Body, Soul, and Spirit. The Body returneth unto the Earth, the Soul unto God or unto the Devil, and the Spirit hath its period determined by its Creator, that is to say, the Sacred Number of Seven Years, during the which it is permitted to wander hither and thither in any direction; at length it taketh its decision,[211] and goeth straightway unto the place whence it came forth (at the beginning). To change the condition of the Soul is impossible, but the Grace of the Lord, for many causes and reasons which it is not here permitted unto me to make manifest, hath been willing to permit that, with the aid of the Spirits, we may force the Spirit to return and to conjoin itself again with the Body, so that for the space of Seven Years it can operate any matter. And although this Spirit and the Body joined together can perform all the functions and exercises which they used to execute when the Body, the Soul and the Spirit were together, yet is it only an imperfect Body, being in this case without the Soul.

This Operation is, however, one of the greatest, and one which we should only perform in extraordinarily important cases; seeing that in order to accomplish it the Chief Spirits have to operate.

Nothing else is necessary than to be attentive to the moment when the Man is just dead, and then to place the Symbol upon him towards the Four Quarters of the World;[212] and at once he will lift himself up and begin to move himself. He should then be dressed; and a Symbol similar to that which hath been placed upon him should be sewn into his garment. Know also that when the Seven Years be expired, the Spirit which was conjoined with the Body will at once depart, and that we cannot further prolong the period of the aforesaid Seven Years. I made proof of this Operation in the Morea for the Duke of Saxonia, who had only children who were minors, and the eldest was between twelve and thirteen years of age, unfit for the government and management of his estate, the which his own relatives would have seized upon and appropriated unto themselves; and by this means I provided (against the contingency), and prevented that estate from falling into other hands.

Chapter XIV. (The Twelve Symbols for the Twelve Hours of the Day and of the Night, to render oneself Invisible unto every person.)

To render oneself invisible is a very easy matter, but it is not altogether permissible, because that by such a means we can annoy our neighbour in his (daily) life, for we can easily employ the same for producing various effects, and we can also work an infinitude of evils (herewith). But, honestly speaking, we must not do the latter, such being expressly forbidden by God. This is wherefore I entreat you to avail yourself hereof always for a good and never for an evil end! You have in this Chapter Twelve Symbols, for Twelve different Spirits submitted unto Prince MAGOT, who are all of the same force. You should put the Symbol (upon the top of your head) under the hat or bonnet, and then you will become invisible; while on taking it away, you will appear visible again.

---

211   " Se resont," in the MS. "Resoudre," like our word "resolve," also may imply to reduce to its chemical constituents. These three parts of the person, which Abraham calls Body, Soul, and Spirit, are designated in the Qabalah by the respective terms of "Nephesch," i.e., the animal part; "Neschamah," or the Soul, that is to say, the Higher Aspirations, and "Ruach," i.e., the Mind or Spirit. But besides these, the Qabalists also recognise certain higher principles, p. 146 of which Abraham the Jew does not here speak, nor yet of the faculty of reincarnation of those principles. Reincarnation is a subject much treated of by the Oriental Sacred writings, and was undoubtedly a fundamental doctrine of the Ancient Egyptian Magic, from which, be it well remembered, the Hebrew Qabalah has been derived. The Esoteric Buddhists divide the personality into Seven Principles, instead of the Three given above.

212   I.e., The Four Cardinal Points,

Chapter XV. (For the Spirits to bring us anything we may wish to eat or to drink, and even all kinds of food that we can imagine.)

As for this Symbol, and all like ones appertaining unto this Chapter, when you shall wish to make use of them, you shall put them between two plates, dishes, or jugs, closed together, on the outside of a window, and before a quarter of an hour shall have passed, you will, find and will have that which you have demanded. But you must clearly understand that with such kind of viands you cannot nourish men for more than two days only; for this food, although it be appreciable by the eyes and by the Mouth, doth not long nourish the body, which hath soon hunger again, seeing that this (food) giveth no strength to the stomach. Know also that none of these (viands) can remain visible for more than twenty-four hours, the which period being passed, fresh ones will be requisite.

Chapter XVI. (To find and take possession of all kinds of Treasures, provided that they be not at all magically guarded.)

Should you wish to discover or to take possession of Treasure, you must select the Symbol which you wish, whether it be of a common or of a particular Operation, and the Spirit will at once show it unto you, of whatsoever kind, or after whatsoever fashion, it may be. Then shall you place the Symbol which is referable unto it thereon, and it will no longer be possible for it to disappear into the ground, nor for it to be carried away. Furthermore, the Spirits destined unto the Guard of this Treasure will flee, and you can then dispose of it as you wish, and take it away.

Chapter XVII. (To fly in the Air and travel anywhere.)

Name the place whitherunto you wish to travel, and place the Symbol upon your head, under the bonnet or the hat; but take well heed lest the Symbol fall from off you through negligence or want of caution. Do not journey at night-time unless necessity or some pressing reason thereto compelleth you, but select the day-time, and that serene and calm.

Chapter XVIII. (To heal divers Maladies.)

Undo the bandages of the sick person, and clean them, and having applied the unguent and the compresses, put them again upon the sick person; and place the Symbol upon them,[213] and leave it thus for about a quarter of an hour, then take it away and keep it (for use on another occasion). But if it be an internal malady, you shall place the Symbol upon the bare head of the patient. These Symbols may be seen and examined without any danger, howbeit it is always better that they should neither be seen nor handled by any other person than yourself.

Chapter XIX. (For every description of Affection and Love.)

And

Chapter XX. (To excite every description of Hatred and Enmity, Discords, Quarrels, Contentions, Combats, Battles, Loss, and Damage.)

On request, and by the intermediary of the Spirits, we can obtain love, goodwill, and the favour of Princes and Sovereigns, on this wise: Name aloud the person or persons by. whom you wish to be loved, and move the Symbol answering to the class under which they fall; because if you be operating for yourself in matters falling under the heads of love, friendship, etc., you should absolutely name aloud the person, and move the Symbol. But if you name or operate for two other persons, whether it be for love or for hatred, you should expressly name both, and move the Symbols answering to the classes under which they fall. Also, if it be possible, you can touch them with the Symbol, whether it be general or particular. Under this heading are included all classes of goodwill, among the which the most difficult by far is to make yourself beloved by religious persons.[214]

Chapter XXI. (To transform oneself, and take different Faces and Forms.)

213   I.e., the bandages.

214   In the Original MS., " despersonnes religieuses". This expression would include monks, nuns, and also people bigoted in religion.

In this Transmutation, which is rather a Fascination, the method of operating is as follows: Take the Symbol in your left hand, and with it stroke your face. Now were it some (ordinary) Necromancer who was transformed by the working of some Diabolical Art, he would soon be discovered (by you). It is certain, however, that if he who operateth be instructed in the True and Sacred Magic, like yourself, that he[215] could produce no effect upon you; because against the Grace of the Lord, by whomsoever received, no Operation can take effect, whether for Good or for Evil; but should such be Diabolical Operations by express pacts and similar Sorceries, it is certain that you would soon bring them to shame.

Chapter XXII. (This Chapter is only for Evil, for with the Symbols herein we can cast Spells, and work every kind of Evil; we should not avail ourselves hereof.)

All these Symbols are to be either buried in the ground, or placed under doors, steps, or buried under paths and other places by which people do pass, or whereon they lean; in this latter case it is sufficient merely to touch (such places) with the Symbol. It must be here remarked that we can work much evil against our enemies, and if you know for a certain fact that they are attempting your life, there is no imaginable sin in availing yourself of (these Symbols for protection). But should you do this to please some friend, you would not escape easily with impunity from (the disapproval of) your Guardian Angel. Use then this Knowledge as a Sword against your Enemies, but never against your neighbour, which would be without any result but that of bringing hurt to yourself.

Chapter XXVI. (To open every kind of Lock, without Key, and without making any noise.)

Should you wish to open anything locked, such as ordinary Locks (Bolts)[216] Padlocks, Coffers, Cupboards, Boxes, and Doors, you shall touch them with the side of the Symbol which is written upon, and immediately they will open without any noise, without being in any way damaged, and without exciting any suspicion of their having been broken open. When you wish to again close them, you shall touch them with the back of the Symbol, that is to say, with the part thereof not written upon, and at once they will refasten of their own accord. And in no way should this Operation be employed in Churches, or for the committing of Murder. Also (remember) that this Operation can be used for all manner of wicked ends; wherefore we should obtain (permission) first from our Guardian Angel, so as not to irritate him, and abuse the Grace of God, which we have received. Neither should this (Operation) be employed to aid in the commission of Rapes and Violation of Women; but only for (laudable) effects, and other (permissible) ends.

The Child of whose services you avail yourself for the conclusion of this Operation should not be more than Seven Years of age; it should be able to speak clearly, it should be active, and should comprehend what you teach it to do, in order to serve you. And fear not that this Child may be able to reveal and tell unto others anything of what he doeth; also he will not in the least remember that which he shall have done, and you can make trial thereof yourself by interrogating him after the seven days be past, and you will find that he will be able to tell you nothing of that which hath passed; the which is a very remarkable thing.

When you shall have thoroughly decided to give this present Operation unto any, and which should only be given as a free gift, as I have already said; remember to make such person give you Seven Florins, the which you shall distribute unto Seven poor persons with your own hand, And such poor persons must genuinely be in want. Them shall you straitly charge, to repeat for Seven days the Seven penitential Psalms, or the Pater and Ave seven times a day, praying unto the Lord for the person who hath given (the florins) unto you to distribute unto them, that He would deign to come unto his assistance, and to grant unto him for ever such strength that he may never transgress His Holy Commandments.

While in the performance of the Operation, be certain that each person (undertaking the same) is subject unto very great temptations to prevarication, and in particular unto great disquietudes

---

215   I.e., such Evil Magician.

216   " Serrures," which implies bolts as well as locks.

of mind, to force the abandonment of the Operation. For the Mortal Enemy of Man is grieved that he should make the acquisition of this Sacred Science, the which also he receiveth from God Himself, Who hath by this means closed the way against the DEMON, this being the only object and end of this Sacred Science. For the Enchantments whereof the Evil Enchanters and Sorcerers make employ, are in no way wrought by the true method, and they only have power to execute their end in proportion to the Tributes, Sacrifices, and Pacts, rendered in return, which latter evidently bring about the loss of the Soul, and very frequently that of the Body as well.

Consider that it is the pride of (the DEMON) which hath chased him out of Heaven, and think what a heartbreaking thing it is for him to see a Man, made of vile earth, command him who is a Spirit, and who was created noble, and an Angel (as well); and also that it is necessary that he should submit himself unto Man, and obey him, not of his own free will, but by force, and by a power of command which God hath given unto Man, to whom he is forced to humiliate himself, and to obey, he, who had the greatest difficulty in submitting himself unto his Creator. And yet, notwithstanding all this, he is obliged by his most profound humiliation, and by his most severe suffering, to submit himself unto Man, for whom further is destined that Heaven which he himself hath lost for an Eternity.

Wherefore you should continue the Operation, and have recourse unto the Lord, and in no way be troubled, for you shall vanquish every difficulty, seeing that the Lord never faileth those who put all their confidence in Him.

You may only give this Sacred Operation unto two persons; and in the case of your giving it unto a third, it would hold good for him, but you yourself would be for ever deprived of it. I beseech you in grace to well open your eyes, and thoroughly examine him unto whom you shall give so great a Treasure, so that he be not one who will make use of the same to make a mock of God, which is a sin so great, that we Jews are a living proof thereof. For since our predecessors began to make use of this Sacred Magic for Evil, God hath granted it unto so few among us, that in my whole lifetime, ourselves included, we be but the number of Seven persons who by the Grace of God possess the same.

When the Child shall warn you that your Guardian Angel hath appeared, then shall you, without moving from your place, repeat in a low voice Psalm CXXXVII., which beginneth: "Confitebor Tibi Domine, in toto corde meo," "I will give thanks unto Thee, O Lord, with mine whole heart," etc. And, on the contrary, when you shall convoke for the first time the Four Chief Spirits, you shall say Psalm XC.: "Qui habitat in adjutorio Altissimi," "Whoso dwelleth in the defence of the Most High," etc.; and this not in a low voice as in the preceding case, but (aloud) as you usually speak, and standing where you happen to be.

Chapter XXVIII. (To have as much Gold and Silver as one may wish, both to provide for one's necessities, and to live in opulence.)

And whereas I have allowed the Twenty-eighth Chapter to pass without notice, I now refer hereto. Place the Symbol of the Money you require in your purse, let it remain there for a short time, then put your right hand in your purse, and you will there find Seven pieces of the class of Money which you have intended to obtain. But take heed to perform this Operation only thrice in the day. And the pieces of Money whereof you have no longer need will disappear at once. This is why when you have need of small change you should take heed at the same time not to ask for large pieces. I could have here set down other values and Symbols, but I have only given those which I have found the most necessary for a beginner, and partly also to avoid confusing you. And also it is not right that I who am only a mortal man should give further instructions hereon unto you who are about to have an Angel for Master and for Guide.

We have already said that providing he recogniseth a God, any Man, of any Religion soever, may arrive at the possession of this Veritable Wisdom and Magic, if he employ right and proper ways and means. Now I say further that unto whatever Law[217] he who operateth may pertain, he can observe the feasts, etc., thereof, provided that they hinder not the Operation, with a firm and true conviction that he shall have from his Angel greater lights as to the points wherein he may be liable to err. Wherefore you shall be ready and willing to correct your faults, obedient in all things, and on all occasions, unto his precepts. And you should observe exactly and inviolably from point to point, everything touching the regimen of life, the practice, and other counsels given in this Book.

As we have already said, if by chance some slight indisposition should overtake you after the commencement of the Operation, you shall observe that hereinbefore laid down; but should the illness become very much worse, so that remedies become necessary unto the health of the body, and that you have to undergo blood-letting; then do not harden yourself against the Will of the Lord, but having made a brief prayer, thank Him for having visited you in this manner. And having made use of remedies which oblige you to leave off the Operation already begun, so as not to become as it were your own murderer, and notwithstanding that it grieveth you to the heart to be forced so to do, yet nevertheless conform yourself unto His Holy Will. And when you shall have regained your accustomed health, in His own good time shall you return unto the Operation, feeling sure that He will grant you His aid. Such a forced desistance doth not hinder you from awaiting a fitting time, when you may recommence; seeing that such interruption is not in any way voluntary, but forced by necessity. Whereas, had this interruption occurred through pure caprice, you ought never to think further of (recommencing), because we must not make a Mock of God.

There be two kinds of sins which are infinitely displeasing unto God. One is Ingratitude, and the other Incredulity. I say this cursorily, because the Devil will not fail to insinuate a thousand ideas into your head (such as) that this Operation may perhaps be (a real thing) and perhaps not; that the symbols are badly drawn, etc., so as to make you comment upon the subject. This is why you must have Faith, and that you must believe. Neither should you dispute concerning that which you understand not; remember that God out of nothingness hath created all things, and that all things have their being in Him; watch, work, and you will see.

In the Name of the Most Holy ADONAI, the True and Only God, we have finished this Book in the best order and with the best instruction which has been possible to me. Know also that it is only in God that you will find the sole and certain Way to arrive at the True Wisdom and Magic, but yet also by following out that which I have written down in this Book with such exactitude. Still, however, when you shall have put anything into practice, you shall, manifestly know how great and immeasurable hath been my paternal affection;[218] and in truth I dare to say that I have done for love of you what no one in our times hath undertaken, and in especial in that I have declared unto you the two Symbols, that of the Child, and your own particular one, [219]without the which I swear unto you by the True God that out of an hundred persons who might undertake this Operation, there would be only two or three who would actually attain unto it. I have, however, removed most of the difficulties, (therefore) be now tranquil, and despise not my counsel.

It need not appear strange unto you that this Book is not at all like unto so many others which I have, and which are composed in a lofty and subtle style; because I have composed this (work) expressly in order to spare you so much labour, and to enlighten therein the difficulties which you

217   I.e., Religious denomination.

218   Here Abraham the Jew is evidently especially addressing himself to his son Lamech.

219   These two Symbols are probably those which are placed at the extreme end of the Third Book, i.e., the Magical Squares with the Names ADAM and URIEL returned therein, and of which the Squares of numbers above are evidently intended for the reverse sides; ADAM being applied to the Child, and URIEL to the Guardian Angel of Lamech.

might (otherwise) have encountered in order to comprehend its meaning. And so that it might not be at all necessary for it to pass into other hands (than your own), in making this Book I have in no way availed myself of eloquent but peculiar expressions, which those who write such works usually make use of, and even then not without mystifications. But I have employed a certain manner of arrangement, making a mixture of the subject matter, and dispersing it here and there in the Chapters so that you may be forced to read and re-read the Book many times, and also the better so to do, to transcribe and imprint it in your memory. Render then your thanks unto the Lord God Almighty, and never forget my faithful advice, even unto the day of your death. Thus will the Divine Wisdom and Magic be your wealth, and never can you find a greater Treasure in the World. Obey promptly him who teacheth you that which he hath learned by his own experience; and I pray and conjure you by that God Who is my God, to observe summarily and inviolably the three following heads which should serve you as guides and limitations until you shall pass the gulf of this Miserable World:--

(1) Let God, His Word, all His Commandments, and the Counsel of your Angel, never depart from your heart and from your mind!

(2) Be the declared enemy of all the Evil Spirits, their Vassals, and Adherents, during the whole period of your life. Dominate them, and regard them as your Servitors.[220] If they make propositions to you, demanding from you pacts, or sacrifices, or obedience, or servitude, refuse them with disdain and menaces.

(3) It is more than evident that God can know the heart of men, the which 'none else can do. You should therefore force yourself to test severely for some time him to whom you intend to give this (knowledge). You shall closely note his method of life and habits; you shall discuss the subject with him, seeking to discover in the clearest way and as far as possible, whether he would use it for Good or for Evil. Also in giving this Operation you shall fast, eating only once a day, and he who shall receive it shall do the same; see also what we have said in the Third Chapter,[221] and elsewhere. It is also true that one who would suffer much in health by fasting in such a manner, may if absolutely necessary supplement the same by paying one or several persons to fast in his stead and to intercede for him.[222] (The whole object and end of) this should be both to give and receive this operation unto the Glory of the Great God, and unto one's own good and that of one's neighbour, whether friend or enemy, and unto that of all things created.

The Ten Florins of Gold[223] shall be distributed by your own hands when you shall have received the money, unto Seventy-two poor persons who know the Psalms, as mentioned in a preceding Chapter; and see also that you fail not in this, for it is an essential point.

Furthermore you shall demand from him to whom you shall give the Operation, some pleasurable gratification which is in harmony with the Operation, at your choice. But see that you demand not money, for for this you would be deprived entirely of the Holy Wisdom.

Every time that you shall desire to make a fresh command,[224] you shall thrice repeat the Psalm XC., "Qui habitat in adjutorium Altissimi," etc., "Whoso dwelleth in the aid of the Most High," etc.-

---

220   Again let the practical Occultist remember that this counsel applies principally to Adepts; for the ordinary man can not command the Demons, seeing that he has not yet learned to understand and control even all his thoughts; and the Adept can only command such beings through the knowledge of his Higher Self, and of his Guardian Angel.

221   I.e. of the Second Book.

222   I think this system of substitution should be very rarely practised. He must be a very spiritless person who would be dissuaded by the prospect of fasting for a day or two.

223   Before alluded to in several places.

224   This would apparently apply to a command given to the Demons, and not to an Aspirant for the Sacred Wisdom.

-because this Psalm possesseth so great a virtue that you will be astonished when you comprehend it. If you know that you, as a man, have offended your Creator, in anything regarding the Tables of the Law; perform no operation until after having made a general confession of your sins unto God; the which you shall observe unto the day of your death. By thus acting the Mercy of the Lord will never depart from you.

Unto the which Lord be Praise, and Glory, and Honour, for the Gifts which He hath granted unto us. So be it!

THE END OF THE SECOND BOOK.

THE THIRD BOOK
OF THE
HOLY MAGIC,
WHICH GOD GAVE UNTO MOSES, AARON, DAVID, SOLOMON, AND OTHER SAINTS, PATRIARCHS AND PROPHETS; WHICH TEACHETH THE TRUE DIVINE WISDOM.

BEQUEATHED BY ABRAHAM UNTO LAMECH HIS SON.

TRANSLATED FROM THE HEBREW.

1458

PROLOGUE

HE who shall have faithfully observed that which hath been taught unto him, and shall have with a good will obeyed the Commandments of God, let him, I say, be certain that this Veritable and Loyal Wisdom shall be accorded unto him; and also that the Perfidious BELIAL can do no otherwise than become his slave, together with all his Pestiferous Generation.

However I pray the True God who governeth, ruleth over, and maintaineth all that He hath created; that thou, O Lamech, my son, or whomsoever he may be unto whom thou shalt have granted this Sacred Operation, mayest work it out, having always before thee the Fear of God, and in no way use it for Evil, because God the Eternal hath wished herein to leave us our free will, but woe unto him who shall abuse His Divine Grace. Yet I say not but that if an enemy should attempt thy life, that it is permissible unto thee if necessary to destroy him; but in any other case lay not thine hand unto the sword, but use gentler methods. Be kind and affable unto every one. One may also serve a friend without harm unto oneself.

David and King Solomon could have destroyed their enemies in an instant, but they did not so; in imitation of God Himself who chastiseth not unless He is outraged.

If thou shalt perfectly observe these rules, all the following Symbols and an infinitude of others will be granted unto thee by thy Holy Guardian Angel; thou thus living for the Honour and Glory of the True and only God, for thine own good, and that of thy neighbour. Let the Fear of God be ever before the eves and the heart of him who shall possess this Divine Wisdom and Sacred Magic.

THE FIRST CHAPTER.

TO know all manner of things Past and Future, which be not however directly opposed to God, and to His Most Holy Will.

(1) To know all things Past and Future in general.
(2, 3) To know things appertaining unto the Future.
(4) Things to happen in War.

(5) Things past and forgotten.
(6) Tribulations to come.
(7) Things propitious to come.
(8) Things past regarding Enemies.
(9) To know the Signs of Tempests.
(10) To know the Secrets of War.
(11) To know true and false Friends.

(1)

M	I	L	O	N
I	R	A	G	O
L	A	M	A	L
O	G	A	R	I
N	O	L	I	M

(2)

T	H	I	R	A	M	A
H	I	G	A	N	A	M
I	G	O	G	A	N	A
R	A	G	I	G	A	R
A	N	A	G	O	G	I
M	A	N	A	G	I	H
A	M	A	R	I	H	T

(3)

D	O	R	E	H
O	R	I	R	E
R	I	N	I	R
E	R	I	R	O
H	E	R	O	D

(4)

N	A	B	H	I
A	D	A	I	H
B	A	K	A	B
H	I	A	D	A
I	H	B	A	N

(5)

N	V	D	E	T	O	N
V	S	I	L	A	R	O
D	I	R	E	M	A	T
E	L	E	M	E	L	E
T	A	M	E	R	I	D
O	R	A	L	I	S	V
N	O	T	E	D	V	N

(6)

S	A	R	A	P	I
A	R	A	I	R	P
R	A	K	K	I	A
A	I	K	K	A	R
P	R	I	A	R	A
I	P	A	R	A	S

(7)

M	A	L	A	C	H
A	M	A	N	E	C
L	A	N	A	N	A
A	N	A	N	A	L
C	E	N	A	M	A
H	C	A	L	A	M

(8)

K	O	S	E	M
O	B	O	D	E
S	O	F	O	S
E	D	O	B	O
M	E	S	O	K

(9)

R	O	T	H	E	R
O	R	O	R	I	E
T	O	A	R	A	H
H	A	R	A	O	T
E	I	R	O	R	O
R	E	H	T	O	R

(10)

M	E	L	A	B	B	E	D
E	L	I	N	A	L	S	E
L	I	N	A	K	I	L	B
A	N	A	K	A	K	A	B
B	A	K	A	K	A	N	A
B	L	I	K	A	N	I	L
E	S	L	A	N	I	L	B
D	E	B	B	A	L	E	M

(11)

M	E	B	H	A	E	R
E	L	I	A	I	L	E
B	I	K	O	S	I	A
H	A	O	R	O	A	H
A	I	S	O	K	I	B
E	L	I	A	I	L	E
R	E	A	H	B	E	M

NOTES TO THE CHAPTERS OF MAGICAL SYMBOLS
BY
S. L. MACGREGOR-MATHERS.

THE following Notes to these Chapters I have classed under various heads for greater convenience of reference, thinking that besides the explanations of most of the Magical Names employed in the Symbols, it would also be of assistance to the Occult student to be able to see at a glance briefly stated at the end of each Chapter, the substance of the information especially referring thereto, given by Abraham the Jew in other parts of the work, notably towards the end of the Second Book:--

Under (a) therefore I have stated by what Powers the Symbols of each particular Chapter are manifested.

Under (b) the Names of the Sub-Princes of the Evil Spirits who are the especial overseers of the execution of the effect desired.

Under (c) whether the Operations of the Chapter in question can be to an extent performed by the "Familiar Spirits," or not.

Under (d) an abridgment of any especial instructions given by Abraham in other parts of the work.

Under (e) I have given the meanings of most of the Names employed in the Squares, as far as possible, and also any additional remarks which seemed necessary.

These Magical Symbols of this Third Book consist solely of Squares of Letters, which may be roughly divided into four distinct classes.

(1) Those in which the whole of the Square is occupied by Letters. In this form the double Acrostic arrangement is especially marked; though in some few cases it is slightly varied by the introduction of a different name.

(2) Those in which part of the Square is left vacant, the Letters being arranged in the form of what is called in Geometry, a Gnomon.

(3) Those in which the central part of the Square is left vacant, the Letters forming a border round the void part.

(4) Those of more irregular disposition, and in which in some instances single Letters are placed separately in the vacant part of the Square.

It will be remarked that in nearly all cases these Names arranged in the Squares represent generally the effect to be produced, or in other words are simply the Hebrew or other appellations of the result to which the Square is to be applied. At the beginning of each Chapter is placed a numbered list of the effects to be obtained by the use of each Symbol there given, Then follow the Squares themselves.

In the Original MS. these Squares have been also numbered to correspond with the list at the beginning of each Chapter, but from the evident difference in the ink this has been done later, though the handwriting is the same. I think also that in several cases the numbers to the Squares have been misplaced; and though usually the natural Sequence of 1, 2, 3, 4, 5, 6 is adhered to, yet occasionally they are in a more irregular order, as in the 5th Chapter, for example, where they run thus:--3, 4, 5, 6, 1, 2, 7, 8, 9, 10, 11, 12.

The Squares in the Original MS. are all of the same size, subdivided according to the exigences of the case, though convenience of printing has prevented this equality of size being adhered to in the present work. In most instances the Gnomons and Borders are ruled off from the vacant part, but this rule is not adhered to in all cases in the Original MS. The Letters in the Squares are Roman Capitals. In some few instances two letters are placed in the same small Square, or subdivision, of the larger Square.

NOTES TO CHAPTER I

(a) The Symbols of this Chapter are manifested only by the Angels or by the Guardian Angel.

(b) ORIENS, PAYMON, ARITON, and AMAYMON execute the Operations hereof by means of their Common Ministers.

(c) The Familiar Spirits cannot well execute the Operations of this Chapter.

(d) Take the Symbol in your hand, place it under your hat or cap, upon the top of your head, and you will be secretly answered by the Spirit who will execute that which you wish. (This mode of operation will evidently be applicable to many of the Chapters.)

(e) No. 1 is a Square of 25 Squares, and is a complete specimen of double Acrostic arrangement. MILON, though Greek-sounding, has here hardly a meaning if derived from either MILOS, a fruit or other tree; or from MEILON, a precious thing, or article of value.--It seems rather derived from the Hebrew MLVN = a diversity of things, or matters.--IRAGO is perhaps from Greek EIRA a question, or inquiry, and AGO to conduct or decide. Hebrew RGO = to disrupt or analyse.--LA-

MAL, probably from Chaldaic MLA = fulness, entirety. OGARI from Hebrew OGR = a swallow or swiftly-flying thing. NOLIM from Hebrew, NOLIM = hidden or covered things. Whence we may extract the following as the formula of this Square: "Various questions fully examined and analysed, and that quickly, and even things carefully hidden and concealed ". This rule we can apply to discover the formulas of other Squares.

No. 2 is a Square of 49 Squares, and is also a complete Specimen of double Acrostic.--THIRAMA from Chaldee TIRM = strongly-defended places, or Citadels.--HIGANAM from Hebrew or Chaldee GNN or GNM = to defend.--IGOGANA, perhaps from Hebrew GG = a roof or covering or protection from above.--RAGIGAR, perhaps from Chaldaic ROO (it must be remembered that, though I here transliterate the letter Ayin by O, it has really the power of a Gh as well; it is a sound difficult of comprehension by a non-Orientalist); = to break up, or breach.--ANAGOGI probably from Greek ANAGOGE the act of raising or elevating.--MANAGIH from Hebrew MNO to restrain; stop, put a barrier to, or contain by a barrier.--AMARIHT from Hebrew AMRTh = Word or Speech.--The whole idea of this Formula seems to be the making forcible way into a defended place or matter.

No. 3 is a Square of 25 Squares, and again a perfect form of double Acrostic. DOREH, from DVR Hebrew = a habitation.--ORIRE perhaps from Latin ORIOR = to rise or be born.--RINIR perhaps from Hebrew NIR = to renew.--ERIRO perhaps from ARR to curse.--HEROD from Hebrew ChRD = shaking, trembling.

No. 4 is a Square of 25 Squares, and again a perfect double Acrostic.--NABHI from Hebrew NBA = to prophesy.--ADAIH perhaps from Heb. DIH. = a bird of omen. BAKAB from Heb. KAB = in trouble. HIADA from Hebrew IDH = sent forward, or thrown. IHBAN from IHB Hebrew = to give or bring. Hence the formula would be somewhat "To prophesy by omens the troubles to come"; the which is much more applicable to No. 6, "The Tribulations to come"; than to No. 4, which is for "The Things to happen in War".

No. 5 is a double Acrostic of 49 Squares.--NVDETON from Hebrew ND = to remove, and AThN = strongly.--VSILARO from Hebrew BSHL = to ripen, and Chaldaic ARO = the Earth.--DIREMAT from Hebrew DR = to encompass or include, and MT = things forgotten or slipped aside. ELEMELE from Hebrew ALIM and ALH=God of the Mighty Ones.--TAMERID from Hebrew ThMR = straight like a palm-tree, and ID = put forward.--ORALISV = from Hebrew = ORL = superfluous, and ISh the substance.--NOTEDVN, from NTH = to stretch out and DN to contend or rule.

No. 6 is a double Acrostic of 36 Squares.--SARAPI from Hebrew ShRP = to burn.--ARAIRP from Hebrew AR = a river, and RPH = to abate or slacken.--RAKKIA from Hebrew RKK = to become faint, to become softened.--AIKKAR from Hebrew OKR = to trouble or disturb.--PRIARA from PRR = to shatter or break up.--IPARAS from Hebrew PRS = to break in pieces, to divide, or part in sunder. This will give a formula of trouble.

No. 7 is a double Acrostic of 36 Squares.--MALACH from Hebrew MLCh = Salt; also that which is easily dissolved; to dissolve.--AMANEC from MNK = a chain, or from AMN = stability.--LANANA from LNN = to lodge, or take up one's abode.--ANANAL from AN = labour, and NLH, to complete or finish.--CENAMA perhaps from QNM = odoriferous. HCALAM perhaps from HCL = spacious (as a palace).

No. 8 is a double Acrostic of 25 Squares.--KOSEM, from Hebrew QSM = to divine or prognosticate.--OBODE, from Hebrew OBD = a servant.--SOFOS from Greek SOPHOS = wise, learned, skilful.--EDOBO, perhaps from DB = to murmur.--MESOK from Hebrew MSK = to mingle or intermix.

No. 9 is a double Acrostic of 36 Squares.--ROTHER is perhaps from RTT, Trembling, Dread; and HRR to conceive or bring forth.--ORORIE from Hebrew OROR = laying bare, disclosing.--TOARAH from Hebrew ThVRH = Law, Reason, or Order of.--HARAOT from Hebrew HRH to bring forth, or from ChRTh = To inscribe or mark down.--REHTOR from RTT and ThVR = reason for dread.--The whole formula will represent the disclosing of the reasons for dreading any terrible effect.

No. 10 is another double Acrostic of 64 Squares, and No. 11 one of 49 Squares. I have here given a sufficiently careful analysis of the meanings of the combinations formed by the letters in the preceding Squares to give the Reader a general idea of the formulas involved. To avoid an undue extension of these notes, I shall not usually analyse every name contained in each Square, but shall confine myself in most cases to giving sufficient indications of the meanings of the principal words or words only, which are therein employed. The Reader must remember also that in such an Acrostic arrangement of the letters of words, half of those therein contained will simply be inversions of the principal word or words therein contained. For example, in No. 11, REAHBEM is of course MEBHAER written backwards.--ELIAILE reads the same way backwards or forwards, and so does HAOROAH; and BIKOSIA written backwards gives AISOKIB. Yet undoubtedly some of these words are to an extent translatable also, and in this case will be found to have a bearing on the subject-matter of the Square. Hebrew especially is a language in which this method will be found to work with a readiness unattainable in ordinary European languages, from the fact that its Alphabet may be said to be entirely Consonantal in character, even such letters as Aleph, Vau, and Yōd, being rather respectively, a drawing in of the breath than the letter A; V rather than U; and Y rather than I. Also in common with all really ancient languages the system of Verbal Roots from which all the words of the language are derived, has this effect, viz., that the majority of combinations of two or three letters will be found to be a Verbal Root, bearing a definite meaning. Besides all this, in the Qabalah each letter of the Hebrew Alphabet is treated as having a complete sphere of hieroglyphic meanings of its own; whence the most important ancient Hebrew Names and Words can be treated by the Qabalistic Initiate as in fact so many formulas of Spiritual force. I have been thus lengthy in explanation in order that the Reader may have some idea of the reason of the construction and use of these Magic Squares.

THE SECOND CHAPTER.

TO obtain information concerning, and to be enlightened upon all sorts of propositions and all doubtful Sciences.

(1, 2, 3) Generally for the above effect.

(1)

A	L	L	U	P
L	E	I	R	U
L	I	G	I	L
U	R	I	E	L
P	U	L	L	A.

(2)

M	E	L	A	M	M	E	D
E	R	I	P	O	I	S	E
L	I	S	I	L	L	I	M
A	F	I	R	E	L	O	M
M	O	L	E	R	I	F	A
M	I	L	L	I	S	I	L
E	S	I	O	P	I	R	E
D	E	M	M	A	L	E	M

(3)

E	K	D	I	L	U	N
K	L	I	S	A	T	U
D	I	N	A	N	A	L
I	S	A	G	A	S	I
L	A	N	A	N	I	D
U	T	A	S	I	L	K
N	U	L	I	D	K	E

NOTES TO CHAPTER II

(a) The Symbols of this Chapter are manifested partly by the Angels, and partly by the Evil Spirits.

(b) ORIENS, PAYMON, ARITON, and AMAYMON execute the Operations hereof by the means of their common Ministers.

(c) The Familiar Spirits can to an extent execute the Operations of this Chapter.

(d) Take the Symbol in your hand, and name what information you require. (In the Second Book, the remarks given concerning this Chapter are evidently far more applicable to the Third Chapter, and I have therefore given them there instead of here.)

(e) No. 1 is an Acrostic of 25 Squares.--ALLUP from Hebrew ALUP = a Doctor, Teacher, Leader, i.e., a person who at the same time leads and instructs his following. Hence also this word means a Bull as the Leader of the herd.--URIEL, Hebrew AURIEL = Light of God, is the well-known name of one of the Archangels. Pulla in Latin means both a fowl, and also light friable earth; but is probably here derivable rather from the Hebrew PLH, meaning to classify or arrange.

No. 2 is an Acrostic of 64 Squares.--MELAMMED is evidently from Hebrew MLMD = a stimulus or spur to exertion.

No. 3 is an Acrostic of 49 Squares.--EKDILUN may be from the Greek EKDEILON, which means, "not afraid of"; from EK in composition, and DEILON, frightened, cowardly.

THE THIRD CHAPTER.

TO cause any Spirit to appear, and take any form, such as of Man, Animal, Bird, etc.

(1) It will appear in the form of a Serpent.
(2) To make them appear in the shape of any Animal.
(3) In Human form.
(4) In the form of a Bird.

(1)

U	R	I	E	L
R	A	M	I	E
I	M	I	M	I
E	I	M	A	R
L	E	I	R	U

(2)

L	U	C	I	F	E	R
U	N	A	N	I	M	E
C	A	T	O	N	I	F
I	N	O	N	O	N	I
F	I	N	O	T	A	C
E	M	I	N	A	N	U
R	E	F	I	C	U	L

(3)

L	E	V	I	A	T	A	N
E	R	M	O	G	A	S	A
V	M	I	R	T	E	A	T
I	O	R	A	N	T	G	A
A	G	T	N	A	R	O	I
T	A	E	T	R	I	M	V
A	S	A	G	O	M	R	E
N	A	T	A	I	V	E	L

(4)

S	A	T	A	N
A	D	A	M	A
T	A	B	A	T
A	M	A	D	A
N	A	T	A	S

NOTES TO CHAPTER III

(a) The Symbols of this Chapter are manifested only by the Angel or by the Guardian Angel.

(b) ORIENS, PAYMON, ARITON, and AMAYMON execute the operations hereof by means of their common Ministers.

(c) The Familiar Spirits do not execute the Operations of this Chapter.

(d) Take the Symbol in the hand, and name the Spirit desired, who will appear in the form commanded.

(e) It will be noticed at once that of the four Symbols of this Chapter, the first has the name of the Archangel Uriel, and the three others those of three of the Chief Princes of the Demons, viz.;--Lucifer, Leviathan, and Satan.

No. 1 is an Acrostic of 25 Squares.--URIEL from Hebrew AURIEL = Light of God.--RAMIE from Hebrew RMIH = Deceit. IMIMI is either from IMM = the Sea, or great waters, or from IMIM = Mules--EIMAR is probably from AMR or IMR = To speak.--LEIRU is the reverse of URIEL, i.e., Uriel written backwards.--This formula seems to show that the Symbol should be numbered 2 instead of 1.

No. 2 is an Acrostic of 49 Squares.--LUCIFER from Lucifer (Latin) = Light bearer. This Square should probably be numbered 3.

No. 3 is an Acrostic of 64 Squares.--LEVIATAN from Hebrew,= the piercing or twisting Serpent. This Square should probably be numbered 1.

No. 4 is an Acrostic of 25 Squares.--SATAN from Hebrew SHTN an Adversary.--ADAMA from Hebrew ADMH reddish earth.

THE FOURTH CHAPTER.

FOR divers Visions.

(1) For Mirrors of Glass and Crystal.
(2) In Caverns and Subterranean Places.
(3) In the Air.
(4) In Rings and Circlets.
(5) In Wax.
(6) In Fire.
(7) In the Moon.
(8) In the Water.
(9) In the Hand.

(1)

G	I	L	I	O	N	I	N
I							
L							
I							
O							
N							
I							
N							

(2)

E	T	H	A	N	I	M
T						
H						
A						
N						
I						
M						

A	P	P	A	R	E	T
P						
P						
A						
R						
E						
T						

(4)

B	E	D	S	E	R
E	L	I	E	L	E
D	I	A	P	I	S
S	E	P	P	E	D
E	L	I	E	L	E
R	E	S	D	E	B

(5)

N	E	G	O	T
E	R	A	S	O
G	A	R	A	G
O	M	A	R	E
T	O	G	E	N

(6)

N	A	S	I
A	P	I	S
S	I	P	A
I	S	A	N

(7)

G	O	H	E	N
O	R	A	R	E
H	A	S	A	H
E	R	A	R	O
N	E	H	O	G

(8)

A	D	M	O	N
D				
M				
O				
N				

(9)

L	E	L	E	H
E				
L				
E				
H				

NOTES TO CHAPTER IV

(a) The Symbols of this Chapter are manifested only by the Angels or by the Guardian Angel.

(b) ORIENS, PAIMON, ARITON, AMAYMON execute the Operations hereof by means of their Common Ministers.

(c) The Operations of this Chapter can also be to an extent performed by the Familiar Spirits.

(d) No especial instructions are given regarding this Chapter in the Second Book.

(e) No. 1 is a Gnomonic Square of 15 Squares taken from a Square of 64 Squares.--GILIONIN = Chaldaic GLIVNIM = Mirrors.

No. 2 is a Gnomonic Square of 13 Squares out of a Square of 49 Squares.--ETHANIM = AThVNIM, Heb. = Vaults, Ovens.

No. 3 is a Gnomonic Square of 13 Squares out of a Square of 49 Squares.--APPARET, Latin = Let it appear.

No. 4 is a Square of 36 Squares.--BEDSER = Hebrew BTzR a Gold Ornament.--ELIELE = ALI ALI Hebrew = Towards me. SEPPED Hebrew SPD = He struck.--RES DEB = perhaps Hebrew, RSh DB head or chief point of a discourse.

No. 5 is a Square of 25 Squares.--NEGOT = perhaps Heb. NHG, He leads.--ERASO = probably Greek, sec. pers. sing. from EROMAI for EIROMAI, to demand or interrogate. GARAG = perhaps from Heb. GRO, to diminish. OMARE = perhaps Greek, an Assembly or Synthesis.--TOGEN = perhaps from Greek TOGE = Why or Wherefore when used in an adverbial sense.

No. 6 is a Square of 16 Squares.--NASI = Hebrew NSI = My Banner or Symbol.--APIS = the Egyptian sacred bull. SIPA perhaps from SPH = Hebrew to consume.--ISAN = perhaps from Heb. IShN = To sleep.

No. 7 is a Square of 25 Squares.--GOHEN should perhaps be COHEN = a Jewish priest.--ORARE, Latin = to pray.--HASAH, Heb. HSH = to keep silence. ERARO perhaps from Heb. ARR to curse. NEHOG = perhaps Heb. NHG = to lead.

No. 8 is a Gnomonic Square of 9 Squares out of 25 Squares.--ADMON = perhaps from Heb. DMO = Tears but also Liquids or fluids.

No. 9 is a Gnomonic Square of 9 Squares out of 25 Squares.--LELEH Hebrew LILH = Night, Darkness.

THE FIFTH CHAPTER.

HOW we may retain the Familiar Spirits bond or free in whatsoever form.

(1) In the form of a Lion.
 (2) In the form of a Page.
(3) In the form of a Flower.
(4) In the form of a Horseman.
(5) In the form of an Eagle.
(6) In the form of a Dog.
(7) In the form of a Bear.
(8) In the form of a Soldier.
(9) In the form of an Old Man.
(10) In the form of a Moor.
(11) In the form of a Serpent.
(12) In the form of an Ape.

(1)

A	N	A	K	I	M
N					
A					
K					
I					
M					

(2)

C	E	P	H	I	R
E					
P					
H					
I					
R					

(3)

O	I	K	E	T	I	S
I						
K						
E						
T						
I						
S						

(4)

P	A	R	A	S
A				
R				
A				
S				

(5)

R	A	C	A	H
A				
C				
A				
H				

(6)

C	U	S	I	S
U				
S				
I				
S				

(7)

P	E	R	A	C	H	I
E						H
R						C
A						A
C						R
H						E
I	H	C	A	R	E	P

R	I	S	I	R
I	S	E	R	I
S	E	K	E	S
I	R	E	P	I
R	I	S	I	R

(11)

(9)

N	E	S	E	R
E	L	E	H	E
S	E	P	E	S
E	H	E	L	E
R	E	S	E	N

(10)

P	E	T	H	E	N
E					
T					
H					
E					
N					

K	A	L	E	F
A	R	A	R	E
L	A	M	A	L
E	R	A	R	A
F	E	L	A	K

(12)

K	O	B	H	A
O				
B				
H				
A				

NOTES TO CHAPTER V

(a) The Symbols of this Chapter arc manifested only by the Angels or by the Guardian Angel.

(b) ORIENS, PAIMON, ARITON, and AMAYMON execute the Operations hereof by means of their Common Ministers.

(c) The Familiar Spirits can hardly be said so much of themselves to be able to execute the Operations of this Chapter, as under the rule of the aforementioned Spirits.

(d) Each person can have four Familiar Spirits and no more: the first working from Sunrise to Midday; the second from Midday till Sunset; the third from Sunset to Midnight; and the fourth from Midnight till Sunrise. Such Spirits may also be loaned to friends, in which case you can avail yourself of another ordinary Spirit in place.

(e) The Square numbered 1 is not however placed first in Order in the MS., but fifth. It is a Gnomon of 11 Squares taken from a Square of 36 Squares. ANAKIM = Hebrew ONQIM = Giants; the root ONQ also = a necklace or torque. This word "Anakim" hardly appears to have any reference to the form of a lion.--No. 2 is a Gnomon of 11 Squares again, taken from a Square of 36 Squares, and is in the MS. placed sixth in order.--CEPHIR in Hebrew means KPIR a young Lion; and this Square should probably therefore be numbered 1.--No. 3 is a Gnomon of 13 Squares taken from a Square of 49 Squares; and in the MS. occupies the first place in order. OIKETIS, Greek, means a maid-servant or feminine page. This Square therefore should probably be numbered 2.--NO. 4 is a Gnomon of 9 Squares taken from a Square of 25 Squares, PARAS = Hebrew PRSh, a horse, or horseman, while PRS = an ossifrage, a bird of the hawk or eagle kind. This Square is apparently correctly numbered, though in the MS. it is in the second place.--No. 5 is a Gnomon of 9 Squares taken from a Square of 25 Squares. RACAH is apparently from the Hebrew RQH meaning vain, empty; and does not seem to have any particular reference to any of the forms mentioned for the Symbols.--No. 6 is again a Gnomon of 9 Squares, taken from a Square of 25 Squares. It is placed fourth in order in the MS.--CUSIS may be from the dative plural of the Greek word KUON = a dog, but in Hebrew it would mean numbering, computing.--No. 7 is a border of 24 Squares taken from a Square of 49 Squares. PERACHI, perhaps from PRK, Savagery. DB is a Bear in Hebrew.--No. 8 is a Square of 25 Squares. RISIR, perhaps from Latin "RISOR," a mocker or jester. ISERI, perhaps from Hebrew or Chaldaic Root, ISR, to punish or whip. SEKES, perhaps from SChSh = reborn by hope.--No. 9 is again a Square of 25 Squares. NESER = Hebrew, NShR, an Eagle; which seems to shew that this Square should be numbered 5. ELEHE is probably ALHI, Hebrew = My God. SEPES? ShPS = the hair on the lip, the moustache. RESEN = RSN Heb., = a bridle, or bit.--No. 10 is a Gnomon of 11 Squares taken from a Square of 36 Squares. PETHEN = Hebrew, PThN, an Asp or venomous Serpent, whence this Square should probably be numbered 11.--No. 11 is a Square of 25 Squares. KALEF, = KLP, Hebrew, a hammer. ARARE from Hebrew ARR to curse, cursed. LAMAL perhaps means "in speaking" from MLL, Hebrew, to speak.--No. 12 is a Gnomon of 9 Squares taken from a Square of 25 Squares. KOBHA = perhaps Hebrew KBH = to extinguish.

THE SIXTH CHAPTER.

TO cause Mines to be pointed out, and to help forward all kinds of work connected therewith.

(1) To prevent Caves from falling in.
(2) To shew a Gold Mine.
(3) To cause work to be done in Mines.
(4) To make work done in inaccessible places.
(5) To make them tunnel Mountains.
(6) To cause all water to be withdrawn from the Mines.
(7) To make the Spirits bring Timber.
(8) To make them found and purge Metals and separate Gold and Silver.

(1)

T	E	L	A	A	H
E					A
L					L
A					A
A					A
H	A	A	L	E	T

(2)

A	L	C	A	B	R	U	S	I
L								S
C								U
A								R
B								B
R								A
U								C
S								L
I	S	U	R	B	A	C	L	A

(3)

C	A	D	S	A	R
A					A
D					S
S					D
A					A
R	A	S	D	A	C

(4)

P	E	L	A	G	I	M
E	R	E	N	O	S	I
L	E	R	E	M	O	G
A	N	E	M	A	L	A
G	O	M	A	R	E	L
I	S	O	L	E	I	E
M	I	G	A	L	E	P

(5)

K	I	L	O	I	N
I	S	E	R	P	I
L	E	N	I	R	O
O	R	I	N	E	L
I	P	R	E	S	I
N	I	O	L	I	K

(6)

N	A	K	A	B
A				
K				
A				
B				

(7)

K	I	T	T	I	K
I	S	I	A	D	I
T	I	N	N	A	T
T	A	N	N	I	T
I	D	A	I	S	I
K	I	T	T	I	K

(8)

M	A	R	A	K
A				
R				
A				
K				

(a) The Symbols of this Chapter are manifested only by the Angels or by the Guardian Angel.

(b) ASTAROTH and ASMODEUS execute together the Operations of this Chapter.

(c) The Familiar Spirits cannot well execute the Operations of this Chapter.

(d) No especial instructions are given regarding this Chapter in the Second Book.

(e) No. 1 is a border of 20 Squares taken from a Square of 36 Squares.--TELAAH = perhaps from ThVLOH, = a Worm which pierces holes in the ground. No. 2 is a border of 32 Squares taken from a Square of 81 Squares.--ALCABRUSI may mean "supported by planks or props, or beams". If so, probably this Square should be numbered 1.

No. 3 is a border of 20 Squares taken from a Square of 36 Squares. CADSAR perhaps from QTzR = to shorten or abbreviate a matter or work.

No. 4 is a Square of 49 Squares. PELAGIM, Hebrew PLGIM Divisions, strata, etc. No. 5 is a Square of 36 Squares. KILOIN = Hebrew QLOIM, Excavations.

No. 6 is a Gnomon of 9 Squares taken from a Square of 25 Squares. NAKAB = Hebrew, NQB = Piercing. Perforation.

No. 7 is a Square of 36 Squares. KITTIK may mean = "To arrange in a store-place". TINNAT recalls a name used on some of the Gnostic Magical Gems. TANNIT is the name of a Tyrian goddess.

No. 8 is a Gnomon of 9 Squares out of a Square of 25 Squares. MARAK, from Hebrew MRQ = To cleanse, purge, or refine.

· THE SEVENTH CHAPTER.

TO cause the Spirits to perform with facility and promptitude all necessary Chemical labours and Operations, as regardeth Metals especially.

(1) To make all Metals.

(2) To make them perform the Operations.

(3) To make them teach Chemistry.

(1)

M	E	T	A	L	O
E					
T					
A					
L					
O					

(2)

T	A	B	B	A	T
A	R	U	U	C	A
B	U	I	R	U	B
B	U	R	I	U	B
A	C	U	U	R	A
T	A	B	B	A	T

(3)

I	P	O	M	A	N	O
P	A	M	E	R	A	M
O	M	A	L	O	M	I
M	E	L	A	C	A	H
A	R	O	C	U	M	I
N	A	M	A	M	O	N
O	M	I	H	I	N	I

NOTES TO CHAPTER VII

(a) The Symbols of this Chapter are manifested only by the Angels, or by the Guardian Angel.

(b) ASHTAROTH and ASMODEUS together execute the Operations of this Chapter.

(c) The Familiar Spirits cannot well execute the Operations of this Chapter.

(d) No especial instructions are given regarding this Chapter in the Second Book.

(e) No. 1 is a Gnomon of 11 Squares taken from a Square of 36 Squares. METALO from Greek METALLON = in metal, mineral, or mining work.

No. 2 is a Square of 36 Squares. TABBAT, Chaldaic ThIBVTh = Heads or Sections of classification of operations. ARUUCA perhaps from ARUQ, adhering to.

No. 3 is a Square of 49 Squares.--IPOMANO, probably from Greek HIPPOMANES, an ingredient used in philtres, etc., perhaps put here for chemical drugs in general.

THE EIGHTH CHAPTER.

TO excite Tempests.

(1) To cause Hail.
(2) To cause Snow.
(3) To cause Rain.
(4) To cause Thunder.

(1)

C	A	N	A	M	A	L
A	M	A	D	A	M	A
N	A	D	A	D	A	M
A	D	A	N	A	D	A
M	A	D	A	D	A	N
A	M	A	D	A	M	A
L	A	M	A	N	A	C

(2)

T	A	K	A	T
A				A
K				K
A				A
T	A	K	A	T

(3)

S	A	G	R	I	R
A					
G					
R					
I					
R					

(4)

H	A	M	A	G
A	B	A	L	A
M	A	H	A	M
A	L	A	B	A
G	A	M	A	H

NOTES TO CHAPTER VIII

(a) The Symbols of this Chapter are manifested partly by the Angels and partly by the Evil Spirits.

(b) ASHTAROTH executes the Operations of this Chapter.

(c) The Familiar Spirits cannot execute the Operations of this Chapter.

(d) To excite a Tempest, give the Signal above you, and touch the Symbol on the top. To make it cease, touch it underneath.

(e) No. 1 is a Square of 49 Squares. CANAMAL = Hebrew ChNML, i.e., Hailstones of great size.

No. 2 is a border of 16 taken from a Square of 25 Squares. TAKAT, TKO, Hebrew, has the sense of "immersed in, overflowed by".

No. 3. A Gnomon of 11 Squares taken from a Square of 36 Squares. SAGRIR, Hebrew SGRIR a most vehement rain and tempest".

No. 4. A Square of 25 Squares. HAMAG, perhaps from Hebrew, MOK, "to compress, or crush, or press".

THE NINTH CHAPTER.

TO transform Animals into Men, and Men into Animals; etc.

(1) To transform Men into Asses.
(2) Into Stags or Deer.
(3) Into Elephants.
(4) Into Wild Boars.
(5) Into Dogs.
(6) Into Wolves.
(7) Animals into Stones.

(1)

I	E	M	I	M	E	I
E	R	I	O	N	T	E
M	I	R	T	I	N	M
I	O	T	I	T	O	I
M	N	I	T	R	I	M
B	T	N	O	I	R	E
I	E	M	I	M	E	I

(2)

A	I	A	C	I	L	A
I	S	I	O	R	E	L
A	I	E	R	I	R	A
C	O	R	I	L	O	N
I	R	I	L	E	I	A
I	R	R	O	I	S	I
A	L	A	I	N	I	A

(3)

C	H	A	D	S	I	R
H						I
A						S
D						D
S						A
I						H
C	H	A	D	S	I	R

(4)

B	E	D	A	S	E	K
E						E
D						S
A	R	A	M	A	SI	A
S						D
E						E
K						B

(5)

K	A	L	T	E	P	H
A	P	I	E	R	I	P
L	I	L	M	O	R	E
T	E	M	U	M	E	T
E	R	O	M	L	I	L
P	I	E	R	I	P	A
H	P	E	T	L	A	K

(6)

D	I	S	E	E	B	E	H
I	S	A	R	T	R	I	E
S	A	R	G	E	I	R	B
E	R	B	O	N	E	T	E
E	T	O	N	O	G	R	E
B	A	R	O	B	R	A	S
E	R	A	T	R	A	S	I
H	E	B	E	E	S	I	D

(7)

I	SI	CH	AD	A	MI	O	N
S	ER	RA	RE	P	I	NT	O
I	RA	AS	I	ME	L	EI	S
C	RA	TI	BA	RI	NS	I	
H	AS	I	NA	S	U	O	TI	R
A	RI	BA	TI	NT	I	RA	
D	E	MA	SI	C	O	A	N	O	C
A	PE	RU	NO	I	B	E	MI
MI	LI	OT	A	B	U	L	E	L
I	NE	NT	I	NE	L	EL	A
O	TI	SI	RO	ME	LI	R	
N	OS	I	RA	C	I	L	AR	I

NOTES TO CHAPTER IX

(a) The Symbols of this Chapter are only manifested by the Evil Spirits.

(b) ASHTAROTH and ASMODEUS together execute the Signs and Operations of this Chapter.

(c) The Familiar Spirits cannot execute the Operations of this Chapter.

(d) Let the being, whether man or animal, see the Symbol, and then touch them suddenly with it; when they will appear transformed; but this is only a kind of fascination.

When you wish to make it cease, place the Symbol upon the head and strike it sharply with the Wand, and the Spirit will make things resume their ordinary condition.

(e) No. 1 is a Square of 49 Squares. IEMIMEI is evidently from Hebrew IMIM = Mules. A very perfect Acrostic.

No. 2 is a Square of 49 Squares also. AIACILA, Hebrew AILH = a deer.

No. 3 is a border of 24 taken from a Square of 49 Squares.--CHADSIR; Hebrew KZR = Fierce, Savage. ChTzR = perhaps, "the tusk of an Elephant ". But ChZR = a wild boar, whence this Square should perhaps be numbered 4.

No. 4 consists of 24 Squares taken from a Square of 49 Squares; two letters SI are allotted to one Square.

BEDASEK is perhaps from BD, a limb, and SK, covered or protected, as with a strong skin. It may thus stand for the Elephant as having powerful and thick-skinned limbs. If so, this Square should be numbered 3.

No. 5 is a Square of 49 Squares. KALTEPH. The Hebrew word for Dog is KLB. This Square it will be noted is not a perfect Acrostic.

No. 6 is a Square of 64 Squares.--DISEEBEH is probably from ZABH = a wolf.--This Square also is not at all perfect as an Acrostic.

No. 7 is a Square of 144 Squares.--ISICHADAMION, probably from DMIVN = Similitude of; and SIG, Scoria or Lava, or SQ, stone; root of SQL, to stone.

THE TENTH CHAPTER.

TO hinder any Necromantic or Magical Operations from taking effect, except those of the Qabalah and of this Sacred Magic.

(1) To undo any Magic soever.
(2) To heal the bewitched.
(3) To make Magical Storms cease.
(4) To discover any Magic.
(5) To hinder Sorcerers from Operating.

(1)

C	O	D	S	E	L	I	M
O							
H							
A							
B							
I							O
M						O	C

(2)

```
L A C H A T
A       A
C       H
H       C
A       A
T A H C A L
```

(3)

```
P A R A D I L O N
A R I N O M I S O
R I L O R A E I K
A N O T A L A M I
D O R A F A C O L
I M A L A T O N A
L I E A C O R I T
O S I M O N I R A
N O K I L A T A N
```

(5)

```
M A C A N B H
A R O L U S E
D I R U C U N
A L U H U L A
S E R U R O C
U N E L I R A
L U S A D A M
```

(4)

```
H O R A H
O S O M A
R O T O R
A M O S O
H A R O H
```

NOTES TO CHAPTER X

(a) The Symbols of this Chapter are manifested only by the Angels, or by the Guardian Angel.

(b) MAGOTH executes the Operations of this Chapter.

(c) The Familiar Spirits cannot well execute the Operations of this Chapter.

(d) No especial instructions are given concerning this Chapter.

(e) No. 1 consists of 17 Squares containing 18 letters (LI of "Codselim" occupying 1 Square) taken from a Square of 49 Squares.--CODSELIM and COHABIM may be from KSILIM, the foolish ones, and KABIM, the mourning ones (Hebrew).

No. 2. A border of 20 Squares taken from a Square of 36 Squares.--LACHAT, perhaps from Hebrew LChSh = to enchant.

No. 3. A Square of 81 Squares.--PARADILON, probably from Greek PARA, against, and DEILON, perverse, or miserable, or unfortunate.

No. 4. A Square of 25 Squares.--HORAH, from Hebrew ChRH, To be enraged; or HRH, to conceive, or bring forth.

No. 5. A Square of 49 Squares.--MACANEH from Hebrew MChNH, a fortification, castle, or defence. MADASUL, from MATzL, about me, before me, at my side.

THE ELEVENTH CHAPTER.

TO cause all kinds of Books to be brought to one, and whether lost or stolen.

(1) For Books of Astrology.
(2) For Books of Magic.
(3) For Books of Chemistry.
NOTES TO CHAPTER XI
(a) The Symbols of this Chapter are manifested only by the Angels, or by the Guardian Angel.
(b) MAGOTH alone executes the Operations of this Chapter.
(c) The Familiar Spirits cannot execute the Operations of this Chapter.
(d) Many ancient Books of Magic, etc., have been lost or destroyed, in some cases by the wish of the Good Spirits, in others by the machinations of the Evil Spirits. By these Symbols you can have many supposed extinct works brought to you, Abraham states; but adds that he could never copy them, because the writing disappeared as fast as he wrote it; notwithstanding this he was permitted to read some of them.
(e) No. 1 is a Square of 16 Squares. COLI, probably from Hebrew KLI, meaning the whole, in the sense of the whole Universe.

No. 2 is a Square of 36 Squares.--SEARAH, perhaps from Hebrew SORH, a whirlwind; or perhaps from ShORH = terrible, and is also used to express a Kid, or a species of shaggy Satyr-like Demon, from the word being used to signify hair.

No. 3 is a Gnomon of 13 Squares taken from a Square of 49 Squares.--KEHAHEK is probably from Hebrew KHCh, meaning to conceal, obscure, or shut up.

(1)

C	O	L	I
O	D	A	C
L	A	C	A
I	C	A	R

(2)

S	E	A	R	A	H
E	L	L	O	P	A
A	L	A	T	I	M
R	O	T	A	R	A
A	P	I	R	A	C
H	A	M	A	C	S

(3)

K	E	H	A	H	E	K
E						
H						
A						
H						
E						
K						

THE TWELFTH CHAPTER.

TO know the Secrets of any person.

(1) To know the Secret of Letters.
(2) To know the Secret of Words.
(3) To know Secret Operations.
(4) For the Military Counsels of a Captain.
(5) To know the Secrets of Love.
(6) To know what riches a person possesseth.
(7) To know the Secret of all Arts.

(1)

M	E	G	I	L	L	A
E						
G						
I						
L						
L						
A						M

(2)

S	I	M	B	A	S	I
I						
M	A	R	C	A	R	A
B						
A						
S						
I						

(3)

M	A	A	B	H	A	D
A						
A						
B						
H						
A						
D						

(4)

M	I	L	C	H	A	M	A	H
I								
L								
C								
A	D	I	R	A	C	H	I	
M								
A								I
H				E	L	I	M	

(5)

C	E	D	I	D	A	H
E						
D						
I						
D	E	R	A	R	I	D
A						
H	A	D	I	D	E	C

(6)

A	S	A	M	I	M
S					
A					
M	A	P	I	D	E
I					
M					

(7)

M	E	L	A	B	A	H
A						
E						
L						
A						
B						
A						
H						

(a) The Symbols of this Chapter are manifested in part by the Angels, and in part also by the Evil Spirits.

(b) ASMODEUS alone executes the Operations of this Chapter.

(c) The Familiar Spirits can to an extent execute the Operations of this Chapter.

(d) Touch the Symbol, and name aloud the person whose Secret you desire to know, and the Spirit will whisper the answer into your ear.

(e) No. 1 consists of 14 Squares from a Square of 49 Squares.--MEGILLA, from Hebrew MGLH = to reveal or disclose.

No. 2 consists of 19 Squares taken from a Square of 49 Squares.--MARCARA, perhaps from KRH to appear; Hebrew SIMBASI, perhaps from BASh, evil, and ZMH, thought. No. 3 consists of a Gnomon of 13 from a Square of 49 Squares.--MAABHAD, from Hebrew MOBD = a deed or act.

No. 4 consists of 29 Squares from a Square of 81 Squares. MILCHAMAH, from Hebrew MLChMH = War.--ADIRACHI from DRK (Hebrew) = Way, Plan, Idea.--ELIM (Heb.) = Mighty Ones.

No. 5 consists of 25 taken from a Square of 49 Squares. CEDIDAH is either from KDID = a Spark, or from DID, the root of the words; love, delights, breasts.--DERARID from Hebrew DRR = liberty.--HADIDEC from DDIK = thy loves or delights.

No. 6 consists of 16 from a Square of 36 Squares.--ASAMIN from Hebrew ASMIM = treasure houses, garners.--MAPIDE perhaps from PID = oppression, misfortune.

No. 7. A Gnomon of 13 from a Square of 49 Squares.--MELABAH from MLABH = Art or Science.

THE THIRTEENTH CHAPTER.

TO cause a Dead Body to revive, and perform all the functions which a living person would do, and this during a space of Seven Years, by means of the Spirits.

(1) From the Rising of the Sun until Mid-Day.
(2) From Mid-Day until the Setting of the Sun.
(3) From the Setting of the Sun until Mid-Night.
(4) From Mid-Night until the Rising of the Sun.

(1)

E	Z	E	C	H	I	E	L
Z	E	O	F	R	A	S	E
E	O	R	I	A	L	A	I
C	F	I	R	T	A	R	H
H	R	A	T	R	I	F	C
I	A	L	A	I	R	O	E
E	S	A	R	F	O	E	Z
L	E	I	H	C	E	Z	E

(2)   (3)   (4)

A	M	I	G	D	E	Lo
M	O	R	B	R	I	Eo
I	R	I	D	E	R	Do
G	B	D	O	D	B	Go
D	R	E	D	I	R	Io
E	I	R	B	R	O	Mo
L	E	D	G	I	M	Ao

I	O	S	U	A
O	R	I	L	U
S	I	S	I	S
U	L	I	R	O
A	U	S	O	I

P	E	G	E	R
E	T	I	A	E
G	I	S	I	G
E	A	I	T	E
R	E	G	E	P

NOTES TO CHAPTER XIII

(a) The Symbols of this Chapter are manifested in part by the Angels and in part by the Evil Spirits.

(b) ORIENS, PAYMON, ARITON, and AMAYMON, execute by means of their Servitors the Operations of this Chapter.

(c) The Familiar Spirits cannot execute the Operations of this Chapter.

(d) In several places Abraham warns the reader that this is the most difficult Operation of any, because for it to be brought about, the concurrence of all the Chief Spirits must be obtained. Watch for the moment when the person dies, and then at once place upon his body towards the 4 cardinal points the Symbol required. Similar Symbols are to be sewn into the garments he wears. Abraham moreover adds that by this means, one can however only prolong the life for 7 years, and no more.

(e) No. 1 is a Square of 64 Squares. EZECHIEL is from Hebrew IChZQAL, the well-known name of the Prophet, derived from ChZQ, to bind,

No. 2 is a Square of 49 Squares, it will be noticed that a small O is placed at the end of each word in the last square towards the right hand. AMIGDEL is from MGDL, a strong tower.

No. 3 is a Square of 25 Squares. IOSUA, the well-known Hebrew name, signifies "he shall save".

No. 4 is also a Square of 25 Squares. PEGER is from PGR = a dead inactive carcase whether of man or of beast.

THE FOURTEENTH CHAPTER.

THE Twelve Symbols for the Twelve Hours of the Day and of the Night, to render oneself Invisible unto every person.

(1)

A	L	A	M	A	L	A
L						
A						
M	A	T	A	T	A	N
A						
L						
A						

(2)

T	S	A	P	H	A	H
S						
A						
P						
H	I	T	N	E	R	A
A	N	A	O	R	I	S
H						

(3)

C	A	S	A	H
A	D	O	D	A
S	O	M	O	S
A	D	O	P	A
H	A	S	A	C

A	L	A	T	A	H
L					
A	R	O	G	A	T
T					
A					
H					

(5)

C	O	D	E	R
O				
D				
E				
R				

(6)

S	I	M	L	A	H
I					
M					
L					
A	S	I		R	I
H					S

(7)

C	E	H	A	H
E				
H				
A				
H				

(8)

A	N	A	N	A
N				
A				
N				
A				

(9)

T	A	M	A	N
A	P	A	T	E
M				D
A				E
N	E	D	A	C

(10)

B	E	R	O	M	I	N
E						
R						
O						
M						
I						
N						

(11)

T	A	L	A	C
A				A
L				L
A				A
C	A	L	A	T

(12)

A	L	A	M	P	I	S
L						
A						
M						
P						
I	S	I	L			
S						

NOTES TO CHAPTER XIV

(a) The Symbols of this Chapter be manifested in part by the Evil Spirits, and in part by the Good Angels.

(b) MAGOT is said to rule the Operations of this Chapter.

(c) The Familiar Spirits do not execute the Operations of this Chapter.

(d) To render oneself invisible is said by Abraham to be a very easy matter. This Chapter contains Twelve Symbols for Twelve different Spirits submitted unto the Prince MAGOT, who are all of the same force. Place the Symbol upon the top of your head (under your head covering) and then you will become invisible, while on taking it away you will appear visible again.

(e) No. 1 is a Square of 49 Squares, whence 19 Squares are taken which are arranged somewhat in the form of a capital F. ALAMALA is probably from the Greek, ALE wandering, and MELAS = black, darkness; i.e., wandering darkness.

No. 2 consists of 25 Squares arranged somewhat in an F form, and taken from the Square of 49 Squares.--TSAPHAH is from TzPH = a covering or shroud.

No. 3 is a Square of 25 Squares. CASAH implies "formed by coagulation".

No. 4 consists of 16 Squares in an F form, taken from a Square of 36 Squares.--ALATAH signifies "adhering closely".

No. 5 is a GNOMON of 9 Squares taken from a Square of 25 Squares.--CODER = Darkness and Obscurity.

No. 6 consists of 17 Squares, somewhat irregularly disposed, taken from a Square of 36 Squares.--SIMLAH = "involved, to clothe or surround on all sides".

No. 7 is a Gnomon of 9 Squares taken from a Square of 25 Squares.--CEHAH = Restriction, and compression.

No. 8 is a Gnomon of 9 Squares taken from a Square of 25 Squares.--ANANA is a word expressing earnest desire for some then defect to be supplied.

No. 9 consists of 19 taken from a Square of 25 Squares.--TAMAN = "to hide or conceal," and recalls the Biblical name of "Teman". NEDAC means "accumulated darkness".

No. 10 is a Gnomon of 13 Squares from a Square of 49 Squares.--BEROMIN signifies "coverings or shrouds of concealment".

No. 11 is a border of 16 Squares from a Square of 25 Squares.--TALAC = signifies "thy mists".

No. 12 consists of 16 Squares taken from a Square of 49 Squares.--ALAMPIS is the Greek adjective ALAMPES, meaning "without the light of the Sun". ISIL is Hebrew and means "he will dissolve".

It will be remarked that all these names distinctly express some idea relating to Invisibility.

THE FIFTEENTH CHAPTER.

FOR the Spirits to bring us anything we may wish to eat or to drink, and even all (kinds of food) that we can imagine.

(1) For them to bring us Bread.
(2) Meat.
(3) Wine of all kinds.
(4) Fish.
(5) Cheese.

(1)

I	A	I	I	N
A				
I				
I				
N				

(2)

B	A	S	A	R
A				
S				
A				
R				B

(3)

L	E	C	H	E	M
E					
C	N	O	H	A	H
H					
E					
M	E	C	H	E	L

(4)

D	A	C	A	D
A	R	A	F	A
C	A	M	A	C
A	F	A	R	A
D	A	C	A	D

(5)

L	E	B	H	I	N	A	H
							A
							N
							I
							H
							B
A							E
H	A						L

NOTES TO CHAPTER XV

(a) The Symbols of this Chapter are manifested in part by the Angels, and in part also by the Evil Spirits.

(b) ASMODEE and MAGOT together execute the Operations of this Chapter.

(c) The Familiar Spirits cannot well execute the Operations of this Chapter.

(d) As for these Symbols and all like ones appertaining unto this Chapter, when you shall wish to make use of them, you shall put them between two plates, dishes, or jugs, closed together on the outside of a window; and before a quarter of an hour shall have passed you will find and will have that which you have demanded; but you must clearly understand that with such kinds of viands you cannot nourish men for more than two days. For this food although it be appreciable by the eyes, and by the mouth, doth not long nourish the body, which hath soon hunger again, seeing that this food gives no strength to the stomach. Know also that none of these viands can remain visible for more than 24 hours, the which period being passed, fresh ones will be requisite.

(e) This Chapter naturally brings to one's mind the descriptions of the Magic feasts in the "Arabian Nights" and elsewhere.

No. 1 is a Gnomon of 9 Squares taken from a Square of 25 Squares. IAIIN means "Let there be wine". Evidently therefore this Square should be numbered 3, instead of 1.

No. 2 consists of 10 Squares taken from a Square of 25 Squares. BASAR means "flesh".

No. 3 consists of 21 Squares in the form of the Roman Capital Letter E, taken from a Square of 36 Squares.--LECHEM means "bread," CNOHAH implies "corn," and MECHEL means "a cake". Therefore this should evidently be numbered 1, instead of 3. MECHEL also means "a window".

No. 4 is a Square of 25 Squares.--DACAD should be spelt with a G instead of a C; the meaning is "bring forth fish". CAMAC means "meal, or flour". AFARA may be from the Greek adverb APHAR = "straightway or forthwith"; but if taken as a Hebrew root may mean "bring forth fruit".

No. 5 is a Gnomon of 15 Squares and 3 other supplementary ones taken from a Square of 64 Squares. LEBHINAH is from LBA = "milk," and INH "to squeeze".

THE SIXTEENTH CHAPTER.

TO find and take possession of all kinds of Treasures, provided that they be not at all (Magically) guarded.

(1) For Treasure of Silver (or Silver Money).
(2) For Gold Money.
(3) For a great Treasure.
(4) For a small Treasure.
(5) For an unguarded Treasure.
(6) For Copper Money.
(7) For Gold in Ingots.
(8) For Silver in Ingots.
(9) For jewels.
(10) For Ancient Medals (and Coins).
(11) For a Treasure hidden by a particular Person.
(12) For Pearls.
(13) For Diamonds.
(14) For Rubies.
(15) For Balassius Rubies.
(16) For Emeralds.
(17) For worked Gold.
(18) For Silver Plate.
(19) For Statues.
(20) For Specimens of Ancient Art.

(1)

T	I	P	H	A	R	A	H
I							
P							
H							
A							
R							
A							I
H						I	T

(2)

C	E	S	E	P
E				
S				
E				
P				

(3)

S	E	G	I	L	A	H
E	R	A	L	I	P	A
G						
I	L	E	N	L	I	
L						
A						
H						

(4)

N	E	C	O	T
E				
C				
O				
T				N

(5)

M	A	G	O	T
A	R	A	T	O
G	A	L	A	G
O	T	A	R	A
T	O	G	A	M

(6)

A	G	I	L
N	I	L	I
A			
K			

(7)

C	O	S	E	N
O				
S				
E				
N				

(8)

O	T	S	A	R
T				
S				
A				
R				

(9)

B	E	L	I	A	L
E	B	O	R	U	A
L	O	V	A	R	I
I	R	A	V	O	L
A	V	R	O	B	E
L	A	I	L	E	B

(10)

O	R	I	O	N
R	A	V	R	O
I	V	A	V	I
O	R	V	A	R
N	O	I	R	O

(11)

K	E	R	M	A
E				
R				
M				
A				K

(12)

I	A	N	A
A	M	E	N
N	E	M	A
A	N	A	I

(13)

B	I	C	E	L	O	N
I	R	O	L	A	T	O
C	O	R	A	M	A	L
E	L	A	M	A	L	E
L	A	M	A	R	O	C
O	T	A	L	O	R	I
N	O	L	E	C	I	B

(14)

S	E	G	O	R
E				
G				
O				E
R			B	S

(15)

H	E	T	I	S	E	R
E						
T						
I						
S						
E	G	I	N	E	S	E
R						H

(16)

A	S	T	A	R	O	T
S	A	L	I	S	T	O
T	L	A	N	B	S	R
A	I	N	O	N	I	A
R	S	B	N	A	L	T
O	T	S	I	L	A	S
T	O	R	A	T	S	A

(17)

K	O	N	E	H
O				
N				
E				
H				K

(18) (19) (20)

C	A	H	I	L	
A					
H					
I					
L					

A	R	I	T	O	N
R	O	C	A	R	O
I	C	L	O	A	T
T	A	O	L	O	R
O	R	A	C	O	R
N	O	T	I	R	A

O	R	I	M	E	L
R	E	M	O	R	E
I	M	O	N	O	N
N	O	N	O	M	I
E	R	O	M	E	R
L	E	I	N	R	O

NOTES TO CHAPTER XVI

(a) The Symbols of this Chapter are manifested only by the Angels or by the Guardian Angel.

(b) ASTAROT and ARITON both execute the Operations hereof by their Ministers, yet not together, but each separately.

(c) The Familiar Spirits cannot well execute the Operations of this Chapter.

(d) Select the Symbol of the Treasure desired, and the Spirit will then shew it to you. Then place the Symbol at once upon the Treasure, and it will no longer be possible for it to disappear into the ground, nor for it to be carried away. Furthermore any Spirits which may be guarding it will thus be put to flight, and you can then dispose of the Treasure as you wish.

(e) No. 1 is a species of border of 28 Squares of which 18 are occupied by letters, taken from a Square of 64 Squares.--TIPHARAH means "Glory, beauty, a shining thing". ITI is the Chaldaic for "is, are".

No. 2 is a Gnomon of 9 Squares taken from a Square of 25 Squares. CESEP means "Silver". This Square should therefore probably be numbered 1, or 8, or 18.

No. 3 consists of 24 Squares from a Square of 49 Squares. SEGILAH means "Treasure".

No. 4 consists of 10 Squares from a Square of 25.--NECOT means probably stamped money.

No. 5 is a Square of 25 Squares. MAGOT is the name of one of the Sub-Princes.

No. 6 is a Gnomon of 10 from a Square of 16 Squares. AGIL may mean "a heap," but also "a globular drop of dew".

No. 7 is a Gnomon of 9 Squares taken from a Square of 25 Squares. COSEN perhaps means "a golden cup".

No. 8 is a Gnomon also of 9 Squares taken from a Square of 25 Squares.--OTSAR means "restraint".

No. 9 is a Square of 36 Squares. BELIAL is the name of one of the four great chiefs of the

Evil Spirits.

No. 10 is a Square of 25 Squares.--ORION, the celebrated mythological name of the Greek hunter, and of the constellation, is perhaps used here as the name of a Spirit.

No. 11 is a border of 10 Squares taken from a Square of 25 Squares.--KERMA means either "a cutting off" or else "a super-inducing".

No. 12 is a Square of 16 Squares.

No. 13 is a Square of 49 Squares.--BICELON is perhaps from IHLM = Diamonds. The root IChL means "abiding strength and hardness".

No. 14 is a border of 12 Squares from a Square of 25 Squares. SEGOR means respectively "to break forth" and "to shut in," according as the root begins with S or Sh.

No. 15 consists of 20 Squares from a Square of 49.

No. 16 is a Square of 49 Squares. ASTAROT is one of the 8 Sub-Princes of the Evil Spirits.

No. 17 consists of 10 Squares from a Square of 25 Squares. KONEH means "possessions".

No. 18 is a Gnomon of 9 Squares taken from a Square of 25 Squares. CAHIL means "gathered together".

No. 19 is a Square of 36 Squares. ARITON is one of the 8 Sub-Princes of the Evil Spirits.

No. 20 is a Square of 36 Squares. ORIMEL is evidently here used as the name of a Spirit. OIRIN is a Chaldaic word meaning Angelic Watchers over the Kingdoms of the Earth. ORION may also come from this word.

THE SEVENTEENTH CHAPTER.

TO fly in the Air and travel any whither.

(1) In a black Cloud.
(2) In a white Cloud.
(3) In the form of an Eagle.
(5) In the form of a Crow (or Raven).[225]
(4) In the form of a Vulture.
(6) In the form of a Crane.

(1)

T	A	S	M	A
A	G	E	I	M
S	E	V	E	S
M	I	E	A	G
A	M	S	A	T

(2)

A	N	A	N
N			
A			
N			A

---

225   Numbered in this Order in the Original MS.

(3)   (4)   (5)

H	O	L	O	P
O	P	O	L	O
L	O	B	O	L
O	L	O	P	O
P	O	L	O	H

O	D	A	C
D	A	R	A
A	R	A	D
C	A	D	O

R	O	L	O	R
O	B	U	F	O
L	U	A	U	L
O	P	U	B	O
R	O	L	O	R

(6)

N	A	T	S	A
A	R	O	I	S
T	O	L	O	T
S	I	O	R	A
A	S	T	A	N

NOTES TO CHAPTER XVII

(a) The Symbols of this Chapter are manifested in part by the Angels, and in part also by the Evil Spirits.

(b) ORIENS, PAIMON, ARITON, and AMAIMON execute the Operations hereof by means of their common Ministers.

(c) The Familiar Spirits cannot well execute the Operations of this Chapter.

(d) Name the place aloud to which you wish to travel, and place the Symbol upon your head under the bonnet or the hat; but take well heed that it does not fall from you, which would be very dangerous. Do not as a rule travel by night; and select a calm and serene day for the Operation.

(e) No. 1 is a Square of 25 Squares. TASMA implies protection. TRMS is the Hebrew word used in the verse, "Thou shalt go upon the Lion and the Adder".

No. 2 consists of 8 Squares taken from a Square of 16. ANAN means "great labour".

No. 3 is a Square of 25 Squares. HOLOP means "to travel".

No. 4 is a Square of 16 Macquares. ODAC means "to pass on from one place to another".

No. 5 is a Square of 25 Squares. ROLOR is perhaps from ROL "to move hurriedly".

No. 6 is a Square of 25 Squares. NATSA means "to flee or fly quickly".

THE EIGHTEENTH CHAPTER.

TO heal divers Maladies.

(1) To heal Leprosy.

(2) For chapped hands, etc.

(3) For old Ulcers.

(4) For pestilential diseases.

(5) For inveterate Paralysis.

(6) For Malignant Fevers.

(7) For bodily pains.

(8) For Sea Sickness.

(9) For Vertigo (and Giddiness).

(10) For the "Miserere" [226] (a most violent and dangerous kind of colic), accompanied by dreadful vomiting.

(11) For Dropsy.

(12) For all kinds of Wounds.

(1)

T	S	A	R	A	A	T
S	I	R	A	P	L	A
A						
R						
A						
A						G

(2)

B	U	A	H

(3)

M	E	T	S	O	R	A	H
E	L	M	I	N	I	M	A
T	M	A	R	O	M	I	R
S	I	R	G	I	O	N	O
O	N	O	I	G	R	I	S
R	I	M	O	R	A	M	T
A	M	I	N	I	M	L	E
H	A	R	O	S	T	E	M

226   So called from the Latin word "to have pity," because the Psalm " Miserere Mei Domine," "Lord, have mercy upon me," is supposed to be a charm against it.

(4)

R	E	C	H	E	M
E	R	H	A	S	E
C	H	A	I	A	H
H	A	I	A	H	C
E	S	A	H	R	E
M	E	H	C	E	R

(5)

R	O	K	E	A
O	G	I	R	E
K	I	L	I	K
E	R	I	G	O
A	E	K	O	R

(6)

B	E	T	E	M
E	M	E	R	E
T	E	N	E	T
E	R	E	M	E
M	E	T	E	B

(7)

B	E	B	H	E	R
E	R	A	O	S	E
B	A	R	I	O	H
H	O	I	R	A	B
E	S	O	A	R	E
R	E	H	B	E	D

(8)

E	L	E	O	S
L	A	B	I	O
E	B	I	B	E
O	I	B	A	L
S	O	E	L	E

(9)

K	A	D	A	K	A	T
A	R	A	K	A	D	A
D	A	R	E	M	A	K
A	K	E	S	E	K	A
K	A	M	E	R	A	D
A	D	A	K	A	R	A
T	A	K	A	D	A	K

(10)

R	O	G	A	M	O	S
O	R	I	K	A	M	O
G	I	R	O	R	A	M
A	K	O	R	O	K	A
M	A	R	O	R	I	K
O	M	A	K	I	R	O
S	O	M	A	G	O	R

(11)

S	I	T	U	R
I	R	A	P	E
T	A	R	A	G
U	P	A	L	A
R	E	G	A	N

(12)

H	A	P	P	I	R
A	M	A	O	S	I
P	A	R	A	O	P
P	O	A	R	A	P
I	S	O	A	M	A
R	I	P	P	A	H

NOTES TO CHAPTER XVIII

(a) The Symbols of this Chapter are manifested only by the Angels or by the Guardian Angel.

(b) AMAIMON performs the Operations hereof.

(c) The Familiar Spirits can to an extent perform the Operations of this Chapter.

(d) The bandages of the sick person having been undone and cleaned, and the unguent, the compresses, and the bandages having been replaced, put the Symbol upon them and leave it for about a quarter of an hour, then take it away, and keep it for use upon another occasion. But if it be an internal malady, you must place the Symbol (the written part downwards) upon the bare head of the patient.--These Symbols may be seen and examined without any danger, yet it is always better that they should neither be seen nor handled by any other person than yourself.

(e) No. 1 consists of 20 Squares taken from a Square of 49 Squares.--TSARAAT = "a stroke or plague; the leprosy".

No. 2 consists of 4 Squares from a Square of 16.--BUAH signifies to clear away.

No. 3, a Square of 64 Squares.--METSORAH signifies "flowing sores or ulcers".

No. 4 is a Square of 36 Squares.--RECHEM means "closely seizing".

No. 5 is a Square of 25 Squares.--ROKEA signifies general evil.

No. 6 is a Square of 25 Squares.--BETEM = "the internal parts".

No. 7 is a Square of 36 Squares-BEBHER = "in purifying or cleansing".

No. 8 is a Square of 25 Squares-ELEOS, the Greek word HALS = "the Sea from its saltness".--ELOS means "calm still water".

No. 9 is a Square of 49 Squares.--KADAKAT means "vertigo, turning of the head".

No. 10 is a Square of 49 Squares-ROGAMOS from Latin Rogamus, "we pray".

No. 11 is a Square of 25 Squares.--SITUR means "secret".

No. 12 is a Square of 36 Squares-HAPPIR means "to shatter or break".

THE NINETEENTH CHAPTER.

FOR every description of Affection and Love.

(1)

(1) To be beloved by one's Wife (or Husband).
(2) For some especial Love.
(3) To be beloved by a Relation.
(4) For a Maiden in particular.
(5) To acquire the affection of a Judge.
(6) To make oneself beloved by a Married person.
(7) To make oneself beloved by a Widow.
(8) By a girl already promised in Marriage.
(9) By a Maiden in general.
(10) By some especial Prince.
(11) By some especial King.
 (12) To obtain the friendship of some particular person.
(13) To have that of a Great Man.
(14) To be beloved by a Woman.
(15) To make oneself beloved by Ecclesiastics.
(16) To make oneself beloved by a Master.
(17) To make oneself beloved by a Mistress.
(18) To make oneself beloved by Infidels.
(19) By the Pope, by an Emperor,[227] or by Kings.
(20) For Adulteries in general.

D	O	D	I	M
O				
D				
I				
M				

(2)

R	A	I	A	H
A				
I	G	O	G	I
A				
H	A	I	A	H

(3)

M	O	D	A	H
O	K	O	R	A
D				
A				
H				

(4)

S	I	C	O	F	E	T
I						
C	E	N	A	L	I	F
O	R	A	M	A	R	O
F						
E						
T						

---

227   In the Original, it is "by the Emperor," i.e. the Emperor of Germany.

(5)

A	L	M	A	N	A	H
L						
M	A	R	E			
A	A	L	B	E	H	A
N						
A	R	E	H	A	I	L
H						A

(6)

C	A	L	L	A	H
A					
L	O	R	A	I	L
L					
A	G	O	U	P	A
H	A	L	L	A	C

(7)

E	L	E	M
L			
E			
M			

(8)

N	A	Q	I	D
A	Q	O	R	I
Q	O	R	O	Q
I	R	O	Q	A
D	I	Q	A	N

(9)

S	A	L	O	M
A	R	E	P	O
L	E	M	E	L
O	P	E	R	A
M	O	L	A	S

(10)

D	E	B	A	M
E	R	E	R	A
B	E	R	E	B
A	R	E	R	E
M	A	B	E	D

(11)

A	H	H	B
			E
			A
B			R

(12)

I	A	L	D	A	H
A	Q	O	R	I	A
L	O	Q	I	R	E
D	R	I	I	D	E
A	I	R	D	R	O
H	A	F	E	O	N

(13)

B	E	T	U	L	A	H
E						
T						
U						
L	O	S	A	N	I	T
A						
H						

(14)

I	E	D	I	D	A	H
E						
D	I	L	O	Q	A	H
I						
D	O	Q	A	R	C	A
A						
H						

(15)

S	A	Q	A	L
A				
Q				Q
A				
L		Q		S

(16)

Q	E	B	H	I	R
E	R	A	I	S	A
B	A	Q	O	L	I
H	I	O	L	I	A
I	S	L	I	A	C
R	A	I	A	C	A

(17)

E	F	E	H	A
F				
E				G
H				
A	L	Q	A	S

(18)

T	A	A	F	A	H
A					
A					
F					
A					
H					

(19)

S	A	R	A	H
A				
R				
A				
H				

(20)

C	A	T	A	N
A				
T				
A				
N				

NOTES TO CHAPTER XIX

(a) The Symbols of this Chapter are manifested in part by the Angels, and in part also by the Evil Spirits.

(b) Probably BELZEBUD performs this Operation; as those of the Twentieth Chapter are submitted to him; and these two Chapters are classed together by Abraham the Jew in his special instructions, the one being the exact reverse of the other.

(c) The Familiar Spirits can to an extent perform the Operations of this Chapter.

(d) Name aloud the person or persons by whom you wish to be loved, and move the Symbol under whose class they come. But if it be not for yourself that you are operating, but for two or more other persons, whether for love or for hatred, you should still name such persons aloud, and move the Symbols of the class or classes under which they come. Also, if possible, it is a good thing to touch them with the Symbol, on the bare skin, if you can. Under this heading are included all classes of good-will and affection, among the which Abraham says that the most difficult thing is to make oneself or others beloved by religious persons.

(e) No. 1 is a Gnomon of 9 Squares taken from a Square of 25. DODIM means "loves, pleasures".

No. 2 consists of 17 Squares arranged like a capital letter E taken from a Square of 25 Squares. RAIAH means "a female companion".

No. 3 consists of 13 Squares taken from a Square of 2 5 Squares. MODAH = "Adorned as for a bridal".

No. 4 consists of 25 Squares from a Square of 49.

No. 5 consists of 29 Squares taken from 49. ALMANAH = "A virgin"; hence evidently this should be numbered 4 and not 5, while probably No. 4 should be here placed.

No. 6 consists of 26 Squares taken from a Square of 36 Squares. CALLAH means "a married woman, but especially a bride".

No. 7. A Gnomon of 7 from a Square of 16. ELEM means "a widow".

No. 8. A Square of 25 Squares. NAQID = "Remote offspring".

No. 9. This has a strong likeness to the well-known SATOR, AREPO, TENET, OPERA, ROTAS. It is a Square of 25 Squares. SALOM = "Peace". AREPO = "he distils". LEMEL = "unto fulness". OPERA, "upon the dry ground". MOLAS = "in quick motion," or perhaps better "stirring it up into quickness,i.e., life". The former sentence is capable of a rather free Latin translation, thus:--

SATOR = The Creator.
AREPO = Slow-moving.
TENET = Maintains.
OPERA = his creations.
ROTAS = As vortices.

No. 10 is a Square of 25 Squares. DEBAM signifies "influential persons".

No. 11. 8 Squares from a Square of 16. AHHB signifies "to love". BEAR signifies in Hebrew "to waste or consume".

No. 12. A Square of 36 Squares. IALDAH signifies "a girl".

No. 13 consists of 19 Squares arranged like the capital letter F, and taken from a Square of 49 Squares. BETULAH = a virgin.

No. 14 consists of 25 Squares from a Square of 49. IEDIDAH is from a Hebrew Root, signifying objects of Love. DILOQAH means "to eagerly pursue, or to burn as with a fever". DOQARCA = "pierced".

No. 15. 12 Squares from a Square of 25. SAQAL means "a wise person".

No. 16. A Square of 36 Squares. QEBHIR = "a protector".

No. 17. 14 Squares from a Square of 25. EFEHA means "passionate".

No. 18. A Gnomon of 11 from a Square of 36. TAAFAH = "to join together, to connect".

No. 19 is a Gnomon of 9 Squares from one of 25 Squares. SARAH means "powerful, high in authority".

No. 20 is also a Gnomon of 9 Squares from a Square of 25 Squares. CATAN = "to adhere closely".

THE TWENTIETH CHAPTER.

TO excite every Description of Hatred and Enmity, Discords, Quarrels, Contentions, Combats, Battles, Loss, and Damage.

(1) To excite Quarrels and Fights.
(2) For Enmity in general.
(3) For Enmities of Kings and of the Great.
(4) For particular Enmities.
(5) For Enmities among Women.
(6) To cause a General War.
(7) To render any one unfortunate in Combat.
(8) To put Discord in an Army.
(9) For a particular Discord.
(10) To sow Discord among Ecclesiastics.
(11) For every description of Vengeance.
(12) To cause Battles, Losses, etc.

(1)

K	A	N	N	A
A	Q	A	I	
N	A	T	A	
N	I	A	Q	A
A				

(2)

S	E	L	A	K
E				
L				
A	I	A	R	E
K				

(3)

R	O	Q	E	N
O		O		
Q	O	I	O	R
E				
N	E	Q	O	R

(4)

A	T	L	I	T	I	S
T						
L	O	Q	O	S	A	T
I						
T	A	S	O	Q	O	L
I						
S						

(5)

O	T	S	A	M	A	H
T						
S						
A						
M	A	K	A	R	O	S
A						
H						

(6)

S	I	N	A	H
I	R	A	T	A
N				
A	X	I	R	O
H	A	R	O	Q

(7)

S	A	T	A	N
A				
T				
A				
N				

(8)

L	O	F	I	T	O	S
O						
F						
I	K	O	N	O	K	I
T						
O						
S						

(9)

G	I	B	O	R
I				
B	I	L	E	T
O				
R				

(10)

N	O	K	A	M
O	R	O	T	A
K	O	B	A	K
A	T	A	M	O
M	A	K	O	N

(11)

K	E	L	I	M
E	Q	I	S	A
L	I	V	O	K
I	S	O	G	A
M	A	K	A	M

(12)

K	E	R	A	B	A	H
E	M	I	R	U	T	A
R						
A	R	O	Q	O	R	A
B						
A						
H						

(a) The Symbols of this Chapter are manifested in part by the Angels, and in part also by the Evil Spirits.

(b) BELZEBUD performs the Operations hereof.

(c) The Familiar Spirits cannot well execute the Operations of this chapter.

(d) See instructions for Chapter XIX, which serve equally for that, and the present Operation.

(e) No. 1 consists of 19 Squares irregularly arranged, and taken from a Square of 25 Squares.--KANNA means "jealous".

No. 2 consists of 13 Squares from a Square of 25 Squares.--SELAK = "to cast down or prostrate".

No. 3 consists of 18 Squares from a Square of 25.--ROQEN implies "persons in power".

No. 4 consists of 25 Squares from a Square of 49.--ATLITIS is a corruption of the Greek adjective ATLETOS = "insufferable, not to be borne".

No. 5 consists of 19 Squares from a Square of 49.--OTSAMAH = "bodily strength".

No. 6 consists of 21 from a Square of 25.--SINAH = "Hatred".

No. 7 is a Gnomon of 9 Squares from a Square of 25. SATAN is the Name of one of the Chief Evil Spirits and has been elsewhere explained.

No. 8 consists of 19 Squares in the form of a capital F, taken from a Square of 49 Squares.--LOFITOS is evidently from the Greek LOPHESIS, meaning "rest, cessation from action (i.e. in this case military action)".

No. 9 consists of 13 Squares arranged in the form of an F, and taken from a Square of 25 Squares.--GIBOR = "strength, might, severity".

No. 10 is a Square of 25 Squares.--NOKAM = "vengeance".

No. 11 is also a Square of 25 Squares.--KELIK = "for all kinds of things".

No. 12 consists of 25 Squares from a Square of 49.--KERABAH = "assault, attack".

THE TWENTY-FIRST CHAPTER.

(1)

TO transform oneself, and take different Faces and Forms.

(1) To appear old.
(2) To take on the appearance of an Old Woman.
(3) To appear young.
(4) To transform oneself into a Girl.
(5) To appear like a young Child.

Z	A	K	E	N
A			Q	I
K	O	L	A	N
E	Q			
N				

(2)

D	I	S	K	E	N	A	H
I							
S							
E							
K	Q						
E							
N							
A							
H							

(3)

D	I	S	A	K	A	N
I	R	O	Q			
S			Q			
A	Q					
K	U	Q				
A						
N						

(4)

I	O	N	E	K
O				
N				
E		Q		
K				

(5)

B	A	C	U	R
A	Q			
C	O	R	E	C
			Q	A
			A	B

NOTES TO CHAPTER XXI

(a) The Symbols of this Chapter are manifested only by the Evil Spirits.

(b) MAGOT performs the Operations hereof

(c) The Familiar Spirits cannot well execute the Operations of this Chapter.

(d) This is rather a fascination than anything else. Take the Symbol desired in your left hand and stroke the face therewith. Abraham further observes that such an Operation performed by an ordinary Magician would be easily seen through by the possessor of the Sacred Magic; while on the contrary this latter would be safe from detection by ordinary Sorcerers.

(e) The Student will note in these Squares the marked position of the Letter Q, as in many other cases where the effect aimed at seems to be rather a deception of the senses of others.

No. 1 consists of 16 Squares from a Square of 25. ZAKEN means "old".

No. 2 is a Gnomon of 16 Squares with the Letter Q added; from a Square of 72 Squares.-- DISKENAH = "in the likeness of an old woman". It is to be remarked that this Square is rather oblong, 8 Squares long by 9 deep.

No. 3 consists of 20 Squares from a Square of 49.--DISAKAN means "to cover up or hide," but were it DISAKAR it would mean "as one young".

No. 4 consists of 10 Squares from a Square of 25 Squares.--IONEK means "thy dove".

No. 5 consists of 16 Squares from a Square of 25.--BACUR = "a firstborn".

THE TWENTY-SECOND CHAPTER.

THIS Chapter is only for Evil, for with the Symbols herein we can cast Spells, and work every kind of Evil; we should not avail ourselves hereof.

(1) To cast Spells upon Men.
(2) To bewitch Beasts.
(3) To cast a Spell upon the Liver.
(4) This Symbol should never be made use of.
(5) To cast a Spell upon the Heart.
(6) Upon the Head and other parts of the Body.

(1)

Q	E	L	A	D	I	M
E					Q	
L					A	
A						
D						
I	Q					
M						

(2)

B	E	H	E	M	O	T
E						
H		Q	O	E	N	
E	Q					
M						
O						
T						

(3)

M	E	B	A	S	I	M
E		Q				
B						
A	Q				Q	
S						
I						
M		Q				

(4)

C	A	S	E	D
A	Z	O	T	E
B	O	R	O	S
E	T	O	S	A
D	E	B	A	C

(5)

L	E	B	H	A	H
E	M	A	U	S	A
B					
H					
A					
H					

(6)

Q	A	R	A	Q	A	K
A						
R						Q
A						
Q						
A						
K		Q		Q		

NOTES TO CHAPTER XXII

(a) The Symbols of this Chapter are manifested only by the Evil Spirits.

(b) BELZEBUD performs the Operations hereof.

(c) The Familiar Spirits cannot well execute the Operations of this Chapter.

(d) Abraham warns strongly against use being made of this Operation. The Symbols should be either buried or concealed in places where the persons we wish to harm are likely to pass by; or, if possible, we can touch them with the Symbol.

(e) No. 1 consists of 17 from a Square of 49 Squares. QELADIM means "those who creep in insidiously".

No. 2 consists of 19 Squares from a Square of 49 Squares. BEHEMOT = "Beasts".

No. 3 consists of 18 Squares from a Square of 49. MEBASIM = "those that stamp down violently".

No. 4 is a Square of 25 Squares.

CASED, Hebrew (if used in a bad sense) = "overflowing of unrestrained lust".

AZOTE, Hebrew "enduring".

BOROS, = Greek = "Devouring, gluttonous."

ETOSA, = Greek = "idle, useless".

DEBAC, = Hebrew = "to overtake and stick close."

No. 5 consists of 14 Squares from a Square of 36. LEBHAH implies, "Agony at the heart". No. 6 consists of 17 Squares. QARAQAK = "thy baldness," also "thy rending asunder".

THE TWENTY-THIRD CHAPTER.

TO demolish Buildings and Strongholds.

(1) To make a House fall to the ground.
(2) To destroy a Town.
(3) To demolish Strongholds.
(4) To ruin possessions (and Estates).

(1)

N	A	V	E	H
A		Q		
V	Q			
E				
H				D

(2)

Q	A	Q	A	H
A				
Q				Q
A				
H			Q	Q

(3)

C	O	M	A	H	O	N
O						
M			Q			
A		Q				
H						
O						
N						

(4)

B	I	N	I	A	M
I	N	U	U	S	I
N					
I					
A					
M					

THE TWENTY-FOURTH CHAPTER.

TO discover any Thefts that hath occurred.[228]

    (1) Jewels stolen.
    (2) Money.
    (3) Worked Gold.
    (4) Silver Workmanship.
    (5) Effects, such as Furniture.
    (6) Horses, and other Animals.

(1)

K	I	X	A	L	I	S
I	R	I	N	E	Q	I
X						
A						
L				M		
I	Q					
S						K

(2)

Q	E	N	E	B	A	H
E		Q				
N						Q
E						
B						
A						
H		Q				

(3)

Q	E	D	E	S	E	L	A	N
E								
D								
E	M	A	Q	A	Q	A	L	A
S								
E	N	A	Q	I	R	I	Q	A
L								
A							Q	
N								N

(5)

C	A	R	A	C
A	R	I	O	A
R	I	R	I	R
A	O	I	R	A
C	A	R	A	C

(6)

M	O	R	E	H
O				
R	O	S	O	R
E	I			
H				

---

228   The Squares are numbered in the above Order in the Original Ms.

(4)

T	A	L	A	H
A	N	I	M	A
L				
A				
H				

(a) The Symbols of this Chapter are manifested in part by the Angels, and in part also by the Evil Spirits.

(b) ARITON performs the Operations hereof; and MAGOT also; but separately.

(c) The Familiar Spirits can to an extent perform the Operations of this Chapter.

(d) No especial instructions are given by Abraham regarding this Chapter.

(e) No. 1 consists of 22 Squares taken from a Square of 49 Squares. The meaning of KIXALIS is not apparent.

No. 2 consists of 16 Squares from a Square of 49. QENEBAH probably conveys the idea of gain or possession.

No. 3 consists of 35 Squares from a Square of 81 Squares. QEDE-SELAN may signify things of value set apart.

No. 6 (the succession of numbers here is irregular) consists of 14 Squares from a Square of 25 Squares. MOREH means "to rebel against, to disobey".

No. 5 consists of a Square of 25 Squares. CARAC means "to involve or wrap up," also "garments, etc.".

No. 4 is a Gnomon of 13 Squares taken from a Square of 25 Squares. TALAH means "a young lamb," or "kid," according to whether its root terminates with Aleph or He.

THE TWENTY-FIFTH CHAPTER.

TO walk upon, and operate under, Water.

(3)

(1) To swim for 24 hours without becoming wearied.
(2) To remain under Water for 2 hours.
(3) To rest upon the Water for 24 hours.

M	A	I	A	M
A				
I				
A				
M				

(1)

N	A	H	A	R	I	A	M	A
A			Q					
H						E		
A		Q						
R								
I								
A						Q		
M					Q	A		
A								

(2)

B	U	R	N	A	H	E	U
U	L	O	R	I	P	T	E
R	O	M	I	L	A	P	H
N	R	I	T	I	L	I	A
A	I	L	I	T	I	R	N
H	P	A	L	I	M	O	R
E	T	P	I	R	O	L	U
U	E	H	A	N	R	U	B

NOTES TO CHAPTER XXV

(a) The Symbols of this Chapter are manifested only by the Angel, or by the Guardian Angel.

(b) Abraham does not state to what Prince this Operation is submitted.

(c) The Familiar Spirits cannot well execute the Operations of this Chapter.

(d) No especial instructions are given by Abraham regarding this Chapter.

(e) No. 1 consists of 23 Squares taken from a Square of 81 Squares. NAHARIAMA means "a river of waters".

No. 2 is a Square of 64 Squares.

No. 3 is a Gnomon of 9 Squares from a Square of 25 Squares. MAIAM = "Abundant waters such as the sea".

THE TWENTY-SIXTH CHAPTER.

TO open every Kind of Lock, without a Key, and without making any noise.

(1) To open Doors.
(2) To open Padlocks.
(3) To open Larders (or Charnel-Houses).
(4) To open Strong-boxes (or Caskets).
(5) To open Prisons.

(1)

S	A	G	U	B
A				
G	O	R		
U			D	O
B				S

(2)

R	A	T	O	K
A	K			
T				
O			Q	U
K				R

(3)

B	A	R	I	A	C	A
A			Q			
R						
I						
A	Q					
C						
A						

(4)

S	E	Q	O	R
E				
Q		S		Q
O				
R		Q		S

(5)

L	O	H	A	R	A	H	O	S
O								
H			Q					
A		Q			Q			
R								
A								
H		A	Q					
O							L	O
S								S

NOTES TO CHAPTER XXVI

(a) The Symbols of this Chapter are manifested in part by the Angels, and in part also by the Evil Spirits.

(b) AMAIMON and ARITON together perform the Operations of this Chapter.

(c) The Familiar Spirits cannot well execute the Operations of this Chapter.

(d) Touch the lock you wish to open with the side of the Symbol which is written upon, and it will immediately open without noise or injury. When you wish to reclose it touch it with the side of the Symbol not written upon, and it will refasten and shew no trace of having been opened.

(e) No. 1 consists of 14 Squares taken from a Square of 25 Squares. SAGUB signifies "exalted" or "lifted up" (as an ancient portcullis might be).

No. 2 consists of 13 Squares taken from a Square of 25 Squares. RATOK means "a confining chain wreathed or fastened round anything".

No. 3 consists of 15 Squares taken from a Square of 49 Squares. BARIACA = "a place for food to be put".

No. 4 consists of 13 Squares from a Square of 25. SEQOR may mean either "to satisfy" or "to deal falsely," according as it is spelt with Q or K.

No. 5 consists of 25 Squares from a Square of 81.

THE TWENTY-SEVENTH CHAPTER.

TO cause Visions to appear.[229]

(1) To make trellis-work to be seen.
(2) A Superb Palace.
(3) Flowering Meadows.
(4) Lakes and Rivers.
(5) Vines with their Grapes.
(6) Great Fires.
(7) Divers Mountains.
(8) Bridges and Rivers.
(9) Woods and various Kinds of Trees.
(10) Cranes.
(11) Giants.
(12) Peacocks.
(13) Gardens.
(14) Wild Boars.
(15) Unicorns.
(16) Beautiful Country.
(17) A fruit Garden (or Orchard).
(18) A Garden with all kinds of Flowers.
(19) To cause Snow to appear.

(1)

229   Numbered in this Order in the Original MS

(20) Different kinds of Wild Animals.
(21) Towns and Castles.
 (22) Various flowers.
(23) Fountains and clear Springs (of Water).
(24) Lions.
(25) Singing Birds.
(26) Horses.
(27) Eagles.
(28) Buffaloes.
(29) Dragons.
(30) Hawks and Falcons.
(30 Foxes.
(32) Hares.
(33) Dogs.
(34) Gryphons.
(35) Stags.

(2)

H	E	S	E	B
E	Q	A	L	
S				
E		G		
B				

(3)

A	O	D	O	N	I	A
O			Q			
D						
O	Q		L		Q	O
N						
I			Q			
A						

(4)

A	T	S	A	R	A	H
T	O	A	L	I	S	A
S	A	D	O	R	I	R
A	L	O	T	O	L	A
R	I	R	O	D	A	S
A	S	I	L	A	O	T
H	A	R	A	S	T	A

(7)

S	O	R	E	K
O				
R				
E			Q	
K				

(8)

A	K	R	O	P	O	L	I	S
K								
R								
O		Q						
P								
O			Q					
L								
I								
S								

(6)

S	E	L	E	G
E			Q	
L				
E	Q	A	Q	E
G	E	L	E	S

(5)

A	G	A	M	A	G	A
G						
A						A
M						
A						
G					A	
A						

(9)

C	A	I	O	T
A				
I		Q		
O				
T				

(10)

I	A	Q	E	B
A				
Q				Q
E				
B		Q		

(11)

M	E	L	U	N	A	C
E			Q			
L						
U	Q					
N						
A					G	E
C						

(12)

P	E	R	A	C
E	Q			
R				
A				Q
C				

(15)

D	O	B	E	R	A	H
O	R	A				
B						
E						
R						
A			C			
H						

(14)

O	L	E	L	A	H
L					
E					
L					
A					
H					

(13)

K	I	K	A	I	O	N
I				O		
K						
A						
I						
O						
N						

(16)

M	A	K	O	R
A				
K				
O				
R				

(17)

M	I	G	I	R	A	S
I						
G						
I						
R						Q
A	M	I	L	E	S	I
S					Q	

(18)

E	S	A	H	E	L
S					
A					
H					
E					
L	B				

(19)

A	R	I	E	H
R				
I				
E				
H				

(20)

L	I	M	I	K	O	S
I						
M						
I			Q			C
K						
O						
S	O	K	I	M		

(21)

S	A	S	A	S
A	R	I		
S	I	Q		
A				
S				

(22)

K	I	K	I	M	I	S
I			Q			
K						
I		Q				
M						
I	T		Q			
S			Q			

(23)

N	E	S	I	K	E	R
E			Q			
S						
I	Q					
K						
E						
R						

(24)

D	O	B	I	H
O				
B				
I				
H				

(25)

F	U	F	A	L	O	S
U						
F						
A						
L						
O					Q	
S						

(26)

P	A	R	A	H
A				
R				
A				
H				

(27)

G	A	D	E	S	I	R
A						
D						
E					Q	
S						
I		Q				
R						

(28)

F	A	N	I	N
A				
N		Q		
I				
N				

(29)

R	E	E	M
E			
E	Z		
M			

(30)

A	I	I	A	H
I	U	S	E	A
I				
A				
H				

(31)

S	U	H	A	L
U				
H				
A			Q	
L				

(32)

G	I	R	I	P	E	S
I			Q			
R						
I	Q				Q	
P			Q			
E						
S						G

(33)

A	R	N	E	P
R				
N		Q		
E				
P				

(34)

A	I	I	A	L
I				
I				
A				
L				

(35)

K	E	L	E	F
E			Q	
L		Q		
E	Q			
F				

NOTES TO CHAPTER XXVII

(a) The Symbols of this Chapter are only manifested by the Evil Spirits.

(b) ORIENS, PAIMON, ARITON, and AMAIMON, execute the Operations hereof by the means of their common Ministers.

(c) The Familiar Spirits can to an extent perform the Operations of this Chapter.

(d) No especial instructions are given by Abraham regarding this Chapter.

(e) No. 1 consists of 13 Squares taken from a Square of 25 Squares. SELAC means "to cast down," "to cut down or fell" (as trees). Perhaps thus signifying the cut wood with which a trellis is made.

No. 2 consists of 13 Squares from a Square of 25 Squares. HESEB may mean the environs of a place.

No. 3 consists of 19 Squares from a Square of 49 Squares. AODONIA, from Hebrew root ODN = "Eden, a delightful place, etc.".

No. 4 is a Square of 49 Squares. ATSARAH = either "a store-house or treasury" or "to flow," according to its derivation.

No. 7 (the order of the numbering of the Squares is here changed) consists of 10 Squares taken from a Square of 25 Squares. SOREK means "to wind about".

No. 8 consists of 19 Squares from a Square of 81 Squares. AKROPOLIS is a Greek word signifying "citadel".

No. 6 consists of 18 Squares taken from a Square of 25 Squares. SELEG = "Snow," whence perhaps this should be numbered 19 instead of 6.

No. 5 consists of 15 Squares from a Square of 49. AGAMAGA = "pools of water," whence this should probably be numbered 4 instead of 5.

No. 9 consists of 10 Squares from a Square of 25 Squares. CAIOT is probably from CHAIOTH = "Living creatures". It may also mean covert, where living creatures abide. Perhaps it should be numbered 20.

No. 10 consists of 11 Squares taken from a Square of 25 Squares. IAQEB probably means a bird of the crane species.

No. 11 consists of 17 Squares taken from a Square of 49 Squares. MELUNAC = "Thy dwelling-place," and perhaps this should be numbered 21.

No. 12 consists of 11 Squares taken from a Square of 25 Squares. PERAC may mean "flowering gardens". Perhaps this should be numbered 13.

No. 15 consists of 16 Squares taken from a Square of 49 Squares.

No. 14 is a Gnomon of 11 Squares from a Square of 36 Squares. OLELAH may mean "horned animals" or "tusked animals".

No. 13 consists of 14 Squares taken from a Square of 49 Squares. KIKAION = a place where gourds grow.

No. 16 is a Gnomon of 9 Squares taken from a Square of 25 Squares. MAKOR = "places digged".

No. 17 consists of 21 Squares taken from a Square of 49 Squares. MIGIRAS = "a place where productive plants grow".

No. 18 consists of 12 Squares from a Square of 36 Squares. ESAHEL = "rich".

No. 19 should probably be numbered 24. It is a Gnomon of 9 from a Square of 25 Squares. ARIEH = "a lion".

No. 20 consists of 19 from a Square of 49 Squares. LIMIKOS = "savage (animals)".

No. 21 consists of 13 Squares from a Square of 25 Squares. SASAS probably means "Horses," and this Square should probably be numbered 26 instead of 21.

No. 22 consists of 18 Squares taken from a Square of 49 Squares. KIKIMIS = "thistles," and also "some kinds of flowers".

No. 23 consists of 15 Squares from a Square of 49 Squares. NESIKER signifies fluids of various kinds.

No. 24 consists of 9 Squares from a Square of 25. DOBIH = "a bear," and should evidently be otherwise numbered.

No. 25 consists of 14 Squares from a Square of 49 Squares.

No. 26 is a Gnomon of 9 Squares from a Square of 25 Squares. PARAH = "a heifer," but also "fruit, produce".

No. 27 consists of 15 Squares from a Square of 49.

No. 28 consists of 10 Squares from a Square of 25. FANIN is probably from BN, and meaning "Towns and Villages," whence this should probably be numbered 21.

No. 29 consists of 8 Squares from a Square of 16. REEM ="Unicorns," and also beasts of the beeve kind, Buffaloes, etc. Perhaps this Square answers for 15 as well.

No. 30 consists of a Gnomon of 13 Squares from a Square of 2 5 Squares. AIIAH = rapacious birds.

No. 31 consists of 10 Squares from a Square of 25. SUHAL means "a blackish lion," whence this Square should be numbered 24 probably.

No. 32 consists of 18 Squares from a Square of 49. GIRIPES may mean "small beasts that run swiftly".

No. 33 consists of 10 Squares from a Square of 25. ARNEP should probably be ARNEB. It means "a Hare," whence this Square should perhaps be numbered 32.

No. 34 is a Gnomon of 9 Squares from a Square of 2 5. AIIAL probably means "wild goats".

No. 35 consists of 12 Squares from 25. KELEF = "a Dog," whence this Square should probably be numbered 33.

THE TWENTY-EIGHTH CHAPTER.

TO have as much Gold and Silver as one may wish, both to provide for one's necessities, and to live in opulence.

(1) To have coined Gold.
(2) To have coined Silver.
(3) To have Silver in small coins.
(4) To have small change in Copper (or Bronze).

(1)

S	E	Q	O	R
E	Q	A	M	O
Q		S		Q
O			Q	
R		Q		

(2)

K	E	S	E	R
E				
S				
E				
R			K	

(3)

P	E	S	E	P
E	Q			
S	O	R	O	S
E	M	O	Q	
P	E	S		

(4)

M	A	T	B	A
A				
T				
B				
A				

NOTES TO CHAPTER XXVIII

(a) The Symbols of this Chapter are manifested only by the Angels or by the Guardian Angel.

(b) ORIENS alone performs this Operation.

(c) The Familiar Spirits can to an extent perform the Operations of this Chapter.

(d) Place the Symbol of the Money you require in your purse, let it remain there for a short time, then put your right hand into your purse, and you will there find seven pieces of the class of money you have wished for. This Operation should not be performed more than three times in the day. The pieces of money you do not use will disappear, which is why you should not ask for several kinds of money at the same time. And if you spend it, both you and those into whose hands it passes will find it genuine.

In another place Abraham says, that once only in your life you may ask your Guardian Angel for a large sum of money sufficient to represent a fortune; and that he himself had done so and obtained his request.

(e) No. 1 consists of 17 from a Square of 25 Squares. SEQOR perhaps here means money.

No. 2 consists of 10 Squares from a Square of 25. KESER may mean a "collection or heap".

No. 3 consists of 19 Squares from a Square of 25. PESEP should be probably BESPR = "much, many".

No. 4 is a Gnomon of 9 Squares from 25. MATBA probably means "let it be forthcoming, bring forth".

THE TWENTY-NINTH CHAPTER.

TO cause Armed Men to appear.

(1) To cause an Army to appear.
(2) Armed Men for one's defence.,
(3) To cause a Siege to appear.

(1)

M	A	C	A	N	E	H
A						
C						
A						
N						
E						
H						

(2)

M	A	H	A	R	A	C	A	H
A								
H								
A								
R								
A		Q						
C			Q					
A								
H								

(3)

M	E	T	I	S	I	U	R	A	H
E		Q							
T									
I	Q								
S									
U							Q		
R									
A						Q			
H									

NOTES TO CHAPTER XXIX

(a) The Symbols of this Chapter are manifested in part by the Angels, and in part also by the Evil Spirits.

(b) ORIENS, PAIMON, ARITON, and AMAIMON, execute the Operations hereof by the means of their common Ministers. PAIMON also performs this Operation alone.

(c) The Familiar Spirits cannot well execute the Operations of this Chapter.

(d) No especial instructions are given by Abraham regarding this Chapter, by which Abraham says (in the First Book) that he himself had caused armed men to appear.

(e) No. 1 is a Gnomon of 13 Squares from a Square of 49 Squares. MACANEH = "an encampment".

No. 2 consists of 19 Squares from a Square of 81. MAHARACAH perhaps means "an ambuscade".

No. 3 consists of 21 Squares from a Square of 81 Squares.

THE THIRTIETH CHAPTER.

To cause Comedies, Operas, and every kind of Music and Dances to appear.

(1) To cause all kinds of Music to be heard.
(2) Music and extravagant Balls.
(3) For all kinds of Instruments to be played.
(4) For Comedies, Farces and Operas.

(1)

N	A	G	I	N	A	H
A					M	
G				G		
I						
N	G					G
A						
H			Q			

(2)

M	E	K	O	L	A	H
E						
K						
O						
L						
A						
H						

(3)

N	I	G	I	G	I	N
I						
G						
I						
G						
I						
N						

(4)

M	E	C	A	S	E	F
E	P	A	R	U	S	E
C	A	L				
A						
S						
E						
P						

END OF THE[230] SYMBOLS

NOTES TO CHAPTER XXX

(a) The Symbols of this Chapter are manifested only by the Evil Spirits.

(b) MAGOT performs the Operations hereof.

(c) The Familiar Spirits can to an extent perform the Operations of this Chapter.

(d) No especial instructions are given by Abraham regarding this Chapter.

(e) No. 1 consists of 18 Squares from a Square of 49 Squares. NAGINAH = "a stringed instrument".

No. 2 consists of a Gnomon of 13 Squares from a Square of 49 Squares. MEKOLAH = "Singing".

No. 3 is a Gnomon of 13 Squares from a Square of 49 Squares. NIGIGIN = "musical instruments," probably.

No. 4 consists of 21 Squares from a Square of 49 Squares. MECASEF means "enchantment".

This finishes the list of Symbols set down by Abraham the Jew, the which I have given in their entirety; but I must of my own initiative warn any who may endeavour to use these Signs, that unless animated by the purest and best motives they will find them react terribly against them; and that, if the preliminary period of Six Months' preparation advocated by Abra-Melin be not observed, the Symbols will be practically worthless in their hands; for, as will be observed, the Names in the Squares for the most part are simply the statement of the ends desired to be accomplished thereby.

Finally, I will quote the following passage from the "Key of Solomon the King":--

"ACCURSED BE HE WHO TAKETH THE NAME OF GOD IN VAIN! ACCURSED BE HE WHO USETH THIS KNOWLEDGE UNTO AN EVIL END. BE HE ACCURSED IN THIS WORLD

---

230   In the Original MS. these words " Fin des Signes" are written in this manner across and within the two last Squares.

AND IN THE WORLD TO COME. AMEN. BE HE ACCURSED IN THE NAME WHICH HE HATH
BLASPHEMED!"

ESSENTIAL REMARKS UPON THE FOREGOING SYMBOLS

IT is certain that among all the Symbols which I have hereinbefore written down there be many
which one can employ for evil (purposes); and I avow that (at first) I intended not to give them
here at all; but thereafter I did make reflection in myself that I was working no evil; for often the
secret judgments of God permit disgrace, hindrances, infirmities, and other vexing accidents to
happen unto Mortals, either to awake them from the lethargy wherein they be sunk so that they
recognise not their Creator, or else to give them an opportunity by their afflictions of increasing
their merit. And although God can in no way do evil, but always good, nevertheless we cannot
deny that occasionally He permitteth the Secondary Causes to act. Now the Executioners and
Executors of the Divine justice be the Evil Spirits. Whence I conclude that although it may be in
no sense advisable to work Operations for Evil, yet that there may arise, however, certain cases
which do admit of and permit the same; as (for example) when it is necessary to save and defend
one's own life, or to avert some great scandal or evil, or to prevent offensive acts which might
be done against oneself, or to displease God and hurt one's neighbour, as well as in just Wars,
and other like cases. Yet it is always best in such instances to govern yourself according to the
counsel of your Holy Guardian Angel. I have also written these for the reason that God hath
given unto Man free Will both in merit and demerit; for, further, having finished the Operation, if
thou shouldest wish (which I pray God not to permit) to operate for Evil and to abuse the Grace
which God hath granted thee, the Spirits would be only too ready to give and manifest unto thee
the Symbols, and will grant willingly unto thee all that thou shalt demand of them. Concerning
this matter I repeat unto thee,--Fear the Lord, love Him, and respect His Commandments with a
good heart, and thou shalt live happy and contented upon Earth.

If thou considerest maturely what be the essential points of this Operation, thou shalt find that
the first point is to make a firm, veritable, and real resolution to live in a truly edifying condition
of modesty, and in retirement, as far as it shall be possible for thee so to do. For Solitude is the
source of many blessings, such as, to give oneself up to prayer, and unto the contemplation of
things Divine; to flee evil conversations and occasions of sin; to live in oneself; and to accustom
oneself to continuing a life of such regularity. For if one were to go to present oneself before a
King, what would one not do to appear before him with splendour and magnificence; and what
diligence and care would not one put in practice to prepare oneself hereunto. Now we must understand that the enjoyment and vision of the Angels of the Lord be infinitely above the Princes of
Earth, who in fact are but a vanity, a shadow, and vile dust of Earth. Now if to please these Mortal
Princes one would almost commit idolatries; what ought one not to do to appear before the Holy
Angels of God who represent the Grandeur of the Majesty of God. Let each one hold for a thing,
sure and certain that the Grace which the Lord granteth unto us in giving us this Sacred Science
by the means and intermediation of His Holy Angels is so great that none can fitly express it.

It is certain that having obtained this Sacred Wisdom thou mayest dispose of it and communicate it unto three friends; but thou must not exceed this Sacred Number of the Ternary, for in
such case thou wouldest be altogether deprived of it. One of the most meritorious deeds in the
sight of the Lord, is to share with one's neighbour the goods which God hath given unto us; yet
must we take note of that which God commanded unto MOSES, when He ordered him to--give the
Operation unto AARON his brother, namely that he should receive as the Symbol of an Offering
Ten Golden Florins, the which he should distribute unto Seventy-Two poor persons with his own
hands, obliging them to repeat the Psalms which I have already mentioned in the Second Book,
and which should be of the number of Seventy-Two. For if he who receiveth this Operation should

not perform this Alms, the Operation would be void of value for him. Thou, not yet having the Authority to give it, without having received the Ten Golden Florins, thou must act like MOSES, unto whom the Lord granted it on this condition, for him to give it unto his brother AARON.

I have also described the precautions which we must take before granting this Sacred Science unto any; and I repeat here that at least Six Months should transpire during which we should frequently test, and seek by conversations to sound, the inclinations of him unto whom we may be willing to give it; so as to know whether he be a reliable person, and also the object for which he demandeth and is anxious to obtain this Science. Now shouldest thou perceive that such an one is light and inconstant, and that he hath only vague ideas, and habits and manners which be not good, then shalt thou temporise with him for a time, so as to bring up causes, occasions, or pretexts, so as not to give it unto him, even shouldest thou already have promised it to him. For it is better to undergo the displeasure of a Mortal Man than that of an Eternal God, from Whom thou hast received so great a Grace. I have, however, myself made trial hereof, for to my great wonderment (once upon a time) when I was thinking that I was putting it to good use in giving it unto a certain person for whom I had great respect; God Himself intervened and did not permit my intention to be carried out, for that person began of his own accord to wonder whether the matter were true or no, and he doubted it much, believing that it was a fable, and did not have an entire faith therein; and he made me comprehend by his discourse that he was not such an one as I had thought. Furthermore it happened that he fell dangerously ill, and I in my turn was reprimanded by my Angel who blamed me for the choice I had made. The whole machinery of the Universe is maintained by Faith; and he who believeth not, suffereth the chastisement of his perfidy both in this World and in the next. I could here say much more relating to our own selves, but as thou wilt have to pass under the influence of thy Holy Guardian Angel, thou wilt be suffi-ciently instructed in his own good time, and by himself, concerning these matters which be both delicate and to be jealously guarded.

The Evil Spirit is so subtle, so keen, and so cunning, that that which he cannot obtain at the time of the Conjuration, he will seek. to have on other occasions in offering thee his services. This is why the very first action to take especially with thy Familiar Spirits, should be to command them, never to say anything unto thee of themselves, but only to speak when thou shalt interro-gate them, unless it were to warn thee of matters which concern either thine advantage or thine hurt. For if thou dost not limit their liberty of speech they will tell thee so many and so important things, that they will completely overcloud thine understanding, and thou wilt not know what to believe, so that in the confusion of ideas they could make thee prevaricate, and perhaps fall into irretrievable error. Never make thyself to be greatly entreated in any matter wherein thou canst aid and succour thy neighbour, and do not wait until he demandeth assistance from thee, but seek to know to the full his need even though it be concealed, and give him prompt aid. Also trouble not thyself as to whether he be Turk, Pagan, or Idolater, but do good unto all those who believe in a God. Be especially charitable towards those who are in extreme want, prisoners, or sick, and let thine heart be touched, and succour them generously; for God taketh pleasure in beholding the poor succoured.

In the Twenty-Eighth Chapter where it is treated of the way to have Silver and Gold sufficient to supply one's needs on occasion; thou must know that the quantity of Gold or of Silver of which thou hast then actually need, will be at once brought unto thee, and thou canst use it for this occasion only. And if thou usest it not within the twenty-four hours, this sum will disappear and thou wilt no longer be able to avail thyself of . it. Think not, however, that this Gold is but a phan-tasy, for if thou effectually expendest it, and dost not endeavour to hoard the same, he who shall receive it from thine hands can enjoy the same and expend it according unto his desire, and the money will be real both for him and for others.

For once only mayest thou demand of thine Holy Angel the amount of Gold and of Silver which thou shalt judge suitable unto thine estate and conditions. My possessions were few, and I demanded of mine Angel Three Thousand Thousand Golden Florins, and they were granted unto me. Later I made such good use of the Sacred Science, and I understood so well how to augment my goods, that at the present time, after having married three Daughters unto each of whom I gave a hundred thousand (golden florins), as thou wilt see by the testament which I have made, I am leaving in current money more than a Million Golden Florins, besides a large quantity of very valuable furniture. Had I been of noble birth I might have demanded much more and have profited less. When any one demanded of me: "Eh! How have you managed to gain so much?" I would reply thereto that it is a fine thing to know by certain Knowledge how much such or such a thing is worth here, and how much it is worth elsewhere, that this year, wheat, barley, and other crops, will be cheap in Italy, and dear in France, etc., etc.; and that commerce well managed, enricheth any one.

As for what concerneth the manner of treating and commanding the Spirits, it is an easy thing unto whomsoever walketh by the proper paths; and it is a very difficult thing for whomsoever through ignorance submitteth himself unto them. I have heard say that there be some men who pass for being famous herein, such as a certain blind man D'ACALI, a certain BEARLI, a PETER D'ABANO, and many others. Ah! how many of them do but deceive themselves! I do not say that these men did not perform extraordinary things; but it is necessary to note their manner of working, for their Science is imperfect, and their Authority proceedeth not from God by the inter-mediation of His Holy Angels, but proceedeth directly from express Pacts made with the Devil, and (acteth) by means of Consecrated Books full of thousands of Diabolical Conjurations and impious Exorcisms; in one word things which be contrary unto the Commandments of God and the peace of men. And with all this their Operations be destined for certain times and hours, and finally the Demon carrieth away with him their miserable Souls, which thing arriveth only too often. And yet it is the Science of these persons which causeth them to pass for famous Wise Men.

In the First Book I have made mention of those whom I had encountered in my journeyings in Europe. The true Commandment is that which dependeth from God, and in which there is no dependence placed on any Spirit imaginable, for in employing them, if you make unto them the least submission, the slightest prayer, or honour, you are rendering yourselves their slaves, and they are in no way submitted unto you. The Spirits have so great knowledge that they compre-hend very well by our actions what dispositions we have, and understand our inclinations, so that from the very beginning they prepare the way to make us to fail. If they know that a man is inclined unto Vanity and Pride, they will humiliate themselves before him, and push that humility unto excess, and even unto idolatry, and this man will glory herein and become intoxicated with conceit, and the matter will not end without his commanding them some pernicious thing of such a nature that ultimately thencefrom will be derived that sin which will make the Man the Slave of the Demon. Another man will be easily accessible to Avarice, and then if he take not heed the Malignant Spirits will propose unto him thousands of ways of accumulating wealth, and of ren-dering himself rich by indirect and unjust ways and means, whence total restitution is afterwards difficult and even impossible, so that he who is in such case findeth himself ever the Slave of the Spirits. Another will be a man of Letters; the Spirits will inspire him with presumption, and he will then believe himself to be wiser even than the Prophets, furthermore they will endeavour to lead him astray in subtle points in matters appertaining unto God, and will make (that man) fall into a thousand errors, the which afterwards when he wisheth to support he will very frequently deny God, and His high Mysteries. The causes and matters whereof (the Spirits) will make use to cause a man to waver are infinite, especially when the man attempteth to make them submit to his commands, and this is why it is most necessary to be upon one's guard and to distrust oneself, The true Commandment will be that which will be given when he who commandeth shall have maturely reflected and considered who he is in himself, and who he is who should serve and obey him. And if a Mortal Man not having on his side the support of the Power and Will of the Lord shall have sufficient force to command the Spirits and to constrain them to obey him; (they, namely) who have the same virtue and power, which God hath granted unto them, they having lost nothing hereof; and they also being Spirits from God and herein differing from thee who art drawn from the mire, as Gold is from Lead; and that their sin is notorious, for the which they were chased from Heaven; figure also unto thyself, that a Spirit which of his own nature is all vanity, would not be likely to submit himself unto thee without a superior force (compelling him), neither would he wish to obey thee nor to serve thee. He who shall reflect and reason upon these particulars will know that all things come unto us from God, and that it is He Who wisheth and commandeth that the Evil Spirits should be submitted unto us. If then all things depend from the Lord, upon whom wilt thou, O Man, base thyself so as to be capable of thyself (alone) to dominate the Spirits? It is certain that such an enterprise cannot succeed without the loss of thine own soul. Then it is by the virtue of that God Who hath submitted them under thy feet, that thou shalt command them, as will be precisely ordained unto thee by thy Holy Angel. "Donec ponam inimicos tuos scabellum pedum tuorum." "Until I shall make thy foes thy footstool." Also do not familiarise thyself with them; for they be not little pet dogs. Adopt a serious tone and an air of authority, make them obey thee, and be well ware of accepting the least offer which they shall make unto thee of themselves; and treat them as their Master, also without occasion thou shalt never molest them, and order them to execute thy commands from point to point without adding or diminishing in any way imaginable. And when thou canst employ Inferior Spirits (in a matter), thou shalt in no way make thy requests unto the Superiors. Also seeing that all have not the same powers, thou shalt take heed not to command unto one (Spirit) a thing appertaining unto (the office of) another; and because it would be impossible for me to here write down in full the quality, virtue, and office of each Spirit, thou shouldest search this out for thyself and sharpen thy faculties; and in the first demand which thou shalt make unto the Four Spirits (who are) the Supreme Princes, and unto the Eight Sub-Princes; thou shalt demand the most skilful of the Spirits, of whom thou shalt make a register for convenience of the practice which I describe unto thee in this Third Book where also thou wilt find the Symbols of many Spirits. But seeing that the subjects of various erring humours (of mind) and other occasions which arise daily be diverse, each man will procure for himself those (Spirits) which be of his nature and genius and fit for that wherein thou wouldest employ them. And when thou shalt find an extreme resistance unto operating, on the part of any Spirit, after that thou shalt have given him the necessary instructions, and that he cannot execute that which thou hast commanded him; in such case thou shalt convoke the Superior Spirits and demand of them others which may be better capable of serving thee in thy need. And in all cases thou shalt avail thyself of the power and command of thy Holy Angel. Keep ever continually before thine eyes the Fear of God; and seek to obey His Commandments, and those of thy Holy Angel, ever retain in thine heart his holy instructions; never submit thyself unto the Evil Spirits in the slightest degree even should it seem to be to thine own advantage and unto that of thy neighbour (so to do). For the rest, be certain that they will obey thee so perfectly and really, that there will be no operation however great or difficult it may be, that thou shalt not bring unto a glorious termination; the which I myself also have done. As regardeth the service which thou shouldest render unto thy neighbour in his necessities, thou shouldest perform it with zeal, and in no sense wait for him to ask it of thee, and seek also to comprehend his needs unto the uttermost, so as to be able to take sound action (therein). Thou shalt take heed to succour the infirm and the sick and to work for their healing; and see that thou dost not good works to attract praises and to make thyself talked of in the world. Also thou mayest make semblance of performing (thy cures) by prayers, or by ordinary remedies, or by (the recital of) some psalm, or by other like means.

Thou shouldest be especially circumspect not to discover the like matters unto reigning Princes;

and in this particular thou shalt do nothing without consulting thy Good Angel; for there is a certain generation which is never contented, and besides that which ariseth from simple curiosity, these Princes regard such (action) as a duty and obligation. Also it is a certain fact that he who possesseth this Sacred Magic, hath no need whatever of them. Further they are naturally inclined to ask of thee always things prejudicial, the which if granted by thee would offend the Lord, and if not they become your declared enemies. Now my opinion (is that it) would be always (preferable) to render them what services you can from a distance.

There is nothing which is so pleasing unto the Angels as to demand knowledge from them, and for my part I think there is no greater pleasure than that of becoming wise when one learneth from such masters.

I both have exhorted, and do exhort unto a solitary life, which is the source of all good; it is true that it is difficult to accustom oneself thereunto; but once thou shalt have obtained the Sacred Science and Magic the love for retirement will come unto thee of thine own accord, and thou wilt voluntarily shun the commerce with and conversation of men; for the pleasure and contentment thou wilt enjoy when thou shalt be the possessor of this Science will be so great that thou wilt despise all amusements, excursions, riches, and every other thing however attractive such may be.

For once only will it be permissible to obtain property and goods proportionate unto thy degree and estate; the which afterwards are to be used by spending them liberally for thine own needs and those of thy neighbour, sharing with him in his necessity the good things which God shall have given (unto thee); for he who should employ these for evil ends shall render himself incapable of obtaining from God any other grace and benefit.

The Child which one should choose for greater surety and success in (the acquisition of) this Sacred Science should be born of a legitimate marriage, and its father and mother should be also legitimate. It should be from six to seven years of age, vivacious, and witty; it should have a clear speech and pronounce well. Thou shalt prepare it some time before commencing the Operation and have it ready when the time requireth. I myself am of opinion that there should be two (children) in case of any accident which might happen, through sick ness, or death, or other like (hindrance). Thou shalt gain it over to thee by giving it puerile things to amuse it, and have it ready when necessary, but in no way tell it anything of what it is to serve for, so that if it be questioned by its parents it can tell them nothing. And if it be a well-behaved Child, it is all the better. We may be certain that by this means we can arrive at the possession of the Sacred Science; for where he who operateth faileth, the innocence of the Child supplieth (that which is wanting); and the Holy Angels are much pleased with its purity. We should not admit women into this Operation.

All the clothes and other things which have been used during the period of the Six Moons, you should preserve, if you intend to continue in the same house wherein thou hast performed the Operation, because they be always good. But if thou dost not intend to use them more, nor yet the Oratory, thou shalt burn them all, and bury the ashes in a secret place.

It is now necessary to give unto thee a little light, and declare unto thee the quality and value of the Spirits, and in what thou canst exactly employ them with surety of success. Thou must however take note that each Spirit hath a great quantity of Inferior Spirits which be submitted unto him. Also I wish to say that as regardeth things base, vile, and of little importance the Superior Spirit will not execute them, but will cause them to be executed by his Inferiors with all punctuality. And this mattereth not unto him who operateth provided that his commands be fulfilled, and that he be punctually obeyed.

THE ORDER OF THE FIRST HIERARCHY.
(SERAPHIM, CHERUBIM, THRONES.)
THE Spirits of the Seraphim serve to make thee respected and loved for works of Charity, for that which regardeth honours and other similar things. In matters of great importance they

themselves act; but for matters base and carnal, it is their subjects who do serve and operate.

THE ORDER OF THE SECOND HIERARCHY.

DOMINIONS, VIRTUES, AND POWERS.

THE property of the Dominions is to dominate; to procure liberty; to vanquish enemies; to give authority over Princes, and over all kinds of persons, even Ecclesiastics.

The Virtues are proper to give strength and force in all matters whether of War or Peace; and in all Operations concerning the health of men, and in all maladies for which the fatal hour hath not yet been written.

The Powers have the dominion over all the Inferior Spirits; and this is why they can serve in all things in general, good or evil, and they are devoted unto all things in general, good or evil; and they be straight and right in execution, very punctual, very prompt, and exact in their Operations.

THE ORDER OF THE THIRD HIERARCHY.

PRINCES, ARCHANGELS, AND ANGELS.

THE Princes comprise Spirits capable of giving Treasures and Riches, and they or their dependants serve in all the Operations, being a mass composed of different Orders, and they are sufficiently truthful.

The Archangels be proper to reveal all Occult matters, and all kinds of secret things, such as obscure points in Theology and the Law. They serve with great diligence.

The Angels in general do operate each one according unto his quality. There be an infinite number of them. They command the Four Princes and the Eight Sub-Princes in all kinds of Operations. These latter having taken their oath, observe that which they have promised, provided that the Operation one demandeth of them be in their power. To cause the Spirit to re-enter a dead body is a very great and difficult Operation, because in order to accomplish it the Four Sovereign Princes have to operate. Also it is necessary to take great care, and to pay heed unto this warning, namely that we should not commence this Operation until the sick person is really at the point of death, so that his life is absolutely despaired of. It should be so timed as to take place a little while before the sick person giveth up the ghost; and thou shalt carry out all that we have said hereon in the Second Book. But on no account should we perform this Operation to divert ourselves, nor for every class of person; but only on occasions of the very utmost and most absolute necessity. This Operation I myself have performed but twice in my life, namely once for the Duke of Saxonia, and on another occasion in the case of a lady whom the Emperor Sigismond loved passionately.

THE Familiar Spirits are very prompt, and they are able to execute in most minute detail all matters of a mechanical nature, with the which therefore it is well to occupy them; as in historical painting; in making statues; clocks; weapons; and other like matters; also in chemistry; and in causing them to carry out commercial and business transactions under the form of other persons; in making them transport merchandise and other goods from one place to another; also to employ them in causing quarrels, fights, homicides, and all kinds of evils, and malefic acts; also to convey letters and messages of all kinds from one country to another; to deliver prisoners; and in a thousand other ways which I have frequently experimented.

These Spirits should be treated according to their quality, and a distinction should be made between a great Spirit and one of a vile or insignificant nature, but thou shouldest nevertheless alway conserve over them that domination which is proper unto him who operateth. In speaking unto them thou shalt give them no title; but shalt address them sometimes as "you," sometimes as "thou"; and thou shalt never seek out expressions to please them, and thou shalt always have with them a proud and imperious air.

There be certain little terrestrial Spirits that are simply detestable; Sorcerers and Necromantic Magicians generally avail themselves of their services, for they operate only for evil, and in wicked and pernicious things, and they be of no use soever. He who operateth could, should he so wish, have a million such, but the Sacred Science which worketh otherwise than Necromancy in no way permitteth you to employ such as be not constrained by an Oath to obey you.

ALL that hath hitherto been said and laid down should suffice, and it is in no wise to be doubted that he who executeth all these matters from point to point, and who shall have the right intention to use this Sacred Science unto the honour and glory of God Almighty for his own good, and for that of his neighbour, shall arrive with ease at the possession thereof; and even matters the most difficult shall appear easy unto him. But Human Nature is so depraved and corrupted, and so different from that which the Lord hath created, that few persons, if any, do walk in the right way; and it is so easy to prevaricate, and so difficult not to fall in an Operation which demandeth the whole (soul of a) man in (its) entirety. And in order not to intimidate in any way him who shall resolve to undertake this Operation, I am about here to set down in writing the difficulties, temptations, and hindrances which will be caused him by his own relatives; and all this will be occasioned by the Evil Spirits so as to avoid having to submit themselves, and humiliate themselves, and subject themselves unto Man, their greatest enemy, seeing that they behold him in powerful condition arriving at the enjoyment of that Eternal Glory which they themselves have foolishly lost; and their rage is so great and their grief so poignant, that there is in the world no evil which they be not ready to work, if God were to permit them, they being always attracted by the idea of the destruction of the Human Race. Therefore is it necessary to take courage and make a constant resolution to resist in all things with intrepidity, and to earnestly desire to obtain from God so great a Grace in despite of men and of the Demon. Also beforehand thou shouldest arrange thine affairs in such wise that they can in no way hinder thee, nor bring thee any disquietude in the period of the Six Moons, during which time there will occur the greatest possible attempts at assault and damage unto thee which the keen and subtle Enemy will bring to bear upon thee. He will cause thee to come in contact with evil books, and wicked persons, who by Diabolic methods and tricks will seek to turn thee aside from this enterprise, even though it be already commenced, by bringing before thee matters which in appearance will seem of the greatest importance, but which really be only built up on false (and evil) foundations. To such annoying accidents thou shouldest steadily oppose thyself, by following out carefully the ample instructions which I have given thee, thus banishing them from thee with calmness and tranquillity so as to give no chance to the Enemy of exercising his fraudulent tricks to interrupt thee.

Thy relations also, astonished at thy manner of life and thy retirement, will make every effort to attempt to find out the reasons thereof. It will be necessary to satisfy them by words full of affection, and to make them think that time which engendereth change, also causeth men who are not altogether ignorant persons to resolve at times to live by themselves. This hath been the cause why so great a number of good and learned men have retired into desert places, so that being separated from their own relatives and from the world they might live tranquilly in prayer and orisons to render themselves more worthy to obtain through the Grace of the Lord a Gift so great and so perfect.

I FURTHER approve of thy possessing a Bible in the vulgar language, and also the Psalms of David, for thine own use. Some person may here reply: "I understand the Latin, and I have no need of the common language". I answer him that when we pray we ought not in any way to embarrass the Mind by having to interpret the Psalms; for at such a moment we should be as much united as possible to God; and even the Psalms being in the vulgar tongue when one readeth them they imprint themselves better on the memory; and this is the true manner of particular prayer, if the person praying be illiterate, for in saying the Psalms in Latin he would not know what he was asking of God.

IN these Three Books we shall not find the slightest thing which hath not a true and necessary foundation. And we should take the greatest care, and keep ourselves as we would from a deadly poison, from commencing this Operation at all, if we have not made a firm resolution to carry it through unto the end. Because (in the contrary case) some notable evil would befal him who had (carelessly) commenced the Operation, and who would then only too well comprehend that we may not make a mock of the Lord. Should it happen that God by His Will and Commandment should visit thee and afflict thee with some malady which should render thee incapable of finishing the Operation according unto thy wish, thou having already commenced it; then shouldest thou like an obedient servant submit thyself humbly unto His Holy Will and Commandment, reserving His Grace unto the time pleasing unto His Divine Majesty to grant it thee. And thou shalt cease from thine Operation, so as to finish it on another more favourable occasion, and meanwhile thou shalt devote thyself unto the cure of thy body. And such a case ought in no way to afflict thee, for the Secrets of God are impenetrable, and He performeth, permitteth, and operateth all things for the best and for our good, although it may be not understanded of us.

HEREINAFTER Will I set down the Key of this Operation, which is the only thing which facilitateth this Operation to enjoy the Vision of the Holy Angels, by placing the Symbols given hereafter upon the brow of the Child and of him who performeth the Operation, as I have said in the First Book, to which one can easily refer.

I will say even as much as this, that out of an hundred scarcely five or six persons can attain unto the possession of this Sacred Magic without this Key; for reasons which one can in no way disclose.

Also we should repeat the Psalm VI. "Domine, ne in furore tuo arguas me," etc. ("O Lord, afflict me not in Thine Anger").

THERE is nothing in the World which we should so much desire as a true Science, neither is there any more difficult to obtain than this one, because often one dieth before attaining unto it in its entirety.

This is the true and only Way of this Sacred Science and Magic which the Lord hath granted unto us by His pure mercy; and is that which in Six Months maketh us attain unto the most high and Occult gifts of the Lord which we can think of.

This is the True Science which comprehendeth all other Sciences once one is in possession thereof.

Oh! how many books be read among us which seem wonderful!

It is not fitting for me even to reveal a part of this Science and its properties; and to appropriate unto myself that which appertaineth unto a person of a great mind and so far above me. In teaching it even, I have far exceeded that which I should have done, in having given unto thee the two last Symbols, but what will not paternal love and affection do? Endeavour only to obey me and to follow out my precepts from point to point, according to the manner in which I have given them unto thee in writing; keeping alway the Fear of God before thine eyes. Also forget not the slightest thing which I have said unto thee in these Three Books, for with the help of God Who ruleth and governeth all things, and reigneth gloriously in Heaven and upon Earth, and Whose Divine justice shineth in Hell; if thou hast recourse unto Him and puttest all thy confidence in His Divine Mercy, thou shalt obtain this Holy Science and Magic whose power is inexpressible. Then, O my Son! and Whosoever may attain thereunto; remember to praise and glorify the Lord, and to pray unto Him that He may be willing to deign and accord unto me His Holy Glory, the place of veritable rest, whereof to me while yet in this Valley of Misery He hath granted a large share through His Goodness and Mercy; and I pray the sacred Lord also that He may be willing to grant it unto thee also with His Holy Benediction, and unto all those who by thy means will arrive at the possession of this Sacred Magic, and who will use it according unto His Holy Will.

May God deign, say I, to grant unto such all temporal goods, and a good Death in His Holy Kingdom!

SO MAY IT BE!

E N D.

Note.--The above set of four Squares evidently represent the Symbols already referred to in the Second Book (Chap. xx.), and in the concluding pages of this Third Book; as being those to be placed on the head of the Operator and of the Child during the Angelic Invocation. The Name URIEL for the former, the Name ADAM for the latter. But evidently, also, the Squares of numbers above are intended as the reverse sides of the two lower ones. The Latin word HOMO is the translation of ADAM in the sense of Man. The Squares of numbers are not of the ordinary magical class.

www.ingramcontent.com/pod-product-compliance
Lightning Source LLC
Chambersburg PA
CBHW050643150426
42813CB00054B/1166